VULNERABLE CHILDREN

VULNERABLE CHILDREN

Three Studies of Children in Conflict:
Accident Involved Children,
Sexually Assaulted Children
and Children with Asthma

LINDY BURTON

SCHOCKEN BOOKS · NEW YORK

Published in U.S.A. 1968
by Schocken Books Inc.
67 Park Avenue
New York, N.Y. 10016

Library of Congress Catalog Card No. 68-21683

Printed in Great Britain

For Hugh, Virginia and Jonathan

Acknowledgements

At the outset I must acknowledge my considerable debt to all those whose work with children stimulated these present studies. Many of them are quoted in the text, and reference is made to their published work in the bibliography. In particular I should like to thank Professor Dennis Stott, now of Guelph University, Ontario, whose kindness and encouragement I deeply appreciated. My thanks are also due to all those who assisted in the preparation of the original thesis upon which this book is based. In particular I should like to thank Dr Alan Milner whose ideas and planning stimulated the second study in this book.

Contents

Contents

CHAPTER I

Children in Conflict

Conflict in childhood occurs for many reasons. Initially, it may arise through the child's inability to adequately communicate his needs to those in his immediate environment. Frustrations produced in this way may spur the child into greater efforts to express his wants through his behaviour or his verbalisations. He may try out many different methods of requesting help before finally he achieves satisfaction. Further conflict may occur when the child, though able to express his needs, nevertheless finds them unrewarded due to the indifference or opposition of those around him. Again, he may attempt through exaggerations of behaviour to overcome this impasse, and gain the essentials which he requires for survival.

In some cases, conflict of this kind is short-lived, the child quickly finding a solution to his problems. In other instances it is more sustained, and may eventually colour the child's thoughts and substantially alter his general behaviour, the child attempting in various ways to assuage his needs. Bizarre behaviour may result, and in some instances the child may fall back on socially inappropriate methods of communicating his wants. As a result, supposedly 'problem' behaviour may occur. Far from being 'maladjusted' it represents an attempt on the part of the child to wrest satisfactions necessary for his growth from those in the environment.

It is from this standpoint, sympathetic to the child's underlying needs, that the so-called 'problem' behaviour observed in the three studies in this book, is discussed.

Three separate types of situation for acting out are described —road accident involvement, sexual assault, and asthma in childhood—and an attempt is made to relate the observed behaviour to the child's personality needs, and to frustrations in his environment. The difficulties in behaviour are then viewed in many instances as attempts on the part of the child to overcome a conflict between himself and those around him.

From the outset the child is dependent on others for survival. All his physical needs must be met consistently if he is to thrive. Sustained apathy or hostility will almost certainly prejudice his development. Consequently from infancy the child must be capable of expressing his tensions and attracting help from those around him. If he does not meet with immediate satisfaction he must be capable of modifying his methods of communication so that they become more appropriate for the expression of his desires.

Generally, even the least observant of parents can be made to recognise a child's physical needs. It takes little imagination to interpret the sustained crying of a small infant, and such gross behaviour on his part is almost certain to produce some response from those around him. Furthermore expert advice is generally close at hand, and usually readily sought.

More difficult to interpret are the child's emotional needs. Not only is the child far less able to express these, but also they are infinitely more complex and subtle. Attempts to communicate them may be overlooked or misunderstood. Rarely is expert advice requested or even available. Yet from first days the child would seem to need constant reassurance that he is cared for, and that he exists as an independent person.

As R. D. Laing (1960) has expressed it, the child—and later the adult—must:

> experience his own being as real, alive, whole, as differentiated from the rest of the world in ordinary circumstances so clearly that his identity and autonomy are never in question, as a continuum in time, as having an inner consistency, substantiality, genuineness and worth. . .

Perhaps it is the child's total dependence which makes the development of this sense of separate existence essential from the outset. Without it the child would be a straw blown in the wind, totally disorientated by the multitude of differing incidents in which he is involved. Every temporary frustration would be a threat to his survival, and he would be overwhelmed by fears of obliteration. So many complex skills must be mastered, and so many internal and external obstacles overcome, that without encouragement from others and a sense of self-confidence, there seems little likelihood that any real struggle to maturity would take place.

Whatever the reason, it seems essential from the beginning that the child should receive from those around him encouragement and assistance in his development. Such assistance makes it possible for him to correct his responses where they are inappropriate, and so pattern his behaviour into ways which are most suited to his later adult life in the community. Indeed, just as there are innate, genetically determined factors prompting the child to seek out the bodily satisfactions essential for his general development, so also it would seem that there is an equal need on his part to be taught how best to communicate, and thereby discharge, his tensions most efficiently.

Where consistent parental handling has made it obvious to the child not only that his needs will be met, but also that he is capable of communicating these needs effectively, he will receive sufficient self-assurance to develop further. Where, however, parental inadequacy has failed to give him either the certainty that essential satisfactions will be forthcoming, or the knowledge that he is communicating efficiently, he will continue to search for the most appropriate way of relieving his existing tensions. Where the dilemma persists the child will remain in a state of insecurity unable to mature further until he is sure that his behaviour will be acceptable to those upon whom he depends for life.

Obviously therefore from infancy the child must be assured that his behaviour is acceptable to those around him, and appropriate for the release of his tensions. In our culture, the mother's more consistent presence during infancy will make her the first person to whom the infant turns for such reassurance, and if she rewards him in this she will become the object of his first deepest affections. In these days before he can talk or understand speech, every touch or response made by her assumes significance for the child. Where she is relaxed and confident in her handling of him, and appreciative of his presence, he is most likely to be reassured and develop satisfactorily. Where she is inadequate, rejecting, or openly hostile, he may be placed in conflict and consequent exaggerations of behaviour may result.

3

In later childhood the father assumes a more important role than formerly in the learning situation. This comes about for numerous reasons, partly as a result of the child's gradual awareness that his mother is not always able to satisfy his needs, and consequently his resolve to find someone else who is, and partly also as a result of the increasing mobility which brings him into his father's presence more frequently. His father's attitude to him then becomes an important one, and it seems essential that both parents should be positive from the first. Where one parent rejects—no matter how excellent the other —it is more than probable that the child will never achieve real self-assurance.

Where the father's attitude is negative from the outset, whilst not directly in contact with the child, this may be communicated to the child through the mother. She will undoubtedly appear more tense, more ambivalent in her own attitude to him, and less tolerant of any petty frustrations he may cause her. Similarly, her frustration level will be lowered if marital disharmony prevails.

Parental love of the sort required for healthy personality development seems to consist of nothing more than a willingness to assist and enjoy the normal maturation of the child. Where his physical and emotional needs are met consistently and generously in a manner most suited to his level of physical competence he will be assured of his acceptance and develop satisfactorily. This applies both to the supposed crucial training situations of early infancy such as weaning and potting, and to all later strivings to maturity. Where the mother views the situation from the standpoint of the infant, and understands what his needs mean to him, no serious personality disorientation will result—however odd the training method adopted may appear. Where, however, training situations become the battleground for the mother's underlying hostility, an exaggeration of the child's personality problems may take place. Similarly, where strivings for self-assertion are continually blocked, personality distortion will result. Adequate parental affection necessitates the giving of freedom at the appropriate ages.

Where the parents perceive and respond adequately to the child's struggles for self-assurance, the child will normally achieve sufficient maturity to be able to perceive and respond to the complex commands of parents and society. He will modify his behaviour appropriately. Where however, he is still in need of more basic reassurances, because his struggles for self-assertion have been unrewarded, he will remain too pre-occupied with more fundamental conflicts for any real moral development to take place. He may obey parental or social demands in a transitory way, but he will probably be unable either to retain his learning or to draw any conclusions from it.

Some parents, it is recognised, will have extraordinary difficulty in relating satisfactorily to their children. Usually such parents suffered frustration in their own childhood learning experience and were not given adequate approval or opportunity for self-assertion as infants. These parents never obtained sufficient personality integration to give unquestioningly to their own children. They therefore tend to see parenthood as a means of satisfying their own needs (which it may be, but only secondarily) rather than as a means of assisting the infant to maturity. Some parents may endeavour to live vicariously through their children—manipulating their lives rather than leaving them free to be themselves. (So deep-rooted is the normal urge to achieve integration, that frustration in the parent's childhood will result in endeavours to overcome these conflicts throughout life.) Sometimes the parents may exhibit immaturity in handling all their children, sometimes in the handling of one, in either case some warping of the child's personality development might be expected.

Where the mother herself is lacking in self-assurance, difficulties may occur during pregnancy, the insecure woman being unable to face the responsibilities entailed. Some immature mothers will tend to dislike their conceptions, feeling sick and emotionally upset during pregnancy, and having extended and difficult labours. Pregnancy stress of this kind may be transmitted chemically to the child and may have a profound effect on his behaviour even in the womb. After birth, anomalies of infant behaviour may result, intensifying the mother's difficulty, justifying and reinforcing her initial rejection. Whether these represent attempts by the infant to alter his mother's reactions, or merely result from physiological

5

trauma, is a matter for speculation. Neither alternative is inconceivable, but both might from the outset precipitate mother and child into a spiral of unrewarding interactions. The mother has a difficult baby who does not reward her attempts to rear him, her initial dislike is reinforced, and her attitude conveys itself to the child, who increases his resistance at such unlovingness. Many subsequent personality disorders therefore may be traced back to difficulties in infancy, or even during pregnancy.

Some mothers, it may be argued, have difficult infants or difficult pregnancies or labours, without being immature or rejecting in attitude. This is certainly true, but very frequently it seems that these mothers overcome the initial difficulties by making extra efforts to comprehend and meet the infant's needs. Their loving and consistent handling results generally in a normal and happy personality development on the child's part. Some degree of neural and emotional vulnerability may persist, however, remaining dormant as long as the environment is a satisfactory one. Where the child is subsequently stressed by accidental circumstances the tendency to break down is greater. Other individual factors may predispose against normal development, even in children whose mothers are most accepting. These might include brain damage of a more extensive nature and characteristics governed by heredity, such as poor intelligence.

Most environmental stresses, for example death, illness, hardship, or war, may adversely affect normal personality development, but it is suggested that these situations will cause greatest distress to children who are vulnerable either as a result of neural impairment or as a result of insecurity due to deprivation of parental approval.

Where adverse personality development takes place, it is my belief that a full knowledge of parental and environmental conditions, and a genuine attempt to modify any adversity that may be present in these, will almost invariably produce an improvement in the child's behaviour.

It is also my belief that most frequently these behaviour disorders will represent adaptive attempts on the child's part to wrest the assurances necessary for normal growth from the indifferent environment.

As Blau and Hulse (1956) have so ably expressed it:

> In the behaviour disorder one sees that the child has not submitted with a sense of failure and helplessness, but is fighting to save himself as an individual, despite the tremendous odds that he faces. The opposition is in many ways fantastic, unrealistic and futile, but it still means that he has not given up . . .

From this sympathetic standpoint it seems impossible to label such behaviour 'maladaptive'. In many cases the acting out produces the assurances required from the parents, in other cases the behaviour is continued and becomes patterned because of sustained parental hostility. Even when this patterning takes place, and the activity is repeated without any apparent hope of satisfaction, it seems that it may, from the child's view point, create the illusion that he is of significance, that he matters. Whilst the child is able to maintain this illusion, at whatever price, he is at least saved from admitting to himself his apparent lack of value. The behaviour disorder therefore prevents him from losing all self-assurance, and from retreating into a world of phantasy.

This book therefore attempts to show how some form of socially inappropriate behaviour on the child's part may have resulted from his attempt to gain approval and self-assurance. Three separate groups of children were studied, all of whom appear to have been placed in a conflict. They appear to have desired approval and acceptance as independent people, and yet through environmental inadequacy, to have been denied satisfaction of this basic need. This conflict seems to have coloured their whole existence. Their thoughts are filled with their problems, and in their phantasies they seek solutions to their conflict. At home and in school their behaviour betrays their unrest—their struggles for identity exaggerate their responses. Few of them achieve real social or academic success because they are caught in the throes of their struggle for self-integration.

The first group of children to be discussed are the road accident involved children. They are extremely assertive, both in their phantasies and also in their behaviour. They show such a need for acceptance by adults and children outside their own families, that it can only be presumed that they have no real security in this sphere. The conflict they are experiencing is mirrored in their restless and inconsequential behaviour. They attempt to escape their problems by unremitting action. Possibly a major cause of their extreme assertiveness is the assertiveness of their mothers. Many of these women had been subjected to intense environmental and physical stress, and pre-occupation with their own problems left them less able to assist their children in their development. The children through their pranks and escapades not only sought parental attention, but also strove to assert their own independence. To some extent the child's development and his mother's handling of him were hindered by his physical vulnerability from earliest days. All the evidence would suggest that these children were over-reactive because of pregnancy stress and subsequent minimal brain damage.

The second group of children studied had been sexually assaulted. These children were seen twice, with testings a year apart. On both occasions they displayed an exaggerated need for approval and acceptance. This need was obvious both from their behaviour in school, and also from the kind of phantasies which they created. Whilst no investigation of home circumstances was made, it is more than probable that some inadequacy may have existed there, contributing to the children's insecurity. It is also possible that the child's sexual involvement with an adult represented an attempt on his part to gain the approval necessary for personality development.

The final group of children to be discussed is a group of children suffering from asthma. They too appear unable to assert themselves, and this failure makes them depressed and anxious, both at home and in school. Mothers of such children would seem to be narcissistically involved with them, and they attempt to live through their children. The children, in rebellion, act out their need for separation at home, and it seems possible that their illness affords them an opportunity to exist independently.

At the outset, it must be stressed that all three of these studies are retrospective studies, with the usual inherent inadequacies.* Consequently, conclusions as to the aetiology of the child behaviour observed are always viewed as tentative. The studies represent careful attempts to explain how the behaviour

* For a complete discussion of these see Bell (1958).

might have been caused, but they do not offer concrete evidence of its causation. For this, large scale developmental studies would be necessary.

Similarly it should be stressed that these studies deal with only a few of the many possible personality variables, and causative factors, involved in such complex behaviours. My belief that these are the more crucial factors may well result from personal bias or from an inability to enumerate more subtle parent-child interactions.

An attempt has been made throughout the experimental work to evaluate the behaviour observed in a rigorously objective fashion. Every effort has been taken to prevent subjective assessments. Carefully matched control groups were used in each study, and the results of the personality tests were assessed independently by two post-graduate clinical psychologists. These precautions were taken because so much of the theory underlying these areas of child development has been produced in analytical or clinical work and has never been rigorously or objectively assessed. The insights afforded by clinical investigations are considerable, but they are also limited by the fact that such observations are of necessity based on work with small and highly selected samples of patients. These three studies attempt to assess the applicability of such insights to un-selected (that is non-psychiatrically selected) groups of children presenting behaviour problems.

Each separate study evaluates the child's behaviour in school and the personality needs which underlie this behaviour. The accident involved and the asthmatic child's behaviour at home was also studied and in these two studies the mothers' behaviour, avowed attitudes to child upbringing, and underlying personality needs were also assessed.

Four principal research tools were used.

(1) *The Bristol Social Adjustment Guide* (Stott and Sykes 1958) This test is designed to highlight tendencies to emotional unsettledness and maladjustment apparent in the child's behaviour at school. It deals with the child's attitude to his teacher, to his school work, his games and play, and to other children. It also contains items relating to his physique and personal ways. In each section there are many alternative descriptions of behaviour and the teacher is asked to underline

any description which seems true of the child in question. From such observations it is possible to detect consistent patterns in the child's behaviour, which themselves indicate underlying tensions.

(2) *The Thematic Apperception Test* (Morgan and Murray 1935) This test, used both with adults and children, consists of thirty pictures, the majority of which depict life situations involving one or more persons. The subject is asked to make up a story about the picture and about the people in it. He is invited to discuss their needs, feelings and experiences. It is hoped that he will project his own emotions and preoccupations into these phantasy productions, and any consistency of response from story to story is noted as being a possible indicator of the subject's own problems.

(3) *Parent Attitude Research Instrument (P.A.R.I.)* (Schaefer & Bell 1959)
An instrument designed to measure psychologically-damaging attitudes to child-rearing and family life which consists of 115 statements regarding child upbringing. The subject is asked to say whether she 'definitely agrees' with each statement, or whether she 'mildly agrees', 'mildly disagrees', or 'definitely disagrees'. Each response yields a score on one of twenty-three scales (five statements per scale), dealing with one attitude towards family life. For example, there are five statements relating to marital disharmony, and five statements relating to strictness. Twenty sub-scales relate to attitudes considered to be damaging to the healthy development of the child, three sub-scales to satisfactory child-rearing attitudes. Overall it is possible to detect how damaging or encouraging the parent's attitudes are towards the child.

(4) *The Questionnaire* relating to the child's development from conception to the time of the study, devised by the author. This consisted of fifty-seven open-ended questions relating both to the mother's feelings and behaviour towards the child, and also to the child's feelings and behaviour towards his parents and his brothers and sisters. Questions relating to possible stress factors in the environment were also included.

On the basis of the information yielded by these four research instruments as complete a study as possible was made of the child and his environment, and it is these studies which are presented in this book.

Part One

ROAD ACCIDENT INVOLVEMENT IN CHILDREN

CHAPTER II

Road Accident Involvement in Children

Road accidents occur for many reasons. Where they involve a vehicle and a pedestrian, the vehicle may be faulty and become out of control, the driver may be negligent, and the pedestrian careless; or all three may to some extent be responsible.

The reasons for the negligence of driver or pedestrian may again be various. Lack of physical co-ordination, neurological, ophthalmological and physical defect, and unpredicted hazards may singly or jointly be invoked as reasons for the occurrence. Not so frequently mentioned, outside clinical practice, is the notion that the personality of the driver or pedestrian may also have contributed to his involvement in the accident.

It was impossible to estimate the extent to which any or all of these factors had played a part in the road accidents of the twenty children who were studied, all of whom had to go to hospital for treatment of fractures received in the accidents. Instead, this study attempted to estimate the degree to which these children conformed with one another in personality needs, and differed from their peers in this respect.

An attempt was made to relate these needs to the cause of the accident and to explain them in terms of the child's development history, the mother's personality and her avowed attitude to the upbringing of her child. The accident was then seen, not as a chance occurrence, but as an almost predictable part of the child's total development.

Road accidents, rather than other forms of accidental self-injury were selected for study, because they represented accidents in an area in which most children had been instructed to take especial care. To take risks climbing trees is a socially acceded characteristic of childhood, to take a risk on the road is repeatedly stressed as being dangerous, stupid and blame-worthy. Consequently, where carelessness on the roads had been exhibited it was felt that this 'carelessness' was more likely to be caused by unconscious motivations rather than by pure chance.

Another aspect of road accident involvement which makes it a particularly suitable area for acting out from the child's point of view is its dramatic nature. Road accidents cannot be ignored or passed over by those in the environment, as can other, more domestic accidents. Also, by their frequent involvement of another person or piece of equipment, they afford the child a situation in which blame can be placed elsewhere and a semblance of innocence maintained.

The concept of accident involvement, rather than that of accident proneness, was selected for investigation in this study because no accurate estimation of the degree of an individual child's proneness seemed possible. So many accidents to children occur within the home and remain unreported, representing a serious source of error to any investigator, working on the official figures alone (W.H.O. Report 1957), and trying to select, for the purpose of comparisons, groups of high accident and low accident children.

In addition, a pattern of frequent accidents to children at home may well represent careless parents (*Lancet*, 1948, 1.758), (Smid and Logan 1956), or a dangerous environment, rather than a series of specific actings out on the part of the child.

These suggested difficulties in estimating the rate of accident repetition in children may well explain the paucity of studies in this area. By contrast to the well documented field of adult accident proneness (Le Shan 1952), studies of the dynamics of child accident involvement are almost non-existent. A further explanation may lie, as Finch (1951) points out, in the fact that for the adult means of dealing with inner and outer drives and needs have become much more rigid and unchanging than for the child; a pattern of accident proneness must take time to develop. Consequently, one would presume that proportionately fewer children than adults would display such a pattern.

It seems reasonable to suppose that where a long history of accidental self-injury can be traced the chances of discovering morbid psychological causes are greater than where one simply considers an individual who has been involved in one major accident. However, Dunbar (1944) contended that persons who have had one major accident are statistically more likely to have another—i.e. they will be more prone to accidents. This study was therefore begun on the assumption that the personality dynamics precipitating one accident would be essentially the same as those observed in people who were accident prone.

The study subsequently offered some degree of validation for this assumption. In this group of completely unselected fracture cases due to road accidents in school age children, fifteen per cent already had a history of one or more other major road accident, and 25 per cent had had major accidents at school or on the road.

From such a small sample as the one investigated in this study, it would be foolhardy to generalise about the personality dynamics of all road accident victims. However, from the statistics made available for the year in which the study was completed, both by the Royal Ulster Constabulary (1963) and by the Royal Society for the Prevention of Accidents (1963), and from the World Health Organisation Report on accidents in childhood (1957), this sample would appear to be fairly representative in terms of type of accident, the age and sex of the child sustaining it, and the distance from home at which it occurred.

Trends in child road accidents appear to be:

(1) A significantly greater number of boys sustain road accidents than girls.

(2) More children under seven years of age have accidents close to the home, and as pedestrians.

(3) Children over seven years of age have accidents further from home. There is also an increase with age in the number of cyclists injured.

(4) Most child pedestrians sustain accidents between the ages of three to twelve, the greatest number of accidents occurring to six to seven-year-olds. Most child cyclists sustain accidents between six to fourteen, the greatest number of such accidents occurring to fourteen-year-olds.

The personal details of the accident involved children in this group appear to be consistent with those of the larger studies. Of the twenty children, sixteen were male and only four female, a difference which is highly significant (·006, using the Sign Test). All the under seven-year-olds met with accidents close to their own homes and as pedestrians. Of the seventeen children over seven years of age at the time of the accident, thirteen had accidents some distance away from home. Whilst the mean age of the whole group was nine years and nine months, the average age of the seven cyclists in the group was over eleven and a half years, as compared with an average age for the thirteen pedestrians of eight and a half years.

CHAPTER III

Clinical Speculations and Formulation
of Basic Hypotheses

Clinical speculations

In considering the dynamics of personality functioning which make for accident involvement, the clinical literature stresses two major concepts:

(1) accidents which are unconscious self-injuries because of guilt feelings, 'attempts at suicide with insufficient means' (Klein, 1932);

(2) not unrelated to the first, accidents which occur when defences against authority-hostility conflicts fail.

Further and secondary causes are mentioned, for example the avoidance of an unpleasant task, or the gaining of some form of reward, or attention, or sympathy, as the result of an accidental injury.

Suicides with insufficient means. As early as 1914 Freud made the suggestion that an accident might not be due solely to unpredictable and uncontrollable external forces but rather to unconscious psychological factors subserving deep-rooted personality needs.

In the *Psychopathology of Everyday Life* (1914) he quotes numerous examples of accidents, which whilst appearing entirely fortuitous, nevertheless could be interpreted as 'unconsciously purposive' (Menninger, 1936). The following is one example.

A young married woman gave an exhibition of dancing one evening for an intimate circle of relatives. Her jealous husband was greatly annoyed and reproached her by saying that she had behaved like a prostitute. After the incident she spent a restless

17

night and in the morning decided to go driving. She chose the horses herself, refusing one team and demanding another. She refused vehemently to allow her sister's baby with its nurse to accompany her. During the drive she was very nervous and warned the coachman that the horses were getting skittish and finally when the animals really produced a momentary difficulty, she jumped from the carriage in fright and broke her leg, while those remaining in the carriage were uninjured.

As Freud points out, the accident prevented her from dancing for a long time.

Eleven years later in his *Collected Papers* (Volume III), Freud offers further examples of what he then viewed as an 'indirect attempt at suicide'. One of these is the case of Herr K., a former lover of the patient Dora, and latterly the object of her accusations and hostilities, who came one day face to face with her on a street where there was much traffic. Confronted with the woman who had caused him so much pain, mortification and disappointment, 'As though in bewilderment and in his abstraction, he ... allowed himself to be knocked down by a car'.

Further examples of unconsciously purposive accidents were supplied by Abraham. In his *Selected Papers on Psychoanalysis* (1927) he cites the case of a girl who from childhood had an exceedingly strong affection for her brother. She grew to womanhood, measuring every man by the standard of her brother, and had an unhappy love affair which left her depressed. Shortly after this she twice got into serious danger through her own carelessness on a climbing party, much to the wonderment of her friends who knew her to be a good climber, not likely to fall twice in safe and easy places. It appeared later that at the time she was in hospital, she was accustomed to go for a walk about the grounds: there was a ditch dug in the garden which she used to cross by a plank bridge, although she could quite easily have jumped over it. At that time her beloved brother was to be married and this was much on her mind. On the day before the wedding, as she was out walking she sprang over the ditch, instead of crossing by the bridge as usual, and did it so clumsily that she sprained her ankle. 'Later on these self-injuries occurred so frequently that even the attendant began to suspect that there was something intentional in them.

In these minor accidents her unconscious was obviously expressing the intention to commit suicide.'

Neither Freud nor Abraham explicitly state the mechanisms underlying these indirect attempts at suicide, but from the examples selected, it seems certain that the suggested root cause was guilt produced by non-permissible sexual or aggressive longings, ameliorated only by self punishment.

Karl Menninger (1936, 1938) provides one of the fullest expositions of the psychoanalytic idea of indirect suicide. Ranking purposive accidents as focal suicides, he maintains that they occur when the ego refuses to accept the responsibility for self-destruction.

> The guilty act stimulates the conscience to demand of the ego a price. In some instances this price is a (self-inflicted) death penalty. In other instances it seems to be less severe, and we may assume that the local self-mutilation is in some way or other a ransom and protects the ego against the imposition of the death penalty. . . The principle of sacrifice is operative here so that in a sense the individual submits himself to the possibility or certainty of accidents in which he has at least a chance of escape rather than face a destruction which he fears even though it may threaten even in conscience.

Menninger stresses the notion that frequent involvement in accidents may be a periodic payment for the continued indulgence in forbidden erotic and aggressive tendencies, and notes the similarity between this and the obsessive and compulsive techniques used by neurotic patients to offset melancholia.

He quotes the case of a former patient who had twenty-four major disasters in his life, including the accidental poisoning of his own child, and three successive car accidents at the same spot in which each time his car was entirely demolished. He wrecked successively eleven cars. It was possible to discover that his guilt arose in part from terrific unconscious wishes to kill certain members of his family.

Whilst stressing that the essential elements of accidental self injury are those of other forms of self destruction—aggression, punition, and propitiation—Menninger introduces in one of his case histories some suggestion of secondary elements.

He writes of a man who, fearing he had acquired gonorrheal infection of the eye, shaved a splinter of wood into this eye, 'This immediately gave him occasion for more solicitousness, about the eye, more visits to the doctor, more appeals for sympathy, and more justification for aggression.'

That these same motivations might apply with equal force to children was suggested by Melanie Klein (1932, pp. 25–6, 146). She quotes the case of Trude, aged three years and nine months, who after the birth of a sister, 'wanted to rob her pregnant mother of children, to kill her and to take her place in coitus with the father'. Trude exhibited aggressive behaviour towards the parents coupled with extreme fear of retribution, and 'used to manage to hurt herself in some way almost every time before she came for her analytic hour. It turned out that the objects against which she had hurt herself—a table, a cupboard, a fireplace, etc., signified in accordance with primitive and infantile processes of identification her mother or her father who were punishing her.'

Ackerman and Chidester (1936) extend the idea of purposive accidents in children. As do the analysts they stress that accident involved children are not fearless children who can see no purpose in caution, on the contrary 'they often have more fear, but also more unexpressed hatred and guilt than the average child'.

They advance the idea that accidental self injury fulfils two functions in the economy of the child's personality.

Primarily, it serves to disguise the child's own hostility towards another person, and the guilt occasioned by this hostility. They note how even the smallest child is aware of the taboo against expression of interpersonal hostility, and at the earliest ages the desire to hurt becomes converted into activities such as kicking his own feet, pulling out his hair, bumping his head vigorously, biting and scratching himself.

> With older children the expression of this tendency is more subtle and more highly disguised because of the child's increased sensitiveness to the reactions of other people—cutting and smashing fingers, stubbing toes, skinning knees, burns etc., . . .

Ackerman and Chidester maintain that this unconscious, or conscious, disguising of unpermitted hostile feelings is not innate in the child, but acquired from adult precept. At first the child's thinking, like that of primitive man, is animistic, and if he is hurt, he blames someone or something for it, often kicking inanimate objects or toys—the agents of his injury.

He does not excuse others easily; it is only when he himself uses the word 'accident' to excuse his own guilt in the injury of others that he accepts it as a concept. It affords him one means by which to deny magically his own hostility to others, it tends to allay anxiety which emerges from this source.

For the first time in clinical literature these writers make a formal distinction between primary and secondary motives in accidental self injury. The basic motives seem to be that of hurting the self out of guilt, or symbolically hurting others out of revenge. Other secondary motives might be avoiding un-pleasant tasks, gaining some sort of reward, or attention and sympathy. In most cases of self injury they suggest that more than a single motive or purpose is served, the injury playing a many-sided role in the economy of the personality.

They quote the case of a twelve-year-old socially maladjusted girl, educationally retarded, with a history of sexual mis-demeanours, an arm scarred from an accident, and deserted by her mother at six years of age. She hurt herself daily at school.

> She frequently injured herself as an expression of her anger towards another person. She did to herself what she wished to do to another. In addition the self injuries appeared to be a punish-ment for her sexual phantasies for which she felt overwhelmed with guilt. Her conscience would not permit her any form of sexual indulgence without coincident severe punishment.

Authority-hostility conflicts. To Flanders Dunbar (1944) belongs the distinction of focusing attention on the authority-hostility conflict underlying accident proneness. Whilst never ignoring the guilt aroused by sexual and aggressive impulses with con-sequent need for self punishment, she repeatedly stressed that the accident prone person has his area of intense conflict in the realm of authority and that his characteristic means of attempt-ing to solve these conflicts is a striving for independence and autonomy outside authority relationships, and an avoiding of conflict with authority wherever possible, although not by submission.

She found this to be true of 80 per cent of the 1,600 un-selected fractures she studied, and noted:

> By focusing their values on immediate concrete experience, striving to find satisfaction and security outside the authoritarian hierarchy, and avoiding any marked submission or domination in vocational or social roles, accident prone persons get along without serious conflict with authority ... [Whenever these] defences fail and conflict with authority becomes unavoidable, the accident happens. Aggressiveness may break out in an act which appears to punish the victim or those responsible for his frustration or both. Or it may come near enough to the surface to cause the kind of confusion which leaves the person defenceless in the danger situation normally encountered from day to day.

She notes that, unlike depressed persons who consciously attempt suicide, the accident prone individual usually reports no conscious premeditation. It is interesting however that he occasionally reports a dream or a hunch that 'something was going to happen today' or that he was going to have bad luck. Thus far only will his ego permit him to recognise his self destructive tendencies.

Formulation of basic hypotheses

In summary, we may say that the clinical literature on the accident involved child has repeatedly stressed the existence of an inordinate need for aggression or self-assertion. This need to react aggressively against authority is accompanied by a fear of reprisal, an awareness of personal guilt, and a need to make retribution. The accident involved child is consequently thought to be a fearful child, obsessed with the problems of maintaining a truce with the hated figures of authority. The accident is precipitated when open conflict occurs, or seems inevitable. The injury serves both to punish the guilty aggressor and symbolically to punish the authority figure against whom the aggression is directed. Secondly, it subserves the function of gaining attention, sympathy or other rewards.

Whilst no mention has been made of the parents of these children, the repeated stress on the punitiveness of those in authority, and the guilt aroused by sexual and aggressive longings, suggests that the parents of these children have an

22

inordinate need to dominate, punish the child excessively, are much feared by him, and are particularly repressive when faced with their child's aggressive and sexual tendencies. In short, they are not parents most likely to encourage their child's bid for independence.

From these clinical observations, several simple hypotheses concerning the accident involved child and his mother, capable of clear acceptance or rejection, were formulated.

Hypothesis 1. Accident involved children are more anxious, assertive, and guilty than are carefully matched control children. These personality traits will be seen in the significantly higher scores for unsettledness of these children when measured on the Bristol Social Adjustment Guides, and in the significantly greater needs for assertion, the fear of intra-psychic threat, and the portrayal of authority as anxiety-provoking, in their Thematic Apperception Test themes.

These characteristics are seen as arising from repeated conflicts with parent figures; they would result in the child's being seen as significantly more 'problematic' by his mother, and the parent figures being seen as significantly more threatening and unhelpful by the child. The child will also display a greater fear of dominance in his Thematic Apperception Test protocols and report significantly fewer successful outcomes and more evasive action in overcoming the threats of his needs.

Hypothesis 2. This relates to the personality structure of the mothers of accident involved children.

Hypothesis 2 predicts that, compared with the mothers of control group children, the mothers of accident involved children will be more dominant, punitive and repressive. These personality characteristics will be seen in the mother's Thematic Apperception Test themes, which will show significantly higher needs for assertiveness and a greater desire to punish the evil-doer. They will be apparent in the significantly higher scores made by these mothers on the Parent Attitude Research Instrument, particularly on the scores relating to suppression of sex, suppression of aggression, strictness and breaking the will.

Hypothesis 2 also predicts that compared with the control

mothers, mothers of accident involved children will have been initially rejecting in their attitude to childbirth, and their harshness in handling their infant will have resulted from their own feelings of dependence which have never been satisfied. Initial rejection will show up in a comparison of the deviant responses of the two groups of mothers to questions relating to pregnancy and infant handling, and dependency conflicts will be apparent both in the significantly greater 'dependence of mother' score on the Parent Attitude Research Instrument, and in the fear of domination score on the Thematic Apperception Test.

Hypothesis 3. We are concerned here with the relationship which exists between the mother's initially non-accepting attitude, her own need for assertion, the environmental stress, and the child's need for assertion. Several predictions are made:

(1) It is postulated that the accident involved children with more accepting mothers will show less need for assertion than will accident involved children with less accepting mothers—the need for assertion being dependent upon the child's awareness of his mother's rejection, and his consequent struggle to gain acceptance.

(2) It is predicted that children with less assertive mothers, will themselves show less need for assertion, the need for assertion being innately acquired or learnt by the child from his mother. Equally, where the child's bid for freedom is less threatened by the parent, it will be less exaggerated.

(3) It is predicted that children who most need to assert themselves will be the children with most evidence of environmental trauma—the need for assertion results from the environmental stress. In the face of difficulty the child must struggle more decidedly to gain acceptance and independence.

(4) It is predicted that children with high assertive needs will be those children in whose backgrounds exist the greatest evidence of maternal rejection, maternal assertiveness and environmental stress, because the degree of assertiveness depends on general rather than specific environmental frustration.

CHAPTER IV

Previous Work on the Personality of Accident Involved Children

Few empirical investigations have been made into the personality variables of accident involved children, despite the early, and not inconsiderable, theoretical speculation concerning this topic. No studies appear to exist dealing only with the personality needs of children in road accidents, and one may well wonder at the reasons for this surprising lack.

Perhaps, as already mentioned, the root cause lies in the fact that children's personality needs are rarely 'set', and consequently they are not as apparent as those of adults, particularly to casual observers. Further, accident involvement may ameliorate to some extent the personality needs which precipitated it, making them even more difficult to detect.

Equally, the emergency nature of treatment for injuries sustained in road accidents may tend to rivet attention on the physical damage, rather than upon the less obvious personality needs of the victim. There may also be a tendency to avoid attributing any degree of purposefulness to a child's accident involvement. This would only suggest guilt on the part of the child, which would be inappropriate in view of his suffering.

Finally, one may speculate on the part played by public complacency in limiting adequate research into road accident involvement. At the minute, considerable financial assistance is given to road safety campaigns, which receive very adequate publicity. These campaigns work on the premise that children behave reasonably, and with adequate instruction will learn how to behave appropriately on the roads. For the vast majority of children this may be true, but perhaps the small minority of road users who sustain injuries are not temporarily amenable to reason. Their 'carelessness' may result from a personality conflict which formal road safety education would not resolve. They need emotional comfort, and psychological counselling, but these needs may be overlooked because of the public assumption that adequate instruction is being given.

Whatever the cause, few studies exist of the personality needs which underlie accident involvement in childhood. Where studies are available, they tend to describe only observed personality characteristics and to offer little explanation of their causation. No attempt has been made to take a whole view of the child and to relate his personality characteristics to stresses in his home or school background, or to tensions in his relationship with his parents. Because of this, accident involvement tends to be viewed by previous writers as a further example of abnormal behaviour by an already disturbed child, not as an attempt to adapt in order to gain satisfaction from an otherwise indifferent environment, as I would prefer to interpret it.

The first of the existing studies into 'injury prone' children was completed by Elizabeth Mechem Fuller in 1947. Basing her observations on the health records of thirty girls and thirty-one boys of nursery school age, Fuller was able to establish the existence of an accident prone tendency in some members of both sexes. She noticed that 50 per cent of the injuries to girls involved only 14 per cent of the girls, and concluded that girls could be more sharply divided into injury-prone and non-prone than boys.

A further relationship appeared to exist between accident involvement and the tendency to inflict injuries on other children. Those who repeatedly injured others had decidedly higher scores than the children who refrained from hurting others. Similarly those who reported to the nurse with minor scratches, splinters and bumps were usually those with a high incidence of more serious injuries.

Fuller concluded: 'Part of the proneness pattern is the habit of getting into certain injury laden situations which the non-prone child would avoid.'

Marking the children on a behaviour rating schedule, Fuller decided that the injury prone child differed markedly in personality characteristics from the others. No statistical analysis was made of the test results, but the impression gained was that the injury prone child was more impulsive, obstinate, highly strung, overactive, dare-devil, assertive and insolent than other children of his age, He was also a child with slightly more than average problem tendencies.

Birnbach (1948), working in the Center for Safety Education, New York, produced a similar personality profile from studies of fifty-five accident repeating children. Comparing them with forty-eight accident free boys, also from Junior High School, he described the accident group as more aggressive and exhibiting a tendency to control situations by force. Under stress, he found them impulsive and rebellious. They were described by their teachers as less polite, less reliable, less hard working and generally more inadequate than the accident free group. Accident repeating children were physically stronger and with a better health record than the control group, but their knowledge of safety precautions was less, and 20 per cent of them came from broken homes.

Four years later, in 1951, Fuller and Helen Baune completed a second study into injury proneness in children, this time taking as their subjects a class of twenty-two seven- to eight-year-old children, all of whom had received an unusually high number of injuries in their second year at Elementary School.

Analysis of first-aid records revealed that the class under observation had received five times as many injuries as an average class and that a large proportion of the injuries involved conflicts with other children. Sociometric investigations suggested that the children most prone to injury were the least popular members of class—the 'fringers'—that is those on the outside of the group. In addition, as in the Birnbach study, injury prone children were thought to be less well adjusted than average and to have more behaviour problems. They exhibited classroom behaviour incompatible with, and reflecting unhappiness in, the school environment. Adequate control subjects do not appear to have been used in this investigation, and the author freely admits that the group chosen was nonnormal both in terms of intelligence, and in socio-economic status, both of which were well above average.

A more carefully controlled investigation appears to be that made in 1953 by Vita Krall. Taking a group of thirty-two five- to eight-year-old children, all of whom had sustained three or more accidents in the four year period prior to the study, she matched each child with one of comparable age and compared their personality characteristics. Two standardised interviews were used, where the children were asked to make up a story about a doll family living in a doll's house. Both their behaviour and their use of words were noted.

The results suggested that the accident repeaters engaged in significantly more aggression—particularly verbal aggression —in play than the accident free children. They also appeared to show fewer inhibitions, and expressed their aggression more quickly than accident free children. As a group, accident repeaters tended to show more commands, threats and pro- hibitions, and also more affection seeking behaviour than their age mates. They also displayed more activity. In addition, Krall noted that accident repeaters tended to come more frequently than average from larger families and broken homes, to be somewhat later in birth order, and to have transferred school more often than usual. They were also more frequently known to home and school counsellors, suggesting some previous problem behaviour.

Krall noted that these results are in agreement with the clinical assumption that accident repeating children tend to come from homes where there is more parental dominance, less affection and more evidence of physical strength and social disorganisation.

A statistical study of road accidents to children in Great Britain was made in 1955 by A. B. Fitt. After examining the monthly road accident figures for child pedestrians for the eleven years from 1943 to 1953, Fitt noticed that the peak month for road accidents to children is June, which has an accident level twice as high as January, the month showing the lowest level of accidents.

Fitt was unable to explain these figures in terms of weather or school holidays, contending that the figure for fatalities is lower in August, the peak month for holidays, than it is in June. He therefore suggests that the trends may be related to endo- genous or internal factors, and may represent real seasonal variations in accident rate.

In support of this contention the author refers to the con- clusions of several studies of suicide, delinquency, and rioting of prisoners in an American penitentiary, all of which he claims point to the existence of uncontrolled behaviour in the early summer months, and suggest 'real seasonal variations' in behaviour. No explanation is given as to the nature of these mysterious internal influences, nor is any attempt made to exclude—or even discuss—the numerous environmental variables which may have occasioned the behaviour. For example, in the case of the accident involved children, frustrations caused by compulsory homework on light June evenings may well be a contributory factor which would not be present in the later summer months. It is probable that unknown environmental stresses of this kind were of greater importance than the supposed endogenous factors, in the aetiology of road accident involvement.

In 1953 Langford produced a report of the result of a pilot study into child accident proneness. He and his co-workers compared nine accident repeating children with nine accident free controls. They noted very little psychiatric disturbance in either group of children, but suggested that the accident repeating children seemed unable to face up to or deal with problem situations, and after the accident showed a surprising lack of concern regarding their injuries.

Langford noted that accident children were more friendly to the staff than the accident free children, and suggested that this was because they were more used to searching for substitute affection. He considered that the parents of the accident children were significantly less 'in tune' with their children than the other parents.

Basing his conclusions on the nine children studied, Langford suggested that there are at least three types of accident prone child:

(1) An overactive and impulsive child, who reacts poorly to stresses, and becomes disorganised and impulsive. Under stress he disregards or fails to recognise danger signals. This type of child is frequently popular with adults, but not with other children, and over asserts himself to achieve his ambitions.

(2) Another assertive child, but this time one who is immature emotionally and, lacking supervision from his parents, tends to make substitute relationships with other children, often becoming involved in dangerous escapades.

(3) A child who is hostile and resentful towards his parents, and whose home background is rejecting and 'empty.'

Langford's conclusions as to the home background of accident prone children were extended in 1959 by the researches of Backett and Johnston who looked at the family setting of children involved in road accidents. They compared two groups of 101 children for home factors such as: parental health, maternal preoccupation such as going out to work, size of family, family structure, financial level, play facilities, family accommodation, a history of accidents to other members of the family, and intelligence level of the family. Several factors were considered significant in determining accidents. They were:

(1) maternal preoccupation of some kind—work, children, or pregnancy

(2) illness in the mother or in a near member of the family

(3) overcrowding, less protection during play, and possibly even an absence of elementary play facilities.

They concluded that where the standards of the parents were low, accidents were more likely to take place.

Offering further confirmation for the assumption that disturbed parental relationships underlie child accident involvement is the study of Marcus and his colleagues in 1960. After comparing three groups of carefully matched children aged six to ten years, one of which was accident prone, one accident free and one enuretic, they concluded that the accident children were involved in fewer family activities than the other two groups of children, and their parents tended to be anxious and insecure. In contrast to Krall, they suggested that as compared with parents of enuretics, parents of accident children were non-assertive, non-authoritarian and non-punitive. In contrast to the accident free children, only seven of whom had difficulties in adjustment, Marcus found that all the twenty-three accident prone children had problems. In this they resembled the enuretic group. They conclude that underlying the accident are 'a hyperactivity which may be constitutional, a tendency to express tension through physical activity, and disturbed family relationships'. But they suggest that the same emotional stimulus might under different circumstances have produced a different response.

In this, the conclusions reached are similar to that contained in the W.H.O. Report on Accidents in Childhood, produced in 1957. This commented: 'this is probably not a question of "accident prone" character, but one of a temporarily variable state of mind which might render a child more prone to accidents at one time than at another.'

The Group concluded: 'A certain attitude of carelessness and instability of purpose is much more prevalent among those children who have had accidents. Children of this type often come from broken homes or problem families, their recklessness and disregard of consequences is primarily a mental factor which may at times express itself in a physical behaviour, resulting in unforeseen accidents.'

CHAPTER V

The Personality Needs of Accident Involved Children

Hypothesis 1 was concerned with the personality needs of accident involved children. From the clinical material reviewed at the outset of the investigation the assumption was made that these children, as a group, would appear more anxious, assertive and guilty than a carefully matched group of control children.

The testing of this hypothesis proceeded in three stages:

(1) An estimate was made of the anxiety and assertiveness displayed in school by the accident involved and control group children, and measured by the Bristol Social Adjustment Guides filled in by their class teachers.

(2) A comparison of the conflicts and fears underlying the observed behaviours was made by means of an analysis of themes produced by the children in response to twelve Thematic Apperception Test pictures. A specific analysis of the themes relating to parent-child relationships was also made.

(3) A comparison was made of the anxiety-reflecting behaviour displayed by the child when at home. A description of her child's behaviour was elicited from each subject and control child's mother, using a questionnaire.

Subjects

Twenty consecutive admissions to the Children's Surgical Ward of the Belfast City Hospital formed the subject group. These children, suffering in the main from fractured arms and legs, had all been in road accidents. They were selected only in the sense that their ages fell in the school age range five to fifteen years. Children of less than five years, admitted with injuries sustained in road accidents, were excluded from the group

32

because of the obvious difficulties involved in personality testing, and because it was felt that their injury might be more a reflection of the mother's carelessness than that of the child. Children over fifteen years, who had been involved in road accidents, were excluded from the group, because of the difficulty in obtaining adequate controls in cases where the child was no longer at school. Personal details of the subjects are contained in Table I, and the following notes may be regarded as a brief résumé of the circumstances under which the accidents were sustained.

TABLE I

PERSONAL DETAILS OF SUBJECTS IN THE ACCIDENT GROUP

Subject	Sex	Age	I.Q.	Ord. P.	No. Sib.	Father's Occupation
1	F	5	—	1st	3	Van driver
2	M	5	—	5th	6	Father dead—mother cleaner
3	M	5	—	8th	8	Plasterer
4	M	7	—	1st	1	Father legally separated— Mother stitcher
5	M	7	—	3rd	6	Lorry driver
6	M	7	—	5th	6	Garage mechanic
7	M	7	—	3rd	2	G.P.O. engineer
8	M	8	92	2nd	5	Labourer
9	M	7	—	3rd	2	Technical representative
10	M	11	130	1st	1	Father dead (child at Boarding School)
11	M	12	105	1st	3	Father bulldozer engineer (child lives away from home)
12	M	12	84	3rd	2	Sail maker
13	M	13	109	1st	1	Draper
14	M	11	120	2nd	1	Docker
15	M	13	105	4th	3	Civil Servant (child at Boarding School)
16	F	13	98	4th	8	Unemployed labourer
17	F	13	89	1st	5	Unemployed labourer
18	M	13	87	1st	2	Unemployed
19	M	13	103	3rd	2	Butcher
20	F	13	92	2nd	3	Fireplace fitter

Ordinal Position:

Total no. of males = 16*
Total no. of females = 4*
Mean age = 9 years 9 months
Mean I.Q. = 101·15

1st = 7   7th = –
2nd = 3   8th = 1
3rd = 5   Last in family = 6
4th = 2   First in family = 7
5th = 2   (Total of 89 children
6th = –   in 20 families)

* This difference in sexes is significant at .006 level, using the Sign Test

Circumstances Immediately Preceding the Accident

Subject 1. A girl of five years, first of a family of four, who met with her accident whilst playing 'tig' outside the front door. Several cars were parked against the kerb outside the house, and she ran in between them to escape her pursuer. An on-coming car knocked her down and fractured her leg. A month before the accident a third brother had been born, and the child said 'I'm fed up with the boys. There are so many of them. I'm sick with them.'

Subject 2. A five-year-old twin boy who had rushed out after a ball into the road outside his home. He was knocked down by a lorry and fractured an arm. He was a most unsettled child, both at home and in school. After hospitalisation at two years of age for gastroenteritis, he became a persistent rocker and head banger. His father died less than a year before the accident, and the child 'became wild', truanting regularly from school, and appearing completely withdrawn.

Subject 3. A five-year-old boy who, playing chase with other children in his street, rushed out into the road in front of a fruit lorry and fractured both legs.

Subject 4. A seven-year-old boy who rushed out into the road, for no apparent reason, outside his own home, and was knocked down and fractured a leg. The child lived with his mother and grandmother, his father having left home five years previously. The child frequently asked for his father saying 'He mustn't love me—he never comes.' The child's accident took place on the day the mother returned to work after a month's absence due to illness.

Subject 5. A seven-year-old boy who, chased by his brother, ran out into the middle of the road in front of a car. The accident took place one month after the family's removal to a new house. The boy was described by his mother as a 'bad 'un, devilish. He steals off other childer and hides things'.

Subject 6. A seven-year-old boy who liked going to the swings, but who was forbidden to go by his mother. One afternoon he went off on his own, and was knocked down trying to cross the main road on his way home. He fractured a leg.

Subject 7. A seven-year-old boy who was going to do the shopping for his mother, but who was knocked down off his bike by a van near the shops. The mother claims he was well over on

34

his side of the road, and he had just passed a parked car when a van raced up behind him and hit him. He fractured a leg.

Subject 8. An eight-year-old, described by his mother as 'giddy, and senseless' who was knocked down by a motor-cyclist whilst crossing a main road supposedly on a crossing. This was the child's fourth accident in a year. There were three previous road accidents, and only six months before his present accident he had stuck his hand into an escalator, nearly severing it. At the age of eighteen months he had swallowed a bottle of disinfectant and had to be admitted to hospital.

Subject 9. A twin boy aged eight, who sustained his accident when running from a neighbour's house where he had been playing. He was trying to race past his sister and get home first, and he rushed on to the road to overtake her and was knocked down. His mother said he had started nightmares a few weeks before the accident. 'He was frightened for some reason or another. Daddy went in and gave him a smack, but that didn't help. He had to come into our room, or we into his.' The child, who was described by his mother as 'a bit spoiled now, he thinks he's the whole cheese', created unbelievable difficulties in hospital, spitting and kicking at nurses, and refusing treatment.

Subject 10. A boy of eleven, who fractured his leg when knocked from his new bike by a van, whilst he was crossing the road. The boy was considerably distressed immediately before the accident by an emergency illness in the family. An uncle, with whom he had lived since his father's death six months earlier, had been rushed to hospital with a coronary. The boy's father had died in this way, and his father's death had been the 'end of the world for him'. The accident took place only a few days before the boy was to be returned to Boarding School. He had only attended for one term previously and was thought by his mother to be 'desperately homesick'.

Subject 11. A boy of eleven who jumped from a bus at a corner just as it lurched forward. He fractured his right arm. The boy was visiting his parents for the week-end. Normally he lived with his grandmother in the country. This arrangement had been made so that the mother could work full time, but was continued even when subsequently the mother gave up work. The grandmother, with whom the child lived, was described by the mother as 'an awful old nagger. She is the sort who never

35

lets the child out on the street ... She won't let him out past the garden gate'. During the course of my interview with this mother, she yelled and threatened to beat her children for so much as the merest movement on their part.

Subject 12. A boy of twelve who had sustained three road accidents in six months. In the two previous ones he had been knocked off his bike by a car and a lorry. In the third accident he had a football in a bag on his handlebars, and it caught between his legs and he fell off his bike and fractured two arms. He had a history of minor accidents at school, and was described by his mother as 'very quick tempered, and a bit reckless'.

Subject 13. A boy of twelve who was knocked down off his bike by an overtaking car when he was on his way to pick up his pony from the blacksmith's. The boy scored 98/100 in a Highway Test and insists he did nothing wrong. He fractured his leg.

Subject 14. A boy of twelve who was riding his bike with no hands, when he ran into a kerb and was knocked off and fractured his jaw. He later confided that he knew it was reckless, but he didn't think he would get hurt. The boy, described by his mother as 'very quiet and queer', was said to 'go into a mousehole' when she scolded him. When his sister saw him after the accident she rushed upstairs to be sick, and then fell downstairs and had to be taken off in a different ambulance.

Subject 15. A boy of thirteen who went to get some sweets, but found the shop was shut; he borrowed a neighbour's bike, without asking permission, and cycled down to the village. He was knocked off the bike whilst in the village by a van pulling out from the pavement, and he fractured a leg. He had been forbidden by his parents to borrow the bike, and he was not allowed one of his own. The accident occurred just before he was to leave home to attend boarding school for the first time.

Subject 16. A girl of thirteen who stepped off the pavement in front of a pedal cycle and was knocked down and cut her face. She was described by her mother as jealous and frequently asserted 'it's always me that gets shouted at'.

Subject 17. A girl of thirteen who was knocked over by a car and fractured her leg. She had gone for a walk to church with a girl friend and was knocked down whilst crossing the road. Her mother said it was most unusual for her to be out as she 'never goes out anywhere now'.

Subject 18. A boy of thirteen who was knocked down by a car and broke two legs. This was his second road accident, and he had such a history of minor accidents, including falling into a large river, that his mother called him her 'miracle boy'. A wanderer from earliest days, at three years of age he was lost five miles from home.

Subject 19. A boy of thirteen who, cycling home from school, put his head down over the handlebars and ran into the back of a bus. This boy was very anxious about success in school and would refuse to go if he had not been able to complete all homework the night before.

Subject 20. A girl of thirteen who rushed off the pavement in front of a police car, and fractured her leg. She was out shopping for a birthday present for her baby brother's party at the time. It was the first party the family had ever had, and it was to celebrate the baby's recovery from pneumonia. The child did not openly resent her baby brother, but since his birth she had suffered nightmares in which he had died and she had killed him. She would also cry over child torture stories in the Sunday papers, and told her mother she didn't want any children of her own when she got married, but she and her husband would live in a big house with lots of adopted babies to look after.

Several complete histories are given later in this chapter, but at this stage it is interesting to note the large proportion of children in the subject group who had either had an unsettling or frustrating experience immediately before the accident, or who were already in such a hyperactive state that mishap might almost have been expected. Very few children seemed to meet with their accident 'out of the blue' and several mothers commented sincerely that they had always known 'something would happen' to the child in question.

The Control Group

In order to ascertain whether any observed personality needs were specific to the accident involved children, and not general to all children with similar personal characteristics, a control group was selected for comparison.

Twenty children were chosen to form this control group.

They were children with no history of road accident involvement, and each child was matched individually to a member of the subject group. The variables considered to be important in selecting a control child were:

(1) age—within six calendar months of the accident involved child

(2) sex

(3) equal I.Q. (as measured by Raven's Progressive Matrices, and used with children over eight years) and/or equality of school achievement, as rated by their teachers

(4) comparable socio-economic status and religion

(5) exact similarity of ordinal position and approximate similarity in number of siblings.

The selection of the control group was made through the school attended by the accident involved child. The head teacher was approached by the author, and the nature of the study explained to him; his co-operation was then obtained in selecting a control child matched in terms of the specified variables.

Unsettledness and maladjustment displayed in school

In order to assess differences in degree or pattern of unsettledness displayed by accident involved children in school, the class teacher of each subject-control pair was asked to fill in a Bristol Social Adjustment Guide for each child. At the outset care was taken to select control children from the same classes as the accident involved children, and so avoid a possible source of error in rating B.S.A.Gs. Only in one instance were the children from different forms (S.10 and his control, who attended a small private boarding school) and in this case the Head Teacher, who knew both boys well, filled in the Adjustment Guides himself.

Twenty pairs of Adjustment Guides were returned, and a statistical analysis of the differences between groups was made, using the Wilcoxon Matched-Pairs Signed Ranks Test. Exact details of scores obtained are available elsewhere (Burton 1964). Five of the fourteen unsettledness syndromes were seen to yield significant differences between the groups.

The accident involved group were rated by their teachers as

significantly more restless (·01 level), inconsequential (·03 level), and affection seeking, both towards adults (·005 level), and towards children (·05 level). Control children by contrast were seen as significantly less forthcoming (0·5 level).

The sum of scores for the syndromes of hostility to adults and hostility to children, whilst not significantly different, were in the predicted direction: the accident involved group obtaining higher ratings.

In addition to this straightforward comparison of groups, a further statistical analysis was made of the differences between the number of respondents in each group scoring any individual B.S.A.G. item. The Sign Test was used, but no items yielded differences between groups significant at the ·05 level or better. However the results of several items suggest that a slightly larger sample might have produced significant differences. For example, accident involved children were seen as more frequently sidling up to or hanging round their teacher. They were also seen as more frequently bragging to other children.

From all the results obtained on the Bristol Social Adjustment Guides, it would appear that accident involved children as seen by their teachers, are significantly more distractable, more inclined to show off to other children, and less able to assess the results of their behaviour. In addition, they show a significantly greater desire for attachments, possibly to compensate for insecurity in their family setting. The high hostility scores, both hostility directed towards adults and other children, further indicate that a defect in parent-child relationships existed, so that the child no longer considered it important to hang back from foolhardy, and possibly blameworthy acts. The child's restlessness might be due to his preoccupation with conflicts about affection and hostility, for to quote Stott (1964): 'One suspects that certain deprived children, who have never been able to establish permanent adult attachments, come to terms with their deprivation by taking nothing in life seriously.'

Alternatively the significant differences found in the Inconsequential, Restless, and Affection seeking syndromes might well indicate a greater degree of neural impairment in this group, possibly due to sustained stress during the latter stages of pregnancy. These children's affection seeking might then be viewed as part of an inordinate need for stimulation, their high hostility scores as a greater vulnerability to stress, and their restlessness and inconsequentiality as an inability to react rationally, due to neural impairment.

Two brief portraits of accident involved children may highlight the personality characteristics of this group, as observed by teachers in school. Each of them is typical of many of the children studied. They show a variability of behaviour, very much dependent on mood—sometimes open and outgoing, sometimes depressed and hostile. At times they will sidle up to the teacher or pander to him, at other times they will ignore him. Similarly, sometimes they seek attention from their class mates, fooling around, taking unnecessary risks or attempting any challenge in an effort to get praise. At other times, they are surly and hostile, and squabble, fight, or make insulting remarks. Behind their behaviour lies quite obviously a need for affection, and a desire to be thought important or worthwhile. Because of their uncertainty concerning acceptance, they are restless and find it difficult to settle to any task. They are obviously trying children to teach, and probably have difficulty absorbing information.

The first school adjustment profile is for S.8, an eight-year-old boy called James, who attended a small, very over-crowded primary school in a slum area of Belfast. James has already been described earlier in this chapter as 'giddy and senseless' at home and had already sustained four major accidents in the year before the study. At school he was liked by his teacher who said he 'reminds me of an under-privileged William Brown. He has an attractive personality, even though he occasionally exasperates!' Small, dark-eyed James was very quick in all his movements and speech. His mood in school was very variable, sometimes he was eager, sometimes he did not bother. He varied very noticeably from day to day. He was frequently destructive, defacing his work with scribbling, and was very 'rough and ready' in his habits. He was always getting dirty and rarely attended for long. He was too restless to heed correction, and sometimes spoke in thick, mumbling, inaudible speech. In school, he associated mainly with other unsettled types, and was thought to be 'over-brave', taking unnecessary risks. He was frequently late for school, and was known to have truanted on several occasions.

Mary (S.17), a girl of thirteen, appeared very depressed at home, rarely going out anywhere. In school she tended to be very emotionally unstable. Sometimes she was described as being very 'forward'. Sometimes she was very sulky. At times she 'mumbled awkwardly' and her teacher could not 'get a word out of her'. She appeared completely apathetic, having 'no life' in her, and would just sit, rarely indulging in active play. She was resentful of her teacher's advice and would mutter about it to herself. She would only work if she was watched and compelled, and she appeared resentful of other children. At times, however, very briefly, she tended to brag to her class-mates, and to find excessive excuses for engaging her teacher. Obviously, her need to gain affection and approval was not entirely lost.

Underlying personality needs, threats and emotions

The assumption was made at the outset of the investigation that accident-involved children would perceive their environment as significantly more threatening than would the control group. They would also exhibit a significantly greater feeling of personal guilt. Feelings of sadness and conflict would predominate in their stories, and outcomes to stories would be significantly less successful than would those of the controls. The heroes of their stories would tend to resort to more evasive action to overcome threats to their needs, than would control children's heroes.

In addition, it was suggested that an analysis of themes relating only to parent-child relationships would show a significantly greater number of stories portraying parents as punitive and unhelpful.

To test this section of Hypothesis 1, each child in the subject and control groups was individually shown twelve T.A.T. pictures taken from Murray's standard set. Testing was done principally in the child's school, although a few subject children, whose injuries were more extensive, were seen in hospital.

The pictures were administered individually, and the test was prefaced by my asking the child to draw himself, and his mother and father, on foolscap sheets of paper. This procedure was adopted as a 'warm up', and as a means of fixing the child's attention on himself and his family. It also gave the child time to assess me—and was accompanied by frequent but not too obvious exclamations of praise and encouragement on my part. This was found to be an excellent way of luring the child from other preoccupations and involving him in the test.

All the children, both subject and control, were instructed: 'I am trying to find out a little bit more about the sort of stories that children of your age can make up. I have some pictures here of people doing different things, and I will give them to you one at a time. I want you to look at the picture carefully for a minute, and then tell me a story about the people in it. Try to imagine what is happening to them, what they have been doing before the picture, and what they are going to do, or would like to do. This is not a test, and there are no right or wrong answers. I just want you to tell me what you think is happening, or is going to happen. You can take as long as you like over each story.'

When the instructions were not complied with after a minute or two, they were repeated more slowly, and with pauses where it was considered that these were necessary. The instructions were repeated until each child knew exactly what was required.

No time limit was imposed on the child, and many children exceeded the five minutes generally considered as adequate for the production of each story. Where, however, the story related by the child was extremely brief, and encouragement to continue ignored, a couple of minutes were allowed to elapse before the presentation of the next picture.

Three refusals were encountered in the subject group. S.2, the five-year-old boy who had 'rocked' from infancy, and who was so withdrawn in hospital that he was referred for psychiatric attention. At home, and in school, I managed to persuade him to draw for me, but not to respond to the T.A.T. pictures. S.9, the boy whose behaviour in hospital was described in another chapter as excessively hostile and hyperkinetic, refused to talk to me on three consecutive hospital visits. His only comment being 'Lady, go home'. Eventually, some weeks later, he returned to hospital complaining of non-diagnosable stomach pains, and was again seen by me and co-operated willingly. S.16, a teenage girl, refused to talk to me on three consecutive hospital visits and was not seen subsequently, either at home or in school. In neither of the other two studies in this book were refusals noted, and I felt that these unexpected occurrences might result either from the shock of the accident, from a refusal to co-operate due to the visit to hospital* or from the child's general need to assert himself against authority.

The control children for S.2 and S.16 were not tested with the T.A.T. cards and the scores for the remaining thirty-six children were analysed by means of a one-tailed Wilcoxon Matched-Pairs Signed Ranks Test.

The results appear essentially to validate Hypothesis 1. As compared with the control children, the accident involved children told significantly more stories of a hostile emotional tone (·006 level). They showed an inordinate need for assertion (·001 level), and a significantly greater fear of the external environment (·05 level), particularly the domination of others (·05 level). They tended to use significantly more negative, anti-social (·001 level) or evasive (·02 level) action to overcome threats to their needs and they tended to see their stories as ending significantly more often in modified failure (·025 level). By contrast the control group children told significantly more stories of a happy, or positive nature (·05 level). They also showed significantly greater need for security (·05 level) and for achievement (·005 level), and took more positive or socially approved actions to overcome threats to their needs (·001 level). Their stories had more satisfactory endings (·005 level).

In only one aspect were the results at variance with Hypothesis 1.

No statistical evidence was found for the existence of a greater load of personal guilt in the accident involved children. The sum of scores was certainly in the predicted direction:

---

* In this context, it is interesting to note Anna Freud's (1952) comment that children who have built up strong defences against passive leanings oppose the enforced regression implied by physical illness, by becoming difficult, intractable patients. In this way they do not allow themselves to sink back into the helpless infant emotion.

Thesi Bergmann (1945), working in an orthopaedic ward, noted the rages and temper tantrums which appear in immobilised children when chance deprivations, outside the expected medical procedure, are added.

accident involved children appeared more guilty than the controls. But so much emphasis has been laid in the clinical literature on the accident as a form of propitiation or alleviation of guilt that this score seems surprisingly low.

One possible explanation is that the accident served as a form of propitiation, as clinically predicted, and that an overload of guilt was immediately removed from the child, and therefore at the time of the T.A.T. testing was not of great importance in the economy of the child's personality.

An alternative explanation is that guilt does not at any time play a major role in the personality structure of these children and that, whatever the motivation behind the accident, self-punishment is not a pre-eminent cause.

Two complete T.A.T. protocols are now given to illustrate the assertiveness to be found in the stories of the accident involved children. As described above most stories are hostile in tone and show a willingness on the part of the heroes to resort to violence to overcome threats to their needs. They show a very real fear of domination by other people, and a considerable sadness in the face of this domination.

The first protocol is that of James, the restless, inconsequential, eight-year-old, whose school behaviour was described earlier in this chapter. His stories appear to mirror the hostility and assertiveness shown in his behaviour. Later, Mary's protocol is given and mirrors very closely the depression and quiet desperation noted in her behaviour at school. There is also a considerable need for affection and understanding running through her stories.*

These protocols are very representative of those told by other accident children, and were selected as examples because they highlight the close link between the child's phantasy productions and his observed behaviour in school.

James who sustained four road accidents, told the following stories:

(2)† 'Once upon a time there was a man who was working in the

---

* It should be noted that not all the stories centre on the subject's need for assertion or approval, but the *preponderance* of these themes indicates their importance to the subject.

† The T.A.T. cards are numbered from one upwards; (bm) refers to their suitability for use with boys and men, (gf) with girls and women.

field, ploughing it up. The lady at the tree was watching him, and the girl was going to school. It was a hot day and the man worked from morning to night at the field, and at night he sat down in the field and read books, and at two o'clock he would go to bed and in the morning he would get out for work.'

(3) 'There was this boy, no, man, who said to another man "Let's be friends, and we will be pals and do robberies." But this night they went to this lad's house and they shot him, and he was lying on the chair, and they left the gun beside him. Next morning the mother found him and she called the police and they found the two men and hung them.'

(4) 'Once upon a time there was a man and he was working and one day when he was going home from work he went into a pub and got drunk and started a fight with another man and killed him, and he was going to kill another person but his wife stopped him, and the other man called the police and the police came and brought him away and put him into prison.'

(5) 'Once upon a time there was this woman and one morning she woke up and came into the kitchen, and she turned on the light and she watered her flowers, and at that minute the door opened and a man came in and killed her, and she was lying dead and they brought him into court and he was hung.'

(6bm) 'Once upon a time there was this man who was always shouting at his Granny, and this day he came in to say he was sorry, and his Granny was looking out of the window, and the man said he was sorry for shouting at her, and she said it was alright, and the man kissed his Granny.'

(7bm) 'Once upon a time there was these two men who said "Come on, we will rob the bank," and they said "All right", and they decided to rob the bank. They got their guns, and they went out this night and broke into the bank, and a policeman came to see what they were doing. They shot him and they ran off in a car, and the police were looking for the car, and they found it outside the door, and they went in and brought one of the men to Court and found him guilty, and he was the wrong man, and he got put in prison and hung, and then they found the two guilty ones and they got hung.'

(8bm) 'Once upon a time there was these two men and they were coming down the road, and they had a knife and a rifle, and they killed a man, and this wee lad saw them and rang for the police, and they got their rifle and shot at him, and shot at him, and the police heard the shots and ran after them and they couldn't find them. And they killed the two what was in the house for not letting them in, and they couldn't find them, and they escaped through and got into the country, and the police brought Alsatians with them to get them, and some of the policemen went on, and some stayed behind and grabbed them and bring them away and put them in prison.'

(10) 'This man and this woman is planning to get married, and he said "We shall get married on Sunday" and they got married on Sunday, so they did, and when they were coming out, they got shot, so they did, and his wife was there, and she proved him guilty, so he phoned for his solicitor and he said "Would you try and get me free?", and his solicitor said "I'll try my best"—so his solicitor went to the Court, and he went to the Court, so he did—and he tried his best to get him free, but he was finded guilty and he was hanged.'

(13b) 'There is a wee boy at the door of his house and he has no one to play with. They are all at school—he is waiting outside the school door for them to get out, and he is sitting down. The door is made of wood and it is dark inside and he is in his bare feet.'

(14) 'It is very dark in the room. There is a man waiting in a woman's room to kill her when she comes in. She is a policewoman, 'cause he does not like the police. He is looking out the window. He sees her coming up in her car. She is getting out of the car and she comes in to the hotel. She asks for her key to open her door, and she went in and he was going to kill her, and another policeman came in and stopped him, and he got brought to Court, and he got summonsed and his wife came to see him. "What did you try to do, Johnnie?" '

(16) 'There is a lady in the picture and there is bandits, and she is watching them, and they go into a cafe, and there is this blind man and he listens to them talking, and he goes to the police and they beat him up, and this lady sees them. She phones for an ambulance and they bring the lady to court, and two of the bandits are there, and one of the bandits wants his solicitor, and his solicitor comes to Court and tries to get him free, and the other man went to another country, and the police were after him too and he made a tree house up a tree—and one of the police caught him and he was brought back to London and they were both shot.'

(18) 'This man had been found killed 'cause someone had shot

him twice, and they had stole all his money and his wallet. His name was on the wallet, and the other two men shared the money between them, and they took the keys of the bank out of his pocket, and they broke into a gunshop and they stole guns, and they robbed the bank that night, and they got everybody and were looking for the man who done it. They searched everybody on boats and trains and the two men—one of them got on the train and one of them he went in where the parcels are, and there was a policeman and a dog waiting there, and they brought him back to prison. The other man hid in a graveyard, and he was hiding in where nobody could find him, and they asked the other man where was his hide-out, and he said he didn't know, and the CID officer—and the man said he did not know all the time. And they tried to find the other man but they couldn't find him, and they searched everywhere, but they could not find him. He got a whole lot of other friends and they both robbed the train, and some of them got caught, and some of them haven't been caught yet. They escaped to Mexico, and the one who planned it is not caught. He is hiding in the woods, and he is breaking into a whole lot of shops and bakeries and gun shops, and he had been killing a whole lot of policemen, and the reward is £500 for anybody who catched him. He had been killing everybody who is trying to stop him, and they caught him one day, and they put him in the electric chair.'

Mary, the thirteen-year-old who 'never goes out', told these stories:

(1) 'About a girl being very sad as though somebody was shouting at her, because she wasn't working properly. She's out in the wilderness.'

(3gf) 'A girl crying because she's locked in her room because she did something very wrong—she was working and she didn't do it properly—it was her wicked employer who locked her up.'

(4) 'It's a man and he's angry with someone and he wants to fight and there's his wife, and she's very sad for him, and she's trying to stop him, but he won't listen to her.'

(5) 'A girl coming into her room to find it upset. She feels someone has been burgling it and has stolen some of her things. She's very sad looking and she phones the police when she knows what is missing.'

(6) 'The girl is sitting in her room and a strange man comes in and

47

threatens her if she does not do what he says, and he tells her to kill somebody—a rich person—and steal their money, and bring it to him—and if she did not do it, he said he would kill her. The girl has a dream and she calls out what she has heard the man saying that day, and someone hears her, and they went to the police and as she's about to do what the man told her the police turn up.'

(7gf) 'It's a little girl with no parents—she's fretting and that is a nurse sitting beside her trying to comfort her—but she doesn't pay any attention and in the end she's adopted and becomes very happy.'

(8gf) 'It is a wife in the olden days. She's living in a very dirty house. She doesn't bother to clean it. She just sits there gazing out of the window—and her husband comes home. He beats her and yells at her for not getting the house tidy and his supper ready. He leaves her and she's on her own for the rest of her life.'

(9gf) 'It's a rich girl being taught private lessons, and she's with her teacher. She gazes out at the scene and decides to run away. She comes out of her room and jumps down into the sand. The muddy water and muddy sand, and her teacher comes down after her and tries to stop her, but it is no use. By the time the teacher gets down the girl is swept away in the sea, and her body is found a few weeks later.'

(10) 'Is that an old lady? It's an old lady and she's very sad. Her husband is trying to comfort her; he puts his arms around her and she puts her head on his shoulder and asks her what is bothering her, and she said her big cat she had for so many years had died and her husband told her not to worry that she could have another cat. So the next day her husband took her and brought her another kitten and she reared it till it was a big cat, just like her last one.'

(14) 'It's a burglar. He's breaking into a house. He puts his hand out and turns on the light. Unfortunately, there is a policeman hiding and can see him. The policeman waits until he gets in and then gets in after him. When the policeman seen him lifting something he was able to charge him with stealing and took him down to the police-station and charged him with stealing.'

(16) 'The baby in the picture is crying in the corner of a room—it is yelling but its father and mother can't hear it. They're gone out and left an old lady to sit with it but she is a little deaf and can't hear it crying. It's crying because it's hungry—it has to wait

48

till its mother comes in to make it a bottle. The old lady did not sit with the baby again.'

(18) 'An old lady who is very angry with her daughter for not helping with the washing up—the girl makes for the stairs but her mother pulls her back and swears she will beat her if she does it again. The girl does not disobey her mother again.'

Themes relating to parent-child relationships

A further analysis was made of the themes relating to parent-child interaction to be found in the T.A.T. protocols of the thirty-six children. Hypothesis 1 predicted that accident involved children would perceive their parents as significantly more threatening and unhelpful than would the controls.

Nine scoring categories were devised: one miscellaneous, and eight relating to parent-child interaction: parent helps child, parent punishes child, parent worries over child's health, parent worries over child's behaviour, child helps parents, child fears parental separation, child fears parent's illness/death, child wants to escape but fears.

Differences between the two groups of children were compared for each of the nine categories, using a one-tailed Wilcoxon Matched-Pairs, Signed Ranks Test.

From the results it appears that Hypothesis 1 is substantiated. Significantly more of the accident involved children saw their parents as punitive (·05 level), whilst significantly more of the controls saw their parents as helpful (·05 level).

Whilst no significant differences exist between the groups for the other six characteristics, a non-statistical comparison of the sum of scores for the two groups suggests a further substantiation of the hypothesis. Controls told more stories in which the child helped the parent, whilst accident involved children told twice as many stories in which the child feared parental separation, parental illness, or death, or wished to escape from the parents. The greater preponderance of such themes is a further suggestion that the child feels insecure in his relationship with his parents, and may see escape as the solution to his problems. The greater preponderance of themes relating to fear of parental illness and death amongst the accident involved children might be interpreted by the analysts as the child's unconscious need to defend himself against his hostile intentions towards his parents. The child denies his wishes, and fears their end result. An alternative explanation is that the preponderance of these themes may represent a very realistic fear of parental ill-health or death on the child's part.

The following are typical of many stories concerning parent-child interaction, which were told. The first story is told by Maurice (S.18) who had already sustained one road accident, and several minor accidents before going to hospital at the time of the study.

> Maybe a wee boy and he's had an argument with his mother, and he's sitting thinking, and he's sorry he done it, and he's wondering if he should go back and say sorry—might have been arguing about his dinner. He didn't like it and his mother said he had to take it, and he ran out and now he's sorry.'

The following is a story told by Michael (S.19), a thirteen-year-old boy who had ridden into the back of a bus, whilst crouched over the handlebars of his bike:

> 'Looks as if his mother and father have hit him or else he's asleep. Can't see his face, his expression. Maybe he was playing with scissors, cutting something up. He feels in a huff going to bed—very angry—won't speak to whoever hit him.'

Peter (S.4) told the following three stories. His father had left home five years before, and on the day of the accident his mother returned to work after a month's absence in hospital. His stories clearly reflect his unhappiness in parental relationships.

> 'He's sad. He's sitting down. He has his arm on a stool and he's sitting on his foot, and he's got his knee crossed and he's got a gun. He's hiding his face, and he's black hair. Perhaps his mother is dead. I think his mother must be dead or he shot her. He's going to stop crying.'

> (8bm) 'They're going to kill a man with a knife and it's the boy's father and the boy looks as if he wants him killed, and the big thing is sticking up and he's got a tie and shoulders and eyes, and a mouth, and black eyes, and there are four windows. I think the boy's father was bad to him.'

> (12) 'A wee boy and he's sitting down on the doorstep, and the

door's opened and he's in the dark and he's sitting on his bare feet and he has his thumb in his mouth. He's thinking about his Mammy or else his Daddy is dead—or he didn't want to go to bed—or his Mammy is in hospital and he doesn't want to go up and see her.'

Finally, a story told by S.20, a girl of thirteen who resented her small brother and her mother's attachment to him. At the time of the accident she screamed for her father and refused to allow anyone to tell her mother:

'I wouldn't know in what way to start that one off. Is that her mother there? and looks as if she's not speaking to her, and her mother is sucking up to her and she's trying sucking up with her doll and trying to get round her, and I think in the end that she could. Maybe her father is ill and she is wishing that he would be there.'

Problem behaviour and areas of parent-child conflict, as reported by the mother

At the outset of the investigation, it was predicted that accident involved children would display a consistent pattern of anxious behaviour as seen by their mothers, before the accident. It was suggested that anxiety-reflecting behaviour of this kind might take the form of night terrors, fears, jealousies (of both siblings and father) and emotional problems. This pattern would not only reflect the child's general insecurity, but present specific areas in which child and parent might conflict, further accentuating the child's anxiety and feelings of being unloved.

Material used in testing this area of Hypothesis 1 was derived from the interview questionnaire used by the author when talking to the child's mother. Twelve questions were considered to be relevant to the testing of Hypothesis 1. They are the questions:

Did you have any special problems in his first year?
Did you have any major problems in his second year?
What was his immediate reaction to the next baby?
Did he change in his attitude to you or the baby later?
Does he like his brothers and sisters?
Does he show any special jealousy?
Is he ever jealous of your husband?
Do you have any problems with him now?

Did he ever have any nightmares as a small child?
Does he ever have any nightmares now?
Was he afraid of anything as a small child?
Is he afraid of anything now?

Differences in patterns of response between the groups for each question were compared using the Sign Test. Only three questions yielded significant differences between groups. Significantly more accident involved children were described by their mothers as having problems during their first year of life (·035 level), during the second year of life (·006 level), and being problematic at the time of the study (·059 level).

A rather crude total anxiety/problematic behaviour score was derived for each child by adding the number of responses indicative of deviant development, and a comparison of the total anxiety/problematic behaviour scores for the two groups was then made, using the Wilcoxon Matched Pairs Signed Ranks Test (one-tailed). A difference significant at the ·01 level was obtained, suggesting that the accident involved children as compared with the controls were thought by their mothers to show more problem behaviour at home.

But whilst the accident involved children appeared to be more problematic than control children, they did not appear to be over anxious. This fact, arising from the questions relating to rivalry amongst brothers and sisters, night-terrors and fears, suggests that, whilst overall accident involved children are more disturbed in their behaviour than control children, they are not essentially 'disturbed children'.

The considerable significance of the difference in the three questions relating to problem behaviour during infancy, the two-year-old stage, and at the time of the testing, appeared interesting, and prompted further investigation. A statistical analysis was made of the responses to each question, using the Sign Test. It appeared that the most frequently reported problem during infancy was the poor sleep pattern of the child (significant at ·035 level). Excessive crying and apathetic feeding were also noted. Problem behaviour at age two took the form of excessive temper tantrums, roaming or wandering, excessive crying, devilish tricks or excessive fighting, poor sleep patterns, rocking and convulsions.

At the time of the study the most significantly different (·008 level) type of problem behaviour reported was impatience, excessively demanding behaviour, and temper tantrums.

All of these behaviours might result from a thwarted need for assertion, and they might be produced as a defence against the postulated punitive handling of the accident involved mother. Equally the results, taken in conjunction with the significantly high scores made by these children on the inconsequential scale of the Bristol Social Adjustment Guide, are consistent with the idea that the problem behaviour may be exaggerated by some degree of minimal brain damage sustained during pregnancy or birth. It is probable that both perceived maternal rejection and neural vulnerability tend to exaggerate a child's normal strivings for independence.

Case histories indicative of the child's problem behaviour at home are given in the next chapter (p. 64).

The child's difficulties in this area appear to be so dependent on the mother's own negative attitudes, that examples of them seem only appropriate after these attitudes have been discussed. Mother and child seem linked in a spiral of unsatisfactory relationships—the child behaving much as the mother expects him to—his lack of co-operation mirroring her own rejection, and providing him with a defence against his own apparent unwantedness.

CHAPTER VI

The Personality Needs of Mothers of Accident Involved Children

The second hypothesis was concerned with the personality needs of the mothers of accident involved children. The initial assumption was that, compared with the mothers of control group children, they would appear significantly more dominant, punitive and repressive.

The testing of this hypothesis proceeded in three stages. First, a comparison was made of the T.A.T. themes produced by the two groups of mothers, in response to twelve pictures from Murray's standard set. Secondly, mothers were asked to complete the Parent Attitude Research Instrument, and a comparison was made of the responses of the two groups to twenty pathogenic sub-scales of this test. Finally, a comparison was made of the answers to questions about intial attitude to pregnancy, pregnancy stress, and birth trauma, contained in the questionnaire, and responded to individually by each mother.

Underlying personality needs, threats and emotions

The prediction was made that compared with control mothers, the mothers of accident involved children would be more dominant, punitive and repressive. These personality character- istics were expected to show in significantly higher scores on the Need for Assertion, and the Need for Punishing the Evildoer scales of the T.A.T. These needs were thought to arise from unresolved dependency needs,* and consequently the mothers of accident involved children were expected to score signi-

---

* That is, unsatisfied needs on the mother's own part to gain acceptance as an independent person.

ficantly more highly on the fear of domination and the fear of rejection scores, obtained from the T.A.T.

Subjects

The mothers of the twenty accident involved children were approached and I told them I was doing a survey of some of the children admitted to hospital, and would appreciate the opportunity to talk about their children as babies and learn something about their attitude to bringing up children. The questionnaire material was discussed first, the Parent Attitude Research Instrument was then read to the mothers, and the T.A.T. material was given last. It was introduced by saying:

'I have already shown some of these pictures to (name of child). He may have told you that I asked him to make up some stories for me about the people in the picture. I would like you to do the same.' Then standard instructions for the administration of the T.A.T. to adults were given.

The only difference in approach to control mothers—the mothers of the children selected by the Head Teachers as controls—was that they were told that the study related to the effects of hospital experience on young children and that their children were selected as not having had hospital experience due to an accident. I stressed the need to see both the mothers of the children admitted to hospital, and the mothers of those children who were more fortunate before suitable comparisons could be made. No refusals occurred.

Testing

All testing was carried out in the mother's own home, when the mother was alone, and at a time when there was least chance of outside interference. By starting with the questionnaire material, and then proceeding by the P.A.R.I., to the T.A.T. pictures, it was hoped first to focus the mother's attention on the individual child, and then, when the mother had relaxed, to extend the scope of the inquiry. Mothers were encouraged to ask questions about the materials used, and to discuss any of their child's attributes and behaviours at any point during the interview. A small minority were seen twice, for interviews lasting

E   55

approximately one hour each, but most mothers were seen once, in an interview lasting one and a half to two and a half hours.

Results

Twelve T.A.T. cards were shown to each mother, and the protocols produced were analysed by a slightly modified form of the Cox and Sargent method (Burton 1964). The differences between groups for each item were analysed statistically, using a one-tailed Wilcoxon Matched-Pairs Signed Ranks Test.

The results suggested that the mothers of accident involved children showed a greater neeed for assertion than the control mothers (difference significant at the ·001 level). In tone their stories were more often negative (·05 level) and concerned with conflict (·05 level), and they resorted more frequently to negative or anti-social action to overcome threats to their needs (·05 level).

Control mothers by contrast showed a significantly greater need for achievement (·025 level). A non-statistical scrutiny of the sum of scores suggested that more frequently their stories were purposeful in nature and they showed a greater need for affection than the accident mothers.

No significant differences existed between the groups for the need to punish the evil-doer, the threat of domination, and the threat of rejection, and this aspect of Hypothesis 2 was rejected in this study. Mothers of accident involved children, whilst significantly more assertive, did not appear to be over-involved with threats of domination, fears of rejection (suggestive of infantile conflict) or the need to conform to socially acceptable standards. This appeared to negate the original assumption that an unresolved need for dependency might be at the root of their assertiveness. In contrast to the mothers of asthmatic children described in the third section of this book no narcissistic moulding of the child seemed apparent.

The following are stories illustrative of the assertiveness and conflict to be found in the themes of the mothers of accident involved children. The first five stories were recounted by the mother of S.18 the 'miracle boy', one of whose T.A.T. stories was given in the last chapter:

56

(3) 'She's crying—I don't know. It could be a result of her having an argument with someone, and he has probably hit her and pushed her down. She looks as if she doesn't care whether she will get up again or not.'

(4) 'This is nice isn't it. She's pleading with him for something he doesn't agree with, and she's trying to get round him, and she's that appealing look in her eye—begging him and he doesn't know what to do.'

(7gf) 'Oh dear! Mother and daughter. She's trying to help her and for some reason she doesn't want to listen to her—trying to give her advice—or could be her grandmother and she's advising her—and she's turned away as if to say "I know what I'm doing". '

(9gf) 'Mother and daughter again, and mother seems to be going to stop her doing something—she is trying to do something—like running away—but the mother is trying to help her and she doesn't want it—she just wants to get away.'

(18) 'Well this picture is as if she has no love for her, as if she could just strangle her—you just get to that stage—as if you could see them far enough. She looks as I feel at times—dead tired. Still the love's in her eyes—but she's very weary looking—as if to say "you could pack it all in and run".'

This story prompted a discussion on how Mrs. C. could escape from her home. She said her husband was weak and drunk and no good, but whilst her family said she should leave him nobody would take her in if she did. 'They wouldn't give me a shilling if I left him'. A considerable amount of her assertiveness was probably due to her domestic stress. Loving her children and demonstrating this love must have been almost impossible in such personally frustrating circumstances.)

The following are two stories by the mother of James, the eight-year-old accident repeater, whose T.A.T. protocols have already been given in the last chapter. The second story suggests a real motive for James' accident involvement, frustration at endless parental restraint.

(4) 'See, he wants to leave her, and she telling him not to—pulling him back—he wants to do something and she's telling him not to.'

(16) 'I'm always thinking of the children—in case they get knocked down. That's why I keep them in so much. James was always kept in, and when he got out he kept getting knocked over —that's why I let him out now.'

The mother of S.20 told the following two stories. They also prompted a discussion of her own relationship with her parents which was bad. She appeared to have little sensibility of her daughter's needs and did not even recognise the girl's resentment of her younger brother.

(2gf) 'Ruth and Naomi there—this girl has walked away from a quarrel and the mother has given her opinion and the daughter doesn't approve and she's walking away—perhaps to leave home —and the father is getting on with his work—not taking part.'

(4gf) 'This is someone who wants to have her own way about something—she's trying to get round him and she's being refused—just like me—to get a big stubborn man—I'd close my fist and let him have it!'

Two stories told by the mother of Mary, the thirteen-year-old whose own T.A.T. protocol was given earlier, give some indication of the difficulties involved in caring for her daughter. Not only is the girl's own moodiness a perpetual threat to peace but also the mother's own fatigue prevents her from coping adequately.

(3) 'Like Mary, when she goes into a tantrum—she's the only one of the nine you have to be so careful about what you say. She goes and bangs the door, and rushes off, and then she's crying. She always does it—I tell her it's because she was wrong. And she doesn't want any one intruding into her piece of life—no one to annoy her.'

(5) 'A mother going into a room to see if everything is in order and if everything is thrown round everywhere and mother will say "What did I tell you. I'm only after tidying it, and it only lasted half an hour"—but I'm passed doing that now. Looks very tired-looking in face—must have been working awful hard and then it makes you cross.'

Finally, Peter's mother (S.4) told the following stories. Married relatively late in life, her husband left when Peter was three years old. She had indifferent health, and lived with her own rather dominant mother. A small autocratic woman, the stories reflect her own tension and conflict.

(2gf) 'This girl wants to be off—she's unhappy here. She wants to get away. Those people don't want her. I think she'll go.'

(3) 'This girl is in despair. She's had a row with her mother. She's been out late. And she's been turned out. I think she'll run away. Nobody wants her there.'

(4) 'This man wants his freedom. He's fed up with this woman. He wants to be on his way. She's clinging onto him. Pleading with him to stay.'

(6) 'These two are having an argument. He wants her to do something and she won't. She's standing up for herself. She won't be bullied into anything.'

(7) 'This little girl wants to go out, and her mother is making her sit and listen to a story. I think that's cruel—children ought to think of stories as treats not punishments.'

(9) 'These two are fighting—the one here is running off—she wants to get away from the other girl. This one is watching to see where she goes—then she'll follow and it will start all over again.'

(14) 'He wants to escape. He's been locked in and he's trying to get out, through the window. I expect they'll hear him and he'll be caught again.'

A Comparison of the Parent Attitude Research Instrument scores

Because of the postulated dominance, punitiveness and repression of mothers of accident involved children, it was expected that they would score significantly more highly on the twenty sub-scales of the P.A.R.I. measuring psychologically damaging attitudes to child upbringing. Especially significant would be the differences on the scales relating to the suppression of aggression, suppression of sex, strictness, breaking the will, and ascendancy of the mother. Hypothesis 2 predicted that this assertiveness was produced by the mother's own unresolved dependency needs and a correspondingly high score on the 'dependency of mother' and 'fostering dependency' scales was postulated.

No difference between groups was expected on the three sub-scales considered by Schaefer and Bell to represent socially approved child rearing attitudes. These are included in the P.A.R.I. for 'padding'.

All mothers were required to select the most suitable response for each item from four categories: definitely agree, mildly agree, mildly disagree, definitely disagree. Scores were obtained for each mother, on each sub-scale, using the centroid values for each sub-scale produced by Schaefer and Bell. A statistical analysis of the differences between groups for each sub-scale was made using the Wilcoxon Matched-Pairs Signed Ranks Test (one-tailed).

As predicted no significant differences were obtained for the three sub-scales measuring psychologically healthy attitudes to child upbringing.

Of the remaining twenty sub-scales, measuring psychologically damaging attitudes to child upbringing, sixteen were found to yield statistically significant differences in the predicted direction. They were:

			level of significance
Sub-scale	6	Fear of harming the baby	·001
	15	Approval of activity	·001
	23	Dependency of mother	·001
	18	Suppression of sex	·005
	20	Intrusiveness	·005
	9	Irritability	·005
	10	Excluding outside influences	·005
	2	Fostering dependency	·005
	16	Avoidance of communication	·01
	22	Acceleration of development	·02
	5	Martyrdom	·025
	3	Seclusion of mother	·025
	11	Deification	·035
	19	Ascendancy of mother	·035
	8	Strictness	·05
	12	Suppression of aggression	·05

On only four sub-scales were no statistically significant differences found between the groups. They were:

Sub-scale	17	Inconsiderateness of husband
	7	Marital conflict
	13	Rejection of home-making role
	4	Breaking the will.

Only one result was completely contrary to expectation. That is, the non-significance of sub-scale 4 'breaking the will'. Substantiating the idea that the accident involved mothers were more punitive and assertive, however, were the scores obtained for accident mothers on sub-scales relating to strictness, irritability, deification, avoidance of communication and ascendancy of mother.

The postulated repression of sexual and aggressive urges was seen in the scores on the sub-scales relating to these topics. The idea that the mother's own assertiveness might be due in part to her own unresolved dependency needs, appeared to be substantiated by the high scores made on the sub-scales relating to fostering dependency, dependency of mother, martyrdom, seclusion of mother, and excluding outside influences.

The significantly high scores obtained by mothers of accident involved children on the sub-scales relating to fear of harming the baby, is suggestive both of maternal defence against the rejection of the infant, and a possible cause of the infant's behaviour. Ferreira (1960) using several sub-scales of the P.A.R.I., including this sub-scale, with a group of 163 mothers in the later stages of pregnancy found a significant correlation between high scores on this particular scale prior to birth, and subsequent infant colic. Wilson Quentin (1960) also noted a similar pattern of P.A.R.I. scores for 'Anxious Mothers'.

An infant who had been upset by either pregnancy stress or inconsiderate handling must have been troubled further by the mother's behaviour which mirrors the sub-scales relating to approval of activity, and to acceleration of development.

The picture which emerges from an analysis of these sub-scales is one of an initially rejecting mother, to some extent unsure of her feminine role. This type of mother compensated for her insecurity by maintaining a rigid, unremitting, irritable ascendancy in the family, repressing all urges which might threaten her defences, excluding all outside influences which might threaten her supremacy, vigilantly watching over her children's lives and thoughts, and encouraging her already hyperactive children into still more activity. It seems little wonder that the children of these mothers were seen as inconsequential and restless in school.

Initial attitude to pregnancy and infant handling

The prediction was made in Hypothesis 2 that compared with control mothers, the mothers of accident involved children would have resorted significantly more often to a rigid pattern of early infant handling. To test this hypothesis, nine questions in the questionnaire were taken as indices of rejecting or deviant behaviour on the mothers' part (for a note on the reasons for selecting these items see Appendix 1). These questions were:

Question 4. 'Did you have an easy pregnancy?' 'No' answers were rated as deviant. Accident involved mothers scored significantly more highly (·055 level).

Question 5. 'How did you feel about conceiving (name)? Were you pleased? Or was he un-planned?' 'Un-planned' responses were rated as deviant. Accident involved mothers scored significantly more highly (·005 level).

Question 7. 'Were you at all emotionally upset during your pregnancy?' 'Yes' answers were rated as deviant. Accident involved mothers scored significantly more highly (·035 level).

Question 8/9. 'A combination of Question 8—'How did you find your delivery?' 'Non-normal' answers being scored as deviant, and Question 9—'How long did your labour take?' 'Twenty-four hours or over' were deemed deviant. There was no significant difference between the two groups, for this item.

Question 13. 'Were you at all nervous at the thought of having to care for (name) alone, or did you like the idea?' 'Nervous' answers were scored as deviant. No significant difference existed between groups for this item.

Question 14/19. A combination of Question 14—'How did you feed him?' and Question 19—'Did you enjoy feeding (name) yourself?' No breast-feeding after two weeks of age or dislike of breast-feeding where it was established were rated as deviant answers. No significant difference existed between groups for this question.

Question 17. 'Did you demand feed or keep to a regular schedule?' 'Regular schedule' was considered to be deviant. There was no significant difference between groups for this item.

Question 18. 'Did you have any feeding problem whilst (name) was a baby?' 'Yes' answers were scored as deviant. Accident involved mothers scored significantly more deviant responses on this item (·035 level).

Question 24. 'Did you have any special problems in his first year, e.g. sleeping?' 'Yes' answers were scored as deviant. Accident involved mothers again scored as more deviant (·035 level).

Responses to all these questions were compared statistically by using the Sign Test. Four of the questions yielded statistically significant differences in the predicted direction. Only one question, 14/19, yielded results not as predicted. As a group, mothers of accident involved children tended to breast-feed longer and had as much satisfaction from feeding as did the control mothers.

From a scrutiny of the additional information supplied by the two groups of mothers concerning these questions it was obvious that accident involved children's mothers had a significantly more stressful pregnancy.* These mothers tended to be excessively sick or tired, and several sustained major operations or were suffering from chronic illness, e.g. tuberculosis or nervous illness, during pregnancy. As a group they were more fearful of having difficult births, and were generally nervous and emotional during pregnancy. More of their deliveries were reported to be difficult or instrumental, though the controls reported a greater number of long non-complicated labours. As a group, accident mothers showed a slightly greater tendency to regular schedule feeding, and they reported a significantly greater number of slow and withdrawn infant feeders. (This difference was significant at the ·008 level, using the Sign Test.) They also reported a greater number of children with sleeping problems. (The difference is significant at the ·035 level, using the Sign Test.)

Finally, an overall deviancy-rejection score for each mother was made by computing the number of deviant responses she had made to these nine questions. The overall scores for each

---

* As a group they reported significantly more symptoms indicative of physical distress (difference significant at the ·02 level, using the Wilcoxon Matched-Pairs Signed Ranks Test). In this they clearly resembled the mothers studied by Backett and Johnston, 1959.

group were then compared using a one-tailed Wilcoxon Matched-Pairs Signed Ranks Test. The difference between groups was significant at the ·01 level, suggesting that mothers of accident involved children were more rejecting in their initial attitude to pregnancy, suffered more stress whilst pregnant and experienced more conflict in subsequent infant handling.

Several short case histories are now given to illustrate this point. In each one of them can be seen a long history of unsatisfactory mother-child relationships. At the outset it would appear that pregnancy was unwelcome and difficult. This 'coloured' the mother's attitude to the baby, and possibly in reaction, the baby proved to be difficult to handle. His problem behaviour frequently increased his mother's initial dislike and far from being able to meet his needs realistically, she considered him more of a problem and treated him with increasing harshness. So, through the years, mother and child became locked in a spiral of unsatisfying interactions.

The first case history is that of Maurice, and his mother, Mrs C. Several of their T.A.T. stories have already been given and contained evidence of the maternal dominance, and also of the child's frustration in his parental relationships.

Maurice C. was thirteen years old at the time of the study and attended an intermediate school. He was described by his mother as a 'miracle boy' because he had wandered five miles from home at three years of age, broken both legs when he was knocked down by a van at eight years of age, and had fallen into a large river, whilst still unable to swim. Maurice was the first of three children conceived shortly after his parents' marriage. The pregnancy was not a desired one, and Mrs C. was worried throughout. She was living at home with her parents at the time and felt in the way. She quarrelled frequently with them, and also with her husband, whom she discovered to be an alcoholic. She became depressed by this and had a 'nervous illness' for which she was given sedatives. Her pregnancy with Maurice was the 'worst of the lot' and she was always in and out of hospital, first with a kidney infection, later with high blood pressure. She later commented 'I don't know how I stuck it. I swore there'd be no more'. Maurice was born

hree weeks before term, the labour being induced in hospital.
The birth took between eight and nine hours, and the baby's
weight was six pounds. Mrs C. was very ill afterwards, and was
advised by her specialist not to breast-feed. She liked the idea
of caring for Maurice herself, however, and experienced no
immediate problems in feeding. At first a regular feeding
routine was adhered to but later feeding was by demand.
Weaning began when Maurice was over a year, and was not
completed until he was over two years of age. Motor milestones
appeared normal, Maurice sat up unaided at six months, stood
up unaided at eleven months, and walked alone at a year.
Toilet training was begun at six to seven months, no punishment was given, and by eighteen months he was thought to be
'very clean'. The only problem during infancy was that
Maurice was 'cross and gurney. He cried all the time, and never
settled. The least noise disturbed him'. This restlessness and
bad temper existed throughout his childhood and was very
much in evidence at the time of the road accident.

From the time that he could walk 'you couldn't keep
Maurice in. He didn't like to be closed in. He liked to be out'.
He roamed far from home on numerous occasions and Mrs C.
spent a lot of time looking for him. This characteristic was still
apparent in his behaviour at the time of the study. Also apparent
from earliest infancy, and persistent until the time of the study
was a pattern of disturbed sleep. Maurice talked and shouted
about the day's events in his sleep; also from infancy he had
been demanding and temperamental. At the time of the study
his mother said: 'He shouts, he's temperamental and he's no
patience'.

Mrs C. herself was excessively stressed by her husband's
alcoholism: 'he neither works, nor nothing'. She managed on
National Assistance, and her small two-bedroomed terrace
house was warm, though not over clean. She admitted that she
was very tired with the effort of bringing up three sons more or
less on her own, and with the worry of wondering what her
husband might do next. She had many times thought of leaving
him, but whilst her family encouraged her in this notion, she
knew that none of them would take her in, if eventually she
left. She and her husband quarrelled frequently, but she tried
to do this when the children were not present. She said that

when Maurice could not get what he wanted from her he would go to his father 'who is softer with him'. She thought she was a bit over-strict, but her method of punishment suggested the reverse. 'I dive at him, but I miss him more times than I catch him.'

The second case history is that of S.10, an eleven-year-old boy called Rodney B. who met with his accident whilst out riding a bicycle. As mentioned in Chapter Five, Rodney was very distressed immediately before the accident by an emergency illness in the family. An uncle with whom he had lived since his father's death six months earlier, had been rushed into hospital with a coronary. The boy's father had died in this way and his father's death had been the 'end of the world to him'. Mrs B. came from a very different social group from Mrs C. Her husband had been a professional man and she herself was a highly qualified private secretary, with a responsible job.

Mrs B. told me that her pregnancy was definitely not planned. She was not long married and wanted a lot more gaiety before she started a family. She was 'dreadfully sick' throughout pregnancy, and was forced to lie down most of the time because she wanted to vomit as soon as she was up on her feet. Labour was very protracted. She was three days in the first stage, and was finally induced. The birth took place thirteen hours later and it was a high forceps delivery. Rodney weighed eight pounds six ounces, and Mrs B. tried to breast-feed. Rodney cried so much during the first week that she abandoned this method of feeding in place of a bottle. Weaning began 'very young, he was only a matter of weeks, I wanted him off the bottle as soon as he was able'. Rodney was completely off the bottle by six months, and the feeding schedule was regular throughout. Rodney cried every evening and was not picked up. He developed a habit of sucking, first his fingers, and later the blankets, and this habit persisted into later childhood. Toilet training began at birth, and Rodney was reported to be clean 'shortly after a year', and dry day and night at two years. Motor milestones were normal; he crawled and stood up unaided at eleven months, and walked alone at fourteen months. As soon as he was mobile he became 'a bit of a wanderer' and the gate had to be securely tied, and the garden fenced in.

No jealousy was reported when his younger brother was born, nor did Rodney appear to resent his father. On the contrary, he appeared to prefer him slightly to Mrs B., and consequently his father's death six months prior to the accident was 'the end of the world for him'.

Rodney had nightmares occasionally throughout childhood, and particularly around the seven- to eight-year-old phase, when his mother said she was too demanding with him. Mrs B. told the story of Rodney, aged three, who had picked up a number of 'dirty words' from a gang of workmen who were laying drains outside his house. When he repeated these words —which he considered very manly—he was smacked and forbidden to say them. Consequently, when asleep, he yelled the words for all to hear.

Throughout infancy and childhood Rodney was 'strong willed', and Mrs B. said that it was like 'dripping away at a stone' to get him to do something. A further problem she felt was his inability to make suitable friends. He would bring home children whom she considered far too tough and unmannerly. At the time of the study she said 'He is far too independent. He insists on making his own friends regardless of advice, and he resents guidance in this and any other matter'. Rodney also resented discipline and the term before his accident—his first term at boarding school—he 'went away perfectly happy, but after a month he resented the discipline, and was desperately homesick and wanted to come back'. The accident occurred only a few days before Rodney B. was due to return to school.

The final history is that of Peter N., an eight-year-old only child, who met with his accident on the day on which his mother returned to work following a month's absence due to illness. T.A.T. stories for Peter and Mrs N. have been given earlier.

Mrs N. had tuberculosis at the time when she conceived Peter. She was also thirty-six, and as he was her first baby she was naturally very worried in case anything might go wrong, either to herself or to the baby. She was pleased that she was pregnant, but during her pregnancy her already strained relations with her husband became even worse. On several occasions she had evidence of his infidelity, and twice, when he returned home drunk, he had tried to strangle her. She was confined a month prematurely and found the birth extremely difficult. It was a forceps delivery and she had no analgesic because of her T.B. Peter weighed five pounds four ounces at birth, and Mrs N. was worried at the thought of caring for him herself because he was so small. For a while he remained in the premature nursery and was put on to a bottle feed. He was demand fed, but would only take small feeds. Weaning was attempted early on, but Peter completely refused to relinquish the bottle and flatly refused to ingest any food offered to him on a spoon. This refusal persisted until he was well over three years of age, and all solids had to be fed through the bottle. Two problems were apparent from the outset. Peter was chronically constipated as a result of his poor feeding, and he slept for less than a half hour at a stretch. 'The least thing wakened him.' Toilet training was begun at eighteen months and Peter was clean and dry during the day at two years of age, and continent during the night by three years of age. His motor development was somewhat ahead of average, and he was able to walk alone at ten months. During early childhood he was particularly prone to temper tantrums, and was particularly malicious towards other children, always hitting them unawares. He was a very restless sleeper. At the time of the study Peter was still very prone to temper tantrums, and showed a complete refusal to do school work, which his mother attributed to 'laziness'. He was said to be very frightened of 'germs' settling on him, and Mrs N. said that in order to control his habit of picking at the wallpaper, she had told him that there were germs hiding behind it and if he was naughty they would pop out. Mrs N. also believed in corporal punishment and admitted that she smacked and sent him upstairs 'quite often', that is, 'certainly more than once a week'.

Mrs N. said that she had been separated from her husband for five years before Peter's accident. He never visited them, not even to see Peter, who had taken to saying 'He mustn't love me, he never comes to see me'. Even before her husband had left home, Peter had seen little of him, for he was a steel erector and his work took him all over the country.

At the time of the accident Mrs N. lived with her mother, who looked after Peter whilst she worked. Their relationship seemed to be moderately good, but Peter had developed a habit of clinging to men who came into the household, for example, male cousins and an uncle.

In these three case histories, typical of many, one can see maternal tension throughout the child's existence, and find substantial evidence to support the contention that accident involvement is part of a lengthy pattern of disturbed behaviour on the child's part, behaviour which in fact was directed towards wresting adequate attention and affection from the mother.

CHAPTER VII

The Relationships between Need for Assertion and Environmental Stress

The third and final hypothesis in this section is concerned with the relationships which exist between the child's need for assertion, his mother's initially non-accepting attitude, her need for assertion, and the environmental stress they have sustained.

Several predictions were inherent in this hypothesis and were tested separately.

First, the relationship between the mother's attitude of acceptance or rejection, and the child's need for assertion was investigated. The suggestion was made that the more rejecting mothers would have the more assertive children, the child's strong need for assertion resulting from his mother's rejection.

The testing of this assumption made use of the replies given by the accident group mothers to the questions which assessed rejection of pregnancy and harshness of early infant handling, mentioned in the previous chapter. The scores obtained from the T.A.T. protocols of eighteen accident involved children were also used. On the basis of these the children were divided into two groups. One group of ten children had mothers who had scored less than four 'rejecting' responses in the question-naire. The other group, eight children whose mothers were thought to be more rejecting in their initial attitude towards pregnancy, and had scored between five and seven 'rejecting' responses to the questionnaire material. The number of T.A.T. themes indicative of a need for assertion was then computed for each child, and the scores for the two groups were compared statistically using a Mann-Whitney one-tailed Test.

No significant difference was found to exist between the groups, suggesting that the accident involved child's need for assertion, as shown in his T.A.T. protocols, is not solely a function of his mother's initially rejecting attitude to pregnancy and subsequent difficulty in handling. This does not mean that sustained rejection does not cause assertiveness. The mother's initial rejection may well have been overcome in this instance by her subsequent acceptance of the maternal role, rejection as such never being perceived by the growing child. It does suggest however, that on the evidence of this study no consistent relationship existed between rejection of pregnancy, early difficulty in handling, and the child's later need for assertion.

Mother's need for assertion in relation to child's need for assertion

The second assumption to be tested was that accident involved children with less assertive mothers would themselves show less need for assertion, the need for assertion being innately acquired or learnt by the child from his mother.

The testing of this assumption utilised the 'need for assertion' scores derived from the T.A.T. protocols of both the accident involved children and their mothers. Two sets of child 'need for assertion' scores were constructed representing the scores of eight children whose mothers were least assertive (that is, they themselves had told no more than three stories indicative of a need for assertion in their T.A.T. protocols) and ten children whose mothers were considered most assertive (that is, they had told between four and seven stories indicative of a 'need for assertion' in their T.A.T. protocols). A statistical comparison was made between the two sets of children's 'need for assertion' scores, using a Mann-Whitney one-tailed Test.

No significant difference was found between the groups, suggesting that the child's need for assertion was not solely a reaction against the mother's domination, or an imitation of her own assertiveness.

The relationships between child's need for assertion and environmental trauma

The questionnaire concerning the child's development contained three questions concerning possibly traumatic family situations. They were asked whether there were any emotionally disturbing deaths in the family before the child's accident, whether the family had moved house, and if there had been periods of separation of the mother and child, particularly where the child was sent to a strange environment, such as a hospital. From answers to these questions, it was noted that more of the accident involved children had sustained emotionally disturbing deaths in the family (amongst others, two fathers and one baby sister),* than had control children. The difference was considered significant at ·046 level, using the Sign Test.

The information about mother-child separation showed no significant differences between the accident involved and control children, either in length, type, or time of separations.

Similarly, no significant difference was found in the number of accident involved children whose families had moved house or in the number of times they had moved although both these scores suggested that accident involved children had experienced greater environmental upsets of this sort.

A total 'environmental trauma score' was obtained for each child based on the number of times he had moved, the number of deaths described by the mother as emotionally disturbing, and whether he had spent more than one month (the mean length of absence for all accident involved children was four to five weeks) away from home up to the age of seven.

The 'need for assertion' scores of the seven children who were thought to have had least environmental trauma were then compared with the 'need for assertion' scores of all eleven children in whose backgrounds was most evidence of environmental trauma, on these three variables. A statistical comparison was made of the two sets of scores using a Mann-Whitney one-tailed Test.

No significant difference was found between the groups, suggesting that need for assertion was not dependent on the three types of environmental stress which were investigated in this hypothesis. Other sources of tension within the child's environment, if they were investigated, might well produce

---

* It is also possible that the parents' permanent separation may be viewed by the child in much the same way as death—thus possibly increasing the significance of this type of environmental trauma which the accident involved children had experienced.

more significant results, e.g. the mother's illness, or separation from the father, particularly if it was accompanied by a sense of guilt within the child because he supposed he was the cause of this occurrence.

At this juncture, it is interesting to refer back to the notes contained in Chapter Five relating to the details of each child's accident.

In ten out of the twenty cases an unsettling or unusual experience had taken place immediately before the accident, e.g. the accident occurring immediately after the child's hearing that his beloved uncle, with whom he lived, had to be rushed into hospital suffering from a coronary thrombosis. Only six months previously the boy's father had been taken to the same hospital suffering from the same disease, and had died. Further examples were the accident occurring on the mother's first day at a new job, which the child resented; the accident occurring immediately after the mother's return home with a new baby which the child actively disliked; and the accident occurring on the child's way back from the swings where the mother had expressly forbidden him to go.

In a further three cases the child had been in other road accidents, and in six of the twenty cases the mother either described herself as 'nervous/excitable' or admitted that she was under active treatment by a psychiatrist. On this variable there was a significant difference, at the ·o62 level, using the Sign Test, between subject and control group mothers.

These factors, whilst extremely suggestive of the reasons for accident involvement, are difficult to compare with each other and perhaps this explains why the cruder measures of separation, death, or removal bear no relationship to the assertiveness of the accident involved child.

The relationship between the child's 'need for assertion' and the general level of environmental frustration

Finally, two sets of child 'need for assertion' scores were constructed, one set for the children in whose background was least general frustration, and one set representing the scores of the twelve children in whose background was most general frustration. The frustration score was compounded from the mothers' rejection score, the mothers' assertiveness score, and th environmental trauma score (Burton 1964). The sets of scor were compared statistically using a one-tailed Mann-Whitne Test, and there was a difference between groups, significant the ·05 level.

This suggested that the degree of assertiveness of accider involved children was the result of stress felt by the mother an in the home generally. The child responded with greater asse tiveness where the general environment was most frustrating.

CHAPTER VIII

Discussion of Present Findings

From our information we may conclude that the accident involved children are more assertive and unsettled than a carefully matched group of control children. This unsettledness was manifested in infancy in poor sleep, excessive crying and apathetic feeding. Later, the accident involved child was described as having more temper tantrums, tending to roam or wander, crying excessively, sleeping badly and getting up to devilish tricks or fighting. At the time of the study the most significant problem behaviour reported at home was impatience, temper tantrums and inordinately demanding behaviour. At school the accident involved child tended to be significantly more restless, was more easily distracted and behaved inconsequentially. He sought attention more often, both from adults and other children, and showed a greater degree of hostility than the control children.

Behaviour showing anxiety, excessive guilt and fearfulness was not apparent in this group however, contrary to the clinical suggestions that accidents may represent 'attempts at suicide' (Klein) due to excessive guilt, and a fearful wish for self-punishment (Ackerman and Chidester, Menninger, Freud). Accident involved and control children reported an equal number of night terrors, fears and jealousies. A significantly greater number of the subject children were thought to dislike their brothers and sisters, but this dislike tended to take the form of 'always fighting', rather than apathetic envy. Accident involved children showed no marked preference for either parent, and, as a group, they tended neither to cling close to the mother, nor to show an inordinate need to escape from her. At school, by comparison with the control children, they were less withdrawn and significantly more forthcoming. In the T.A.T. themes for the two groups no evidence was found to suggest that the accident involved children were more over-burdened by guilt and fear than were the control children.*

Underlying this behaviour however, as predicted and found elsewhere (Dunbar, Fuller, Langford), was an unusual need for assertion, coupled with a significantly greater fear of domination. Considerable hostility was found in the T.A.T. stories of the accident involved children, both in their overall tone and in the negative activities engaged in by the phantasy heroes. Accident involved children were more inclined to perceive the environment as threatening, and to use evasive action to satisfy their needs. They expected 'modified failure' as a result of their struggles. By comparison the controls told significantly more stories with a happy and purposeful content, and showed a greater need for security and achievement. In addition, the controls tended to use more positive, socially approved action to overcome threats to their needs, and to expect their wishes to be successfully fulfilled.

In an analysis of T.A.T. themes relating to parent-child relationships, the accident involved children saw their parents as more punitive than did the controls, and told more stories relating to fear of parental separation or a denial of their own repressed hostility. They more frequently exhibited a wish to escape from the parent-child situation than did the controls, who by contrast, saw their parents as more helpful and showed a corresponding wish to help them.

The subject children's greater need for assertion, suggested by Dunbar as the basic cause of accident involvement, was seen in this study to relate to the general level of environmental frustration and stress. Children whose mothers were initially

* In this lack of guilt, the children closely resembled the accident involved child described by Beres (1952). He attributes this lack of guilt to in-adequate superego functioning, and comments 'Evidence of disturbed ego functioning were the demand for immediate gratification, the inability to postpone gratification, disregard of the demands of reality (though there was no disturbance of reality testing) and poor work at school. There was minimum evidence of superego activity in this boy, such as guilt, self-criticism, formulation of ideals and moral demands. The quality of this behaviour as it impressed the examiner, was its lack of goal directedness, its diffuse nature. The absence of guilt reactions, the purposelessness of the behaviour, suggested the activity of non-neutralised aggressive energy directed primarily against the self . . .'

most rejecting, subsequently most assertive and who were most subject to environmental stress, showed the greatest need for assertion. No simple relationship was found to exist solely between any one of these stressful variables and the need for assertion.

This finding suggests that the restless, unthinking, assertiveness of accident involved children is produced in response to a combination of maternal stress, rejection, excessive dominance, and unsettling environmental experiences.

Certainly considerable stress existed in the subject children's backgrounds. Significantly more of their mothers had rejected their pregnancy, and had been more frequently sick or emotionally disturbed during it. To some extent, all of these observed differences may have resulted from the fact that more of these mothers were suffering from a chronic—frequently, nervous—illness before the child's conception. The presence of this chronic illness might explain both the mother's very marked unwillingness to be pregnant and also her strong physical reaction to her pregnant condition. It might also explain the high scores made by these mothers on the P.A.R.I. sub-scales relating to 'dependency on mother'. For example, the frequently observed agreement to an item such as 'No woman can be expected to look after a baby alone', which scores very highly in this sub-scale, might be explained by illness, which rendered the woman unable to manage her household without a home help, or to do her shopping for fear of becoming dizzy or faint.

Similarly the mother's illness probably prevented her from assuming the principal role in the home, and possibly explains the greater part played in the home by accident children's fathers. In contrast to the controls, more fathers of accident children were reported as having the greater say in the child's activities. (This was particularly suggestive as at least four of the fathers of the accident involved children were dead, separated, or working away from home, as compared with only one control.) Fathers of accident children appeared to share equally with their wives the discipline of the child, decisions in the home and the child's affections; this suggests both a healthy willingness on the mother's part to share the responsibilities of bringing up the child, and that adds further weight to the idea of necessity—and despite a strong sub-cultural reverse trend

—the sick woman could not play the major role in her child's life.

The marital relationships of the subject child's parents appeared to be good. There was no difference between subject and control groups in their responses to the P.A.R.I. sub-scales relating to 'inconsiderateness of husband', 'marital conflict' and 'rejection of home-making role'. Similarly, few of these mothers had difficult births with the children being investigated, suggesting no real rejection of the feminine role.*

In addition, there was no significant difference between subject and control mothers on the questionnaire items relating to rigidity of infant handling. Indeed, accident mothers tended to breast-feed longer than control mothers, and showed slightly greater satisfaction from feeding.

The picture that emerged therefore from this study was one of a group of mothers whose pregnancy had been unwanted and stressful because of their own poor health or nervous disposition. No evidence was found to substantiate the idea that these mothers were immature or excessively dependent on their own mothers. Indeed, in the T.A.T. stories subject mothers did not differ from the controls in measures relating to fear of dominance or rejection, both of which might be thought to reflect maternal dependency conflicts.

Mothers of accident involved children were significantly more dominant—both in their T.A.T. stories and in their responses to the P.A.R.I. Clearly this dominance did not arise from maternal immaturity, or rejection of the feminine role. How then did it arise? One suggestion springs from the finding that the child's own assertiveness was a result of the general level of frustration in the home. Undoubtedly these mothers were under greater stress physically and mentally than were the controls. Perhaps their need for dominance arose from a reactive, but essentially realistic, need to compensate for their own inadequacy. A perusal of the questionnaire material suggested that over half of the accident involved mothers, at the time of the study, were coping with hardships due to widowhood, separation, or their own physical or mental

* Jones (1942) found that mothers who were neurotically unwilling to shoulder the responsibilities of womanhood had, in the main, more stressful and difficult labours than more mature mothers.

sickness.* Any assertive needs on the child's part, particularly the socially dangerous aggressive and sexual needs, might therefore be clamped down upon in order to maintain the shaky maternal *'status quo'*. The mother's excessive domination might therefore be a realistic reaction to stress, rather than a neurotic need to compensate for supposed personal inadequacy.

Extending this argument, and appraising the other significant scores made by subject mothers on the P.A.R.I., one might conclude that differences on the sub-scale relating to 'fear of harming a baby' and 'fostering dependency' reflected both a denial of initially hostile maternal feelings, and possibly a need to compensate for this original rejection. The greater scores on sub-scales relating to 'seclusion of mother' and 'excluding outside influences' might reflect the mother's inability to cope with situations and people outside the home. The high 'irritability' and 'martyrdom' scores might mirror a threshold to frustration lowered by the extreme stress of the environment.

No logical explanation can be offered for the significance of the 'approval of activity' and 'acceleration of development' scales, unless it be that the mother, feeling inadequate and vulnerable, wished her child, by way of compensation, to assert himself and mature as quickly as possible. As a group, accident involved children tended to crawl, stand up unaided, and walk, earlier than did the controls (Burton 1964). They also tended to respond to pot training at a slightly earlier age. This might reflect both the mother's more assertive attitude, and the higher need for assertion, and greater activity seen subsequently in these children.

Whilst the questionnaire suggested that in certain cases these mothers took a vindictive pleasure in disciplining their children, as a group they did not show up on the questionnaire as more punitive, or in the T.A.T. as having a significantly greater need for punishing the children.† They did however show

---

* In this, the group studied was closely akin to that observed by Backett and Johnston, 1959.

† In this the group was similar to that studied by Marcus in 1960. However, his group, by contrast, and as described in Chapter Four, was thought to be non-assertive. But it is possible that this conclusion was reached by comparing them with the parents of enuretics, who were described as being 'aggressively dominating and over-controlling'.

greater reliance on negative or anti-social behaviour to fulfil their needs, and the tone of their stories suggests more hostility or conflict.

How then do the facts observed in this study suggest modifications to the predictions based on clinical observations?

Firstly, the accident involvement of the children in this study does not seem to represent 'an indirect attempt at suicide' in the sense that some analysts use this expression (Freud, Klein, Menninger). These children do not seem to be burdened excessively with guilt, nor to use the accident as a means of expiation.

If, however, suicidal attempts are seen as a means of getting a greater amount of love (Bender and Schilder 1937, Despert 1951), then these accidents might well represent suicidal attempts. The scores obtained by subject children on the Bristol Social Adjustment Guide suggest considerable anxiety over being loved, and much of their behaviour at school suggested an ambivalence between searching for affection and strongly protesting against its unforthcomingness. From the high 'irritability' and dominance scores of their mothers, it seemed apparent that no real certainty could exist in the children's minds as to their being 'wanted'. From the questionnaire material relating to the details of home circumstances before the accident, it became obvious that many accidents were preceded by events which might well have directed the mother's attention away from the child, increasing his feeling of rejection. Undoubtedly, as a group, these children saw aggressive action as a means of satisfying their needs (comparable to the group studied by Birnbach 1948) and these accidents, involving aggression against themselves, might well represent attempts at wresting sympathy and the required love from the environment.

Unlike Freud therefore, who saw all masochistic behaviour as a response stemming from the primary unconscious need to punish the self for guilt aroused by forbidden impulses, this study agrees with Menaker (1953) in concluding 'that in masochism, the apparent goal of suffering is not the real goal but merely a way station to it . . .'

We might even go further and re-analyse the clinical examples of accident involvement due to guilt, presented by

Freud, Abraham and Klein, and suggest that behind all of them lurked a very real need for affection quite uncoupled with guilt, and an almost adaptive attempt at wresting this from a seemingly hostile environment.

This element of hostility, both in the environment, and within the individual, noted by Ackerman and Chidester (1936); Dunbar (1944); Birnbach (1948); Krall (1953); and Langford (1953) is further observed in this study. These children were aggressive and perceived their environment as hostile. Such aggressiveness, particularly if prevented from free expression, might be directed inwards, a 'trend commonly evident in small children' (Ackerman and Chidester 1936).

The accident would not only afford the child some release for these aggressive feelings, but also give him a real means of punishing those in the environment. By involvement in accidents, and subsequent injury, the child would add further stress to his mother, in a manner which was beyond her control or remonstration. In this way he might punish her quite directly for being unloving.

One might also see these accidents as did Dunbar (1944) as attempts at avoiding conflict or open hostility. In several instances the accident followed immediately upon the child's transgression of a parental command with consequent fear of reprisal. The accident might well then represent 'an avoiding of conflict—although not by submission'.

In almost all essential elements, the accident involved children in this study fit the clinical descriptions of the B-type accident prone adult diagnosed by Dunbar. The essential defences of this accident prone adult were:

(1) His focusing of values in immediate concrete experience. In this study this might be seen in the significantly high Inconsequential scores of these children on the Bristol Social Adjustment Guides.

(2) His striving to find satisfaction and security outside the authoritative hierarchy. In this study this was mirrored by the significantly high affection seeking scores on the Bristol Social Adjustment Guides.

(3) An avoidance of any marked submission or domination in vocational and social roles. This is perhaps apparent in our group in the significantly fewer symptoms of withdrawal

or unforthcomingness as compared with control children

Dunbar noted frequently a lack of planning and general irresponsibility (mirrored by the high restlessness and in consequential scores of our group on the Bristol Social Adjust ment Guide) and marked adventurous and anti-social trends (Our group showed considerable evidence of involvement in pranks and risky escapades in school, and some were described as 'wanderers' and 'fighters' at home.)

Much the same description of the accident-prone child wa given by Fuller (1948, 1951). As in our group, she saw these children as obstinate, disagreeable, impulsive, insensitive to social feelings, hyperkinetic, daredevil, insolent, assertive and with a slightly higher problem tendency. She also noted a tendency for the accident prone child to be more nervous and 'highly strung' than his controls. This might perhaps reflect an especially emotional mother, which was certainly observed in our study.

This element of constitutional predisposition to acciden involvement is suggested by Bender and Schilder's (1937 study of child suicides. They noted that the aggressive tendency observed in would-be suicides in childhood may be 'increased by constitutional factors, and identification with an aggressive parent, or other aggressive members of the family'.

The parents of these accident involved children were indeed dominant, hostile and irritable, severely stressed during pregnancy and undoubtedly surrounded by excessively stressful environments. By imitation, and constitutional inheritance these children might well have a significantly lowered threshold for frustration. With the possible exception of Marcus' study (1960) this constitutional element has been largely ignored in previous work, and appears particularly noteworthy in the present investigation.

As a group, the accident involved children showed considerable evidence of slight neural impairment, due most probably to the significantly high degree of maternal stress in the later stages of pregnancy. This stress supposedly produces excessive emotion, and this in turn is thought to cause secretions which produce an imbalance of chemical agents, which 'may cross the placenta and, though causing no microscopic abnormality may somehow affect those developing neural

tissues of the foetus which govern behaviour in later life'
(*British Medical Journal*, April 1964).

Dysfunction of the hypothalamus has been postulated as a
result of such chemical imbalance (Laufer, 1957) producing an
alteration of the resistance of the synapses, such that the child
responds in a gross way to relatively discrete stimuli. Any
normal tension encountered in infancy produces a response of
considerable urgency and the child may be unable to moderate
his behaviour. This might well explain the restlessness of these
children, both as infants and later, and their excessive activity
as small children.

Whilst many children outgrow this deviant pattern of
maturation (Caplan 1956 and Laufer 1957) in the course of
development, the emotionality, dominance and irritability
observed in the mothers of the accident involved children may
have aggravated the symptoms, producing the restlessness and
inconsequentiality seen later in school.

A further possibility is that the infant, receiving excessive
stimulation in its first months due to minimal brain damage of
this sort, may have acquired a need for such stimulation, and
the subsequent restlessness of his behaviour may reflect his own
strivings to achieve this, long after the postulated neural inco-
ordination disappeared. The accident involved child described
in this study crawled, stood, and walked earlier, slept less,
tended to roam more and became involved in more pranks,
fighting, and affection-seeking behaviour. It is very possible
that all these behaviours represented efforts to replace stimulation once received. The accident might then be seen as an
extension of the child's usual hyperactivity.

Any final assessment of accident involvement in children
must endeavour to combine all the facts. These children undoubtedly showed signs of a constitutional hyperactivity, and a
lowered vulnerability to stress. As a group, they were assertive
and hostile, in need of sympathy and affection, and aware of
their parents as punitive and unloving. Their environments
were particularly stressful. The accident might well represent
an attempt at gaining sympathy, or an effort to punish unloving parents. It might be an expression or extension of the
child's own frustration or a further example of the child's
inordinate need for stimulation.

Whatever the particular reasons in each individual case, one thing is certain, road accident involvement on the part of the child is rarely a chance occurrence. Almost inevitably there is a long previous history of environmental stress and frustration. Before the accident there may well be an event which is so disturbing to the child that it acts as a catalyst rendering imperative the discharge of existing tension. The child behaves impulsively in dangerous circumstances because either he is over-burdened with preoccupations of personal problems, or because unconsciously he wishes to assuage these and satisfy his deep-rooted personality needs.

Part Two

SEXUAL ASSAULT IN CHILDHOOD

CHAPTER IX

Introduction to the Problem of
Studying the Sexually Assaulted Child

The problem of assessing the degree of damage—physical and psychic—sustained by the child victim of a sexual assault is a problem which appears increasingly to occupy the time of the courts. Conclusions as to the degree of physical damage caused can generally be reached by a simple medical examination. An assessment of the psychological damage is not so easily obtained.

No simple tests are as yet to hand to assess how far-reaching, or short-lived, the results may be, and expert advice is rarely sought. Instead a highly subjective rating is made, usually in the Court itself.

Inevitably the picture presented by such a subjective assessment is the popularly accepted cliché of an innocent child harmed irreparably by the wayward behaviour of a mentally unbalanced adult. No account appears to be taken of the degree of co-operation given by the child to his adult seducer, nor of the effects of any such co-operation on his subsequent psychosexual development.

Legally, this picture of abused innocence is a satisfactory one. Man has a horror of imprecise limits (Lafon 1961) and the clear distinction made between attacker and victim enables the Court to attribute blame solely to the adult. Psychologically, such a clear distinction may also have advantages, at least, from the child's point of view. By implying that the child is quite guiltless, it allays parental hostility, and does much to decrease the child's anxiety in the situation.

Ethically, the adult is at fault in abusing the child's youth and lack of moral judgment, and frequently children are involved in sexual episodes quite unwittingly and without any premeditation on their part; but a clear distinction between attacker and victim seems rarely possible.

The consensuality found in many sexual assault cases has long been recognised (von Hontig 1941; Lafon 1961), and the fact that the courts ignore this element of mutuality belittles justice, and renders impossible a true understanding of the personality dynamics underlying this behaviour. Hartogs (1951) has observed this: 'Without exception, sex offenders were affection starved youngsters in their childhood'. Many studies of the child victims of such offenders have suggested that they also share these deprivations of affection. Many such children, in search of substitute affection, unconsciously provoke attacks by befriending strangers, or by returning again and again to the house of an adult from whom they have received some form of sexual stimulation.

As Reifen (1958) observed:

> ... sexual play, at pre-puberty and puberty age, particularly if not involving genuine sexual intercourse, is a source of attraction and satisfaction to many. For these reasons child victims of sexual offences often continue to participate and influence their friends to do likewise.

Reifen notes that many offenders are supplied with victims with no exertion on their own part, and yet the children involved can certainly not be regarded as 'moral defectives'.

How then can such participation be viewed—whether active or passive? From the clinical material, and from the results of the empirical investigations into the personality needs of sexually assaulted children, (below p. 114), it appears to us that underlying such behaviour is a strong need for affection, caused by real or imagined rejection by the parents. What on the surface appears to be an example of aberrant sexual acting out, may then be thought of as a means of wresting the satisfactions necessary for personality growth from an indifferent environment.

Clearly, retrospective studies can never prove that affection seeking needs precipitated the child into the sexual affair—such affection seeking might have arisen subsequently from the child's fright and confusion at his premature sexual involvement. But the recognition of such needs—where they exist following the attack—and an attempt by persons in the environment to meet them, might offset any further personality difficulties on the child's part.

For many children the legal proceedings involved in the committal of the offender may have a singularly traumatic effect. Coming as they do months after the actual offence, and frequently involving the child in giving evidence and being subjected to cross examination, they may seem more frightening to the child than the experience itself: As Reifen (1958) has observed: 'Sometimes, it is only the Court appearance and cross-examination which make him realise that he was the victim of a sexual offence'.

This study therefore is an attempt to investigate the subsequent personality development of a group of sexually assaulted children—most of whom had to assist in Court proceedings against their attackers. As in the other two sections of this book, care has been taken to match the subject children to a group of carefully chosen control children, in order to ascertain that the conclusions reached are applicable only to the children with aberrant sexual experience and not to all children of the same age, sex and level of intelligence.

The structure of this section of the book is, therefore, comparable to that of the other two sections. First, we present a summary of the relevant psycho-analytic literature from which several simple hypotheses are derived. Then follows an account of such empirical work as has been done to date on the problems of the subsequent personality development of sexually assaulted children. Finally follows an account of the present experimental study, together with a discussion of the results obtained.

CHAPTER X

Previous Discussion of the Problem

Freud first stated categorically that sexual seduction in infancy would lead to the development of a neurotic personality. In the fourth of his papers, published in French, and appearing in the *Revue Neurologique* (1896) he stated that the cause of hysteria is a passive sexual experience before puberty, that is, a traumatic seduction. This contention was based on the analyses of *thirteen* neurotic adult patients. The age at which such a seduction would have the most disruptive effect was thought to be between three and four; seductions occurring after the age of eight or ten were not thought to lead to a neurosis. Freud believed that one of the essential differences between the psychoneurosis and the obsessional neurosis was that in the former the seduction was undergone with indifference, or perhaps with some degree of disgust or fright, whereas in the latter the sexual experience was pleasurable, actively aggressive, and frequently preceded by a more passive seduction. Seduction in this sense consisted of actual excitation of the genital organs, and not of masturbation by the child itself.

Within two years however Freud's growing realisation that in the unconscious there is no criterion of reality—truth cannot be distinguished from emotional fiction—led him to modify the theory. Actual seduction as a cause of neurosis became secondary to phantasy seduction. As he later wrote:

> The analytic researches carried out by the writer fell to begin with, into the error of greatly overestimating the importance of seduction as a source of sexual manifestations in children and as a root for the formation of neurotic symptoms. This misapprehension was corrected when it was possible to appreciate the extraordinarily large part played in the mental life of neurotics by the activities of phantasy which clearly carried more weight in neurosis than did the external world. (1922)

His modification of the theory of neurosis did not, however, prevent Freud from emphasising repeatedly the importance of infantile sexual life to subsequent sexual development. After a careful investigation of the psycho-sexual development of his patients he postulated a diphasic theory of sexual development. The widespread sexual sensations present at birth become localised at the three erotogenic areas of the body—mouth, anus and genital—but are repressed as a result of fear of castration in boys, and a result of parental inability to provide 'love' (penis, or baby) in girls. The child is then in a sexually quiescent or latency stage, and only emerges to full awareness of sexuality at puberty.

Complete latency was regarded by Freud as a theoretical extreme or:

> From time to time a fragmentary manifestation of sexuality which had evaded sublimation may break through; or some sexual activity may persist through the whole duration of the latency period until the sexual instinct emerges with greater intensity at puberty. (1905)

Freud emphasised two points which appear particularly relevant to our study:

(1) All children experience sensations of sexuality from the outset. 'Only very few children would seem to escape some kind of sexual activity and sexual experiences before puberty' (1907), and sexual phantasies and longings are certainly part of the mental life of most children. 'It is my conviction that no child —none, at least who is mentally sound, still less one who is mentally gifted, can avoid being occupied with sexual problems in the years before puberty.' (1908)

(2) Specific sexual experiences will modify later sexual development but will be of less influence than the extensive phantasy productions in which some children indulge. Freud's final conclusion on the significance of actual sexual seduction was contained in his article on female sexuality published in 1931.

> Seduction may have the effect of hastening and stimulating to maturity the sexual development of children, and it is quite possible that other factors operate in the same way; such, for instance, as the child's age when brothers and sisters are born or

when it discovers the difference between the sexes, or again, its direct observations of sexual intercourse, its parent's behaviour in evoking or repelling its love, and so forth.

Clearly, the effect of sexual seduction in childhood is a vague and unspecific one, and to be thought of as no more traumatic than many childhood experiences. This view was shared by Abraham (1907) who maintained that: 'Infantile sexual traumas are brought about by an unconscious wish on the part of the child'.

He noted that the majority of children could escape from the sexual situation if they wished, and maintained that the silence shown by some children following seduction could be explained in terms of their own feeling of guilt in yielding to a forbidden attraction.

An extension of Freud's theories of infantile sexuality, particularly those concerned with the explanation of female sexuality, was made by Melanie Klein (1932). Unlike Freud, Klein did not see the girl child's turning from unsatisfying mother to equally unsatisfying father as a passive occurrence. Her supposed awareness of her parents' sexual relationship with one another and her own inability to possess her father's penis resulted in extreme feelings of hatred and resentment. The child consequently experienced sadistic phantasies of attacking and destroying her mother's inside and depriving it of its contents. Owing to the fear of retaliation, such phantasies quickly become the basis for the deepest anxieties. The child fears retaliatory attacks on her own body, called 'aphanisis', or destruction of capacity to obtain libidinal gratification. Some of this fear of the mother may transfer to the non-satisfying penis itself which then becomes a 'bad penis' with accompanying sadistic phantasies.

A conflict exists in the child between its conception of its parents as 'good' and 'bad' objects; and to maintain a satisfactory balance—that is a preponderance of 'good' images—the child must be receiving some parental satisfaction for its non-sexual needs.

A further result of this ambivalence, in Klein's estimation, is that the girl will strive to counteract her fear of the 'bad' or sadistic penis by introducing a 'good' one in coitus. In other words, the child will test out in reality her own phantasy pre-conceptions. This in Klein's opinion, 'will be a further incentive to her to undergo sexual experience in early childhood and to indulge in sexual activities in later life, and will add to her libidinal desires for a penis'.

One way in which the child may ascertain whether her fears are well grounded or not is by having sexual relations with a brother, which Klein believes to be a frequent occurrence. Relationships of this kind also gratify the child's libidinal cravings, intensified as they are by oedipal frustrations, and enables the child to alleviate some of its anxiety.

Klein notes:

> I have repeatedly found that if such sexual objects have acted in addition as helping figures, early sexual relations of this kind exert a favourable influence upon the child's relations to her objects and upon her later sexual development. Where an excessive fear of both parents, together with certain external factors, would have produced an Oedipus situation which would have prejudiced her attitude towards the opposite sex and greatly hampered her in the maintenance of the feminine position and in her ability to love, the fact that she had sexual relations with a brother or *brother substitute** in early childhood and that that brother has also shown real affection for her and been her protector, has provided that basis for a heterosexual position in her and developed her capacity for love.

Of further benefit in such a relationship is the fact that it provides the girl with proof that her vagina is not something destructive—hatred of her mother's vagina in its relationship with her father had produced such fears—and assurance through satisfactory experience would prevent her from becoming frigid, or succumbing to other sexual disturbances in later life.

Klein recognises however that all childhood sexual experiences will not be of such a satisfactory kind, and some may lead to disorders in sexual functioning and personality development.

> If her sexual relations with another child serve to confirm her deepest fears—either because her partner is too sadistic or because

* Our italics.

performing the sexual act arouses yet more anxiety and guilt in her on account of her own excessive sadism—her belief in the harmfulness of her introjected objects and her own id will become still stronger, her super-ego will grow more severe than ever, and as a result, her neurosis and all the defects of her sexual and characterological development will gain ground.

As a footnote to this discussion, she adds: 'This is still more the case where the child has been seduced or raped by a grown up person. Such an experience, as is well known can have serious effects upon the child's mind'.

Given that rape and seduction are unwanted by the child, and of a very brutal nature, this conclusion seems inevitable, not only on the basis of her arguments, but also on the basis of a far more straightforward learning theory. But some seductions appear to be actively desired by the child, and where they do not entail violence, or excessive guilt, it might be logical to conclude that they would not assume any greater significance for the child than helpful relations with a brother-substitute. Adopting the Kleinian standpoint, Susan Isaacs (1933) believed that seduction might lead to increased masturbatory activity.

Where the sexual experience was sadistic the child's fears of aphanisis are increased (Isaacs, like Klein, believed that all children have such fears due to their sadistic phantasies of parental intercourse) and the child seeks 'magical reassurance' in autoerotic activities. Where the anxiety is great, so also she believes autoerotic activities will be most manifest.

Of real danger to the child's subsequent development are actual sexual relations with adult members of the family group. From the Kleinian standpoint this would be explained by the enormous amount of anxiety aroused by fear of retaliation that this would engender. Ferenczi (1932) further stressed the psychic damage which may result from the child's awareness in this situation of the guilt which the behaviour has occasioned in the adult:

> The most important change produced in the mind of the child by the anxiety fear-ridden identification with the adult partner, is the introduction of the guilt feelings of the adult, which makes hitherto harmless play appear as a punishable offence . . . When the child recovers from such an attack, it feels enormously

confused, in fact, split—innocent and culpable at the same time, and its confidence in the testimony of its senses is broken.
... The playful trespasses of the child are raised to serious reality only by the passionate, often infuriated, punitive sanctions and lead to depressive states in the child, who until then felt blissfully guiltless.

One supposes that relationships with adults other than the parents, which produce an exaggerated reaction on the parent's part, may also serve as anxiety provoking to the child. The possibly 'Helpful' object is seen for the first time as 'bad', accentuating the child's fear of sexual relations.

The possibility is never dismissed in clinical writings that the parent's disproportionate anxiety or hostility to the child's relationships with an adult, may reflect a guilty parental desire, which the child was acting out.

The position is best summarised by Johnson (1953):

The parent or parents, usually unconsciously, sanctioned and fostered the child's acting out of the parent's poorly integrated forbidden impulses. As the parent achieved vicarious gratification of these impulses, he often at the same time expressed the hostility inherent in his conflicts in a destructive fashion towards the child.

Parental sanctions for such forbidden impulses may be given unconsciously because the parents are themselves unable to satisfy their needs in the adult world, or because their needs have become inordinate due to the stunting experiences of their own early childhood, or because of a combination of both these factors.

Johnson, on the basis of clinical, rather than experimental studies concludes: 'Long and intensive collaborative treatment of sexual aberrations in children and adolescents reveals that in every case a parent had serious problems at the genital level'. (1953)

Mothers defend themselves from their own guilt feelings for these impulses by using the child as a scapegoat (Eissler 1948). They express hostility to the child, as to a criminal, reassuring themselves of their innocence.

Such parental ambivalence is thought by analysts to produce fixations in the child.

To quote Johnson (1953) again:

One gets the impression that at development levels that do not afford enough satisfaction the organism refuses to go further demanding the withheld satisfactions. If the frustration has led to *repression*, the drives in question are thus cut off from the rest of the personality, they do not participate in further maturation and send up their disturbing derivatives from the unconscious into the conscious. The result is that these drives remain in the unconscious unchanged, constantly demanding the same sort of satisfaction, thus, they also constantly provide the same defensive attitudes on the part of the defending ego. This is one source of neurotic 'repetitions'.

Rabinovitch (1952) contributing to a symposium on sexual psychopathy, noted the preponderance of early genital experiences with adults, in children presenting acting-out sexual delinquency. He notes:

In these cases we can recognise a compulsive need to re-experience gratification at a genital level. The need is often inordinate once the pattern has been established and serves as a dynamic force motivating delinquent behaviour. In most of these cases genital contact has occurred many times over a period, one isolated experience does not tend to establish a compulsive need for repetition.

A further recognition of the part played by parental inadequacies or psychopathology in the sexual acting-out of the children is made by many clinicians (Eisner 1945; Powell 1948; Hartogs 1951; Riaboy 1943; Colm 1951; Clothier 1955; Fleck 1956; Blau and Hulse 1956; Litin, Giffin and Johnson 1950; Heiman and Levitt 1960).

Of greatest danger to the girl child is the loss or inadequacy of the father (Gibbens 1957; Kasanin and Handshin 1941; O'Kelly 1955).

Blos (1957) distinguishes two different patterns of psychosexual development in the girl, producing sexual delinquency and attributable to paternal inadequacy.

Maintaining the orthodox Freudian position that all children —male and female—at first assume an attitude of passive dependence on the mother, he notes that the girl's turning to the father in the oedipal situation entails the danger that her passive trivings towards him will reawaken oral dependency, and a return to the stage of primal passivity, which would preclude a successful advancement to femininity. Where the father is inadequate as an oedipal object this danger increases, and the ego striving towards normal maturation reacts against the threat with an exaggerated independence and interest in the opposite sex.

The first type of sexual delinquent is the girl who, aware of her father's inadequacy, and frequently of her mother's dissatisfaction with the father, turns to sexual acting-out in the hope of possessing a partner, 'who serves her to surmount in phantasy an oedipal impasse—but more important than this, to take revenge on the mother who had hated, rejected or ridiculed the father'.

Blos believes that spiteful and revengeful phantasies with reference to the mother abound, and consequently no sexual pleasure is ever obtained. The sexual acting-out is a defensive struggle in which the illusory oedipal situation prevents the child from regressing to a stage of passive dependency.

A second type of female sexual delinquency—as regards behaviour almost identical to the first—arises in those girls who have failed in resisting regression to pre-oedipal passivity. Here the wild display of heterosexuality defends them from recognising their enslavement to the mother. Girls of this type have no relationship with or interest in their sexual partners. In fact hostility to the male is usual. The male is only seen as an object to gratify the girl's insatiable oral needs. Blos maintains that many of these girls are almost obsessed with the desire to have a baby. Presumably they see maternity as a means of freeing themselves from the all embracing maternal relationship. It is interesting to note here the comments of two of the unmarried mothers seen by Fleck (1956). They saw themselves as being pregnant 'all by oneself' and pregnancy as satisfying the desire to have something 'all one's own'.

Gibbens (1957) describing a group of juvenile prostitutes was able to isolate similar features in their personality. He noted: 'an inability to feel any real affection for men, a fear of being dominated by them, and a thinly disguised hostility and contempt for them'.

One possible aetiological factor for such sexual acting-out, was in Gibben's opinion a high degree of parental conflict. This would not only prevent the girl from identifying with the father satisfactorily in the oedipal situation—whatever his essential adequacy—but afford her little satisfaction in the pre-oedipal stage, producing considerable oral frustration and consequent affection seeking behaviour.

Whilst the extreme pathogenicity of Blos' delinquent types must be stressed, theoretically they may help to account for many of the seemingly purposeless, unenjoyed sexual misdemeanours noted by psychiatrists. They may also account for the participation sometimes apparent in sexual assault cases. Here the child is neurotically seeking to assuage a pre-oedipal conflict and trauma, if sustained, will only arise from the guilt of the adults around it, and from the hostility which the child's behaviour occasions, not from the sexual act itself.

It must be stressed that all the foregoing conclusions are at best tentative. They were derived from intensive analytic investigation of small, selected samples of patients, and have never been subjected to wide-scale empirical investigation. I have included them as theoretical suggestions worthy of more careful consideration in the present study. I do not view them as proven facts.

CHAPTER XI

Formulation of the Basic Hypotheses

To summarise the literature, one may say that the sexual assault of children by adults is not thought to lead to subsequent personality problems, except in cases where it has been particularly brutal or sadistic. Here, a degree of subsequent anxiety might be expected, as well as an increase in autoerotic habits.

In some children the seduction may form part of a pattern of sexual acting-out, being either unconsciously sanctioned by the parents, or a reaction to difficulties in relation to the parents. Of especial danger to normal development will be parental rejection—real or imagined—and parental loss, or absence. Other children may unconsciously use the seduction as a form of reality-testing to assuage anxiety occasioned by sadistic sexual phantasies. The seduction will then only be perceived as a guilty act if it is discovered and reacted against strongly by parents.

Several hypotheses based on these clinical speculations were formulated.

Hypothesis 1. Where a group of sexually assaulted children is compared with a group of carefully matched control children on tests measuring unsettledness and maladjustment at school, the only observable difference will be in affection-seeking behaviour displayed by the two groups. Sexually assaulted children will show significantly more affection-seeking behaviour than will the control group.

Similarly, where a group of sexually assaulted children is compared with a group of carefully matched control children on tests measuring underlying personality structure, the only observable significant differences will be in the need for affiliation, the fear of rejection and the awareness of personal guilt.

99

On an analysis of themes relating to parent-child relationships the only significant difference will be in themes relating to parental loss or rejection. Sexually assaulted children will tell significantly more of these stories.

The adoption of this hypothesis at the outset seems justified by:

(1) The popular assumption that children involved in assault cases are victims rather than participants, that is, they represent a random group, and not a group with special personality needs or fears.

(2) The Freudian assumption that genital needs are common to all children, and sexual assaults of a non-sadistic nature will not be deemed especially traumatic by the children involved. Such incidents will not seriously disorientate the child's subsequent personality development.

(3) The existing clinical suggestion that sexual acting-out arises from an inordinate need for affection.

(4) The clinical suggestion that sexually assaulted children will be made to feel guilty by witnessing parental distress or hostility aroused by the incident, or through identification with the adult who is himself guilty. The possibility that guilt may represent a feeling of unworthiness in the face of the postulated parental unlovingness is not ruled out.

The testing of this hypothesis will rely upon the statistical comparison of teacher's ratings for unsettledness and maladjustment, displayed by both groups of children in school, and measured by the Bristol Social Adjustment Guides, and the statistical comparison of the needs, emotions, threats, action patterns and expected outcomes of the two groups of children, as seen in the T.A.T.

Hypothesis 2. Where a group of sexually assaulted children is tested for unsettledness and maladjustment in school, the children whose sexual experience is most recent, will not differ significantly in measures of unsettledness from those whose experience occurred at an earlier age.

This hypothesis tests in another way the assumption that sexual assault by adults does not have an unsettling effect on the child's general personality development.

The testing of this hypothesis will rely upon a statistical

comparison of the unsettledness and maladjustment scores, yielded by the Bristol Social Adjustment Guide, of two groups of sexually assaulted children: those whose experience was most recent, and those whose experience occurred some years before the personality testing.

Hypothesis 3. Where a group of sexually assaulted children is tested for affection-seeking behaviour, the children with below normal intelligence will show significantly more affection-seeking behaviour than will the children with normal intelligence. In comparison, no difference will exist between the groups in underlying need for affection.

This hypothesis assumes that children of low intelligence will find greater difficulty in hiding or controlling their need for affection than will clever children. The need to inhibit affection-seeking behaviour is postulated as arising from the parental disapproval or disgust at the sexual episode. No difference is thought to exist in the underlying need for affiliation seen in the two groups.

Testing of this hypothesis will rely upon the statistical comparison of the affection-seeking scores, seen in the Bristol Social Adjustment Guide, and the need for affiliation scores, measured by the T.A.T., of children with below and above average I.Q.

CHAPTER XII

Previous Empirical Work on Personality
and Subsequent Development

The first study into the later personality development of sexually assaulted children suggested that well over half of them suffered subsequently from their experience. This study was made by Moses (1932) and it traced the development several years later of sixty children, all of whom had been assaulted by adults. At the time of the study eight children were thought to be neurotic, five were tending to masturbate, eight had become 'preoccupied with sexual things', and sixteeen were propelled into heterosexual activities. Moses concluded that the deviant behaviours were the result of their sexual experience. Unfortunately no control group was used and it is therefore difficult to tell whether this conclusion is accurate, or whether children similar in age and general experience would show similar developmental difficulties.

Several factors may account for the observed preponderance of unsatisfactory development in the children studied. First, only twenty-two of the children were supposedly 'normal' at the outset. Twenty-one were said to have been simple children, and the rest had exhibited severe emotional or behavioural problems before the assault. Secondly, only twenty-three of the children were from 'good' families; the rest were from broken homes, were orphans, or came from alcoholic, sexually promiscuous or rejecting families. Children from such unsatisfactory backgrounds might well have experienced difficulty in development, even without the sexual assault. Finally, the majority of the subject children—fifty—had been involved in cases of complete intercourse with the adult. Such cases are generally thought to be unusual, and would naturally have involved the child more completely in the act than the more usual cases of fondling and exhibitionism.

Results completely in disagreement with those of Moses were produced by Augusta Rasmussen in her study of 1934. In this, fifty-four children, aged nine to thirteen years, whose testimony had resulted in court proceedings against a sexual attacker, were interviewed later in life in order to ascertain the degree of psychic damage sustained. Initially, material was taken from court files, and the follow up was done twenty to thirty years later, through the woman's doctor, who rated her mental health and social adjustment in adult life. At the time of the follow up all but eight of the subjects were well adjusted. The author concluded that there was no evidence to link the later personality disintegration of these eight subjects with the attack. Instead the evidence suggested 'an independent constitutional predisposition' to break down.

Like Moses, Rasmussen stressed the large number of assault victims who came from broken and inadequate homes. Twenty-one of the fifty-four in this group were from families in which one parent was absent or inadequate. Rasmussen also emphasised an element of passivity or acceptance of the sexual attack. In thirteen cases the girl had remained completely passive during the act, in a further twenty-two cases the offence had been committed more than once, and in thirteen of these cases a steady relationship had developed between the man and the girl. In four cases the child had offered herself or provoked sexual intercourse.

Rasmussen accounted for the large number of passive or non-resistant children in the sample in several different ways:

(1) Many were lured by money, sweets, or small gifts.

(2) Many of the attackers were acquaintances and had gained the child's confidence.

(3) In many instances the man approached the child carefully taking care not to arouse fear.

(4) Most of the children knew of sexual relationships before the attack, and some desired experience out of curiosity.

In only a few cases had the child been surprised and brutally overcome, and even in these cases no evidence existed to suggest that the child had suffered psychic or physical damage as a result.

Bender and Blau (1937) further stressed this element of consensuality. In a psychiatric assessment of the personality development of sixteen children (eleven female and five male, age range five to twelve years) admitted to the Bellevue Hospital, New York, following sexual relations with adults, they concluded that all the children had co-operated or played an active or initiatory role in establishing the sexual relationship. The child afterwards rationalised acceptance of the sexual act in terms of fear or the enticement of gifts, but these they felt were secondary reasons.

In most cases they discovered the relationship was repeated and not broken until it was discovered by guardians, and in many cases reprimand did not prevent the development of other similar contacts. Furthermore, the children appeared emotionally placid and there was no evidence of anxiety, guilt or psychic trauma. They noted that the emotional reaction of these children was in marked contrast to that manifested by their adult guardians, who were usually horrified, anxious and apprehensive regarding the future of the child.

Bender and Blau noted that the most striking feature of sexually assaulted children was their unusually charming and attractive personalities. This was so noticeable that the authors frequently considered the possibility that the child might have been the actual seducer rather than the one innocently seduced. Bender and Blau emphasised a point made by the two earlier studies, that is, that the assaulted children generally came from stressed family backgrounds. In this study eight of the sixteen children were lacking one or both parents. In two further cases the father was mentally deficient and had committed an offence with the child, showing no further interest in it, and of the remaining six children, four were from large families and usually the youngest.

The authors also stressed that most children displayed educational problems. Their school work became so poor as a result of their sexual preoccupations, and their retardation so marked, that they were considered defective. Indeed two children in the group had I.Q.s below 80 and ten had an average I.Q. of 84. The children were often hyperactive and restless and were frequently rebellious, disobedient and disrespectful towards parents.

Despite these general difficulties, the authors concluded that seven of the sixteen children showed no apparent acute emotional or behavioural response to their sexual experiences. Three of the younger children however tended to masturbate, three of the children who had been abused by parents tended to be bewildered and preoccupied, and one child acquired a pessimistic and callous attitude and despaired of ever being able to control her sexual urges sufficiently to make an adequate adjustment.

Fifteen years later, in 1952, this group of children was again studied, this time by Bender and Grugett. Fourteen children were seen and of these nine had adjusted satisfactorily. Of the remaining children, one who had been seduced by a parent had become psychotic, and four who were intellectually deficient had achieved little personal adjustment.

The results suggested to the authors that sexual preoccupations following a seduction will be abandoned by children when improved facilities allow fulfilment of their individual capacities and their drives towards identification and constructive behaviour. Of the children whose development continued adversely, they commented:

> Their early development had sufficient marked and persistent symptomatology to limit their potential and frustrate normal maturation. Their sexual behaviour in childhood, rather than predisposing to a psychotic adjustment, had been but one aspect of their generally confused reaction to the beginnings of a fundamentally disrupting process.

The first estimate of the incidence of adult-child sexual contacts was given in Kinsey, Pomeroy, Martin and Gebhard's all embracing study of female sexuality (1953). They found that 24 per cent of their sample had sustained pre-adolescent sexual contacts with adult males. The highest frequency of approaches occurred in poorer city communities, and they concluded that the incidence of adult-child contacts would have been greater if their group had been more representative of the lower educational groups. Most children were between ten and twelve at the time of the approach, and exhibitionism, fondling and manipulation of female genitalia were the most frequent offences. Only 3 per cent of the children had been involved in actual coitus. The majority of children—80 per cent—have been involved in only one incident, the remaining 20 per cent had taken part in several episodes, probably because they 'had become interested in the sexual activity'. Kinsey and his colleagues reached no definite conclusions as to the significance of sexual contacts for children's subsequent development. Some subjects reported that it had been pleasurable and involved considerable affection, contributing favourably to later psychosexual development. On the other hand, some 80 per cent of the children said they were emotionally upset or frightened by their contacts with adults. A small proportion had been seriously disturbed, but the authors observed:

> In most instances the reported fright was nearer the level that children will show when they see insects, spiders or other objects against which they have been adversely conditioned. If a child was not culturally conditioned it is doubtful if it would be disturbed by sexual approaches of the sort which had usually been involved in these histories.

The authors expressed difficulty in understanding why any child, except for its cultural conditioning, should be disturbed at having its genitalia touched, or disturbed at seeing the genitalia of other persons, or disturbed at even more specific sexual contacts. They note that the reactions of parents and police may disturb the child more seriously than the sexual contacts themselves, and conclude: 'The current hysteria over sex offenders may very well have serious effects on the ability of many of these children to work out sexual adjustments some years later in their marriages'.

Kinsey's study was followed by that of Weiss, Rogers, Dutton and Darwin (1954, 1955) who again emphasised the dichotomy between accidental and participant victims. Of seventy-three girls studied—all of whom were referred by district attorneys as being the victims of male sex offenders—twenty-one girls were thought to be 'accidental' victims and forty-four to have participated in the affair. In eight further cases no decision about involvement could be reached.

The authors suggested that a participant victim frequently had more than one sexual experience with an adult, the adult was often a friend of the victim, the girl received some type of reward from him for her participation, and the girl kept the relationship a secret from her parents. Frequently participant victims were attractive in appearance, and quickly established superficial relationships with a psychiatrist. Accidental victims, by contrast, were usually younger, had only one sexual experience, the offender was a stranger, and the girl told the parents promptly of the incident.

Noting that twenty-one of the forty-four participant victims came from broken homes, as opposed to seven of the twenty-one accidental victims, the authors suggested that frequently the participant victims' mother was an unhappy woman who had experienced little gratification in her life. Frequently she was jealous of her daughter but felt guilty about the jealousy, and as a result she oscillated between strictness and leniency in the handling of her daughter. This conflict was particularly apparent in the sexual education given to the girl, with the result that it was difficult for the child to develop consistent attitudes towards her own behaviour and hence to develop a stable conscience. Further, the parental conflict made it possible for the child to express anger at her parents by doing things which displeased them, but which they would not fully object to, because of these conflicts. It seemed probable that the child's sexual acting-out was often meaningful as an aspect of her conflict with her parents—the girl expressing defiance of parents, and gaining a feeling of independence through engagement in sexual relations with adult men. This sexual acting-out was not free from remorse and guilt, however, and many participant victims were considered to be burdened by phobias, nightmares and anxieties. Also apparent in the participant group was behaviour indicative of profound emotional disturbance. The girls were sexually promiscuous, stole, played truant from school, ran away from home and were subject to extreme fluctuations of mood. Frequently, they reacted to stress and anxiety with impulsive, often self-damaging behaviour. Whilst nowhere specified, we interpret the authors as meaning that these behaviours were indicative of emotional stress before the assault, the assault being only a symptom of this distress and not resulting from it.

Landis (1956) also attempted to study the degree of participation and characteristics of participant assault victims, in an

American university population. Using a questionnaire on family background and maturation, Landis found that of 1,800 students questioned 30 per cent of the men and 35 per cent of the women reported at least one experience with a sexual deviate. Of these a substantial minority—40 per cent of the men and 35·5 per cent of the women—had had three or more experiences.

The author noted that four out of five males with deviate experience had had homosexual advances made to them, over half of the experiences of the girls had been with exhibitionists, and one-fourth with adults who had fondled them sexually. Landis noted that girls are more likely to be molested by adults as pre-adolescents (41 per cent were under eleven years) while boys are usually older. Young girls, and girls who live in villages or in the country are more likely to be fondled sexually by adults they know, while older girls and city girls are more likely to have experiences with exhibitionists who are usually strangers to the girl.

The authors concluded that in general the great majority of the victims seem to recover rather soon, and to acquire few permanently wrong attitudes from the experience. Only 2·2 per cent of the women with deviate experience and 0·4 per cent of the men felt they had gained undesirable ideas about sex from their experience. Experiences within the primary group were found to be more traumatic for the child than were experiences with strangers. Primary group experiences of girls tended to be with adults who attempted to fondle them sexually, tried to interest them in coitus, or attempted rape. Experiences in secondary group tended to be with exhibitionists.

Of the boys 30·5 per cent, and of the girls 33·8 per cent had known the offenders. The younger the child the more likely he was to know the offender. Older children were generally approached by strangers. Of all the girls, 43 per cent, and of all the boys, 16·5 per cent, reported that they had told their parents about the incident. There was a distinct tendency for children involved in more serious offences not to tell their parents, and Landis suggested that the child is more willing to tell the parents about activities in which implication of participation would not arise, e.g. exhibitionism.

Landis felt that girls who told their parents of the event were likely to be girls who reported fright, shock or emotional upset over it. He suggests tentatively that parental reaction may account in some measure for this subsequent shock and he found that five per cent of the girls who told their parents said they were more shocked by their parents' reaction than by the assault itself.

Landis found that the girls who had been involved in sexual assaults, as compared with the students who had no adult-child sexual contact, were more likely to have distant relationships with their mothers before the age of fifteen. Their mother usually worked full or part time, their fathers were semi-skilled, and the girls were more likely to be non-virgins and experience orgasm before marriage. These distinctions were particularly apparent when the 'possibly participant' victims were compared with the rest, and it was also apparent that the possibly participant group came from the unhappiest homes and slightly less of them had obtained their sexual information from their mothers.

A study made in India by Shahmugan (1958) also suggested that sexually delinquent girls have poor home backgrounds. Of fifty subjects who were referred by the Madras Court's Guidance Bureau for investigation following sexual misdemeanours, forty-five had come from broken homes. None of the thirty controls were from split families. Shahmugan compared the responses of the two groups to fifteen T.A.T. pictures and found that themes of anxiety, separation or rejection, and accident, illness, guilt and conscience, were particularly important in the sexually delinquent group.

Lafon, Trivas and Pouget (1958) also emphasised the poor home background and inadequate personality development of the ninety-eight sexual assault victims they studied. They found that only 9 per cent of the group had an I.Q. higher than 90; 49 per cent had an I.Q. of less than 70; and only 2 per cent were thought to be 'normal' children. The rest were physically handicapped, 'psychologically unstable', 'suggestible', or showing problem behaviour. In 95 per cent of the cases the authors suggested that there was evidence to suggest that the attack was provoked. They suggested that the meaning to the child of this form of sexual behaviour is that it affords her an opportunity of acquiring an adult personality and participating in an adult activity. It means that 'she has been chosen by a man who prefers her to another'. No information is given relating to the girl's subsequent development, and it is therefore impossible to assess the effects of the assault upon it.

Anderson, Kenna and Hamilton (1960), in their study of extra-marital conception in adolescence, give information concerning the subsequent personality development of five girls who conceived following a sexual assault. All the girls appeared to cope satisfactorily with their pregnancy and the subsequent birth of the baby. They expressed no outright regret or strong negative emotion concerning the pregnancy, and the authors concluded:

> By the time we investigated them, there were indications that the initial trauma—if existent—may be much slighter than society wishes to think, nor does it necessarily mean stressful pregnancy or labour or a rejected child. The number of physical examinations, official questions, and emotionally toned adult reactions may well be the more deleterious factor.

Four French studies made in 1961 further emphasised this lack of subsequent disturbance in child victims. Bourdiol and Pettenati noted that in many of the victim's families there was some previous history of illicit sexual relations. Frequently they found there was loose living on the part of a mother or sister. Duc observed some signs of precocious prostitution favoured by the mother in a few of the thirty-six cases he studied. Colin and Bourjade emphasised the poor quality of the relationships of even accidental victims with their mothers. Participant victims were thought by them to be profoundly disturbed emotionally, and to have difficulties arising from the oedipus situation. Lafon, Trivas and Pouget noted that 48 per cent of the 126 victims they studied came from homes broken by divorce, death and separation. Forty-three per cent of the children lived with both parents, but were lacking in guidance, due to the parents' immorality, laziness or feeble mindedness. Two-thirds of the children had been given a particularly rigid sexual education, and only 14 per cent of the mothers and fathers of the assault victims were said to have normal personalities.

As in previous studies, Lafon, Trivas, Faure and Pouget, noted that the majority of victims had a below average intelligence quotient. In 47 per cent of the cases the children's I.Q.s were between 50 and 70, and in a further 42 per cent of the cases it was between 70 and 90. Only 2 per cent of the group were thought to have a 'normal' personality, the rest being opposed to the mother, suggestible, unbalanced, fixated on the father, or very jealous of their brothers and sisters.

In 58 per cent of their cases Lafon, Trivas, Faure and Pouget detected some degree of provocation. Four types of provocation were apparent:

(1) provocation for money
(2) provocation for some other desired object
(3) provocation in the course of escapades
(4) provocation without apparent objective.

They also detected three types of consent. First, true consent by participation in the act; second, impulsive consent in which the act is accepted momentarily against the subject's better judgment, that is, the subject is swept by emotional and instinctive tendencies; finally, passive acceptance, in which the child's defence mechanisms are blocked. The authors concluded that the myth of childhood innocence, perpetuated by generations of adults, was utterly at variance with reality.

Finally, Gibbens and Prince (1963) studied two groups of sexually assaulted children in an effort to see the effects upon them of appearances in Court. One group of eighty-two children was unselected, and the children were contacted by the Federation of Committees for the Moral Welfare of Children. The other group of forty-six children were selected because they had all been involved in prosecutions against their offenders. In the random sample, 85 per cent of the girls, and 71 per cent of the boys could identify their assailant, and in thirteen of the eighty-two cases the indecent behaviour had been going on for some time. Assaults by close relatives and friends came to court more frequently than those involving strangers, and usually had a longer history, and were more serious in nature. Assaults by strangers were frequently of a minor or transitory nature.

Fifty-six per cent of the children in the random sample appeared in Court and a further 10 per cent had to appear in a Higher Court. Children from disorganised or problem families were more often called to appear in Court, possibly because children from apparently respectable homes were more frequently assaulted by complete strangers, whom it was later difficult to trace. Among the problem families the great majority of the assailants consisted of fathers and neighbours. Most of these families were so lacking in recognition of normal social controls and constraint that the event seemed to pass largely unnoticed by the family until some additional crisis drew attention to it.

Gibbens and Prince thought that a very real relationship exists between disturbed backgrounds and involvement in sexual assaults. They suggested that the children assaulted by strangers made the best recovery—56 per cent showed no overt disturbance following the event—though this stability might be explained by better home circumstances. They concluded that the nearer the relationship of attacker to child, the greater the subsequent disturbance—though this again might reflect the fact that children from problem families were more often attacked by relations. Cases coming to Court appeared to have a less satisfactory recovery, although subsequent disturbance might be a reflection of their more disturbed family background and of the seriousness of the violation rather than of the court experience itself.

The authors studied reports of the parents' response to the attack and suggested that in just over a quarter of both groups the parents aggravated the situation. Such families exploited the situation in order to get rehoused or showed some definite psychiatric abnormality.

The literature on the subject of the sexually assaulted child has originated in many different areas of study and has approached the problem with different degrees of scientific exactness, very few studies being satisfactory from this point of view. Generally the conclusions reached must be considered extremely tentative. No distinctions are possible in many of the studies between personality characteristics before the assault, which may have precipitated it, and those seen after the assault, and possibly resulting from it. Generally no information is given about the time lapse between assault and the personality assessment, or about the effect this might have on the observed personality variables. Most often no controls free of sexual assault are used, and without them no reliable assessment can be made of the abnormality of the sexual behaviours or pre-occupations perceived.

Despite these inadequacies, an enormous amount of agreement has been reached. The myth of childhood innocence seems in the main to have been rejected, and some degree of participation in the victim group is accepted by almost all studies. Various suggestions as to the aetiology of this affection-seeking tendency have been made, and the relationship between the existence of this need and subsequent normal development has been investigated, at least in a sketchy fashion.

Clearly there is a need for a well-controlled study of the personality variables of the sexually assaulted child, relating these needs both to possible predisposition to sexual assault, and to subsequent personality development. It is this need which the present study attempts to satisfy.

CHAPTER XIII

The Personality Needs of Sexually
Assaulted Children

The first hypothesis suggested that there would be little observable difference either in behaviour, or in underlying personality structure between a group of sexually assaulted children and a group of control children. Significantly more affection seeking behaviour was expected in the sexually assaulted group, and also a significantly greater need for affiliation, fear of rejection and awareness of personal guilt. On an analysis of themes relating to parent-child relationships it was thought that sexually assaulted children would appear significantly more afraid of losing their parents or of being rejected by them, and would tell significantly more stories centring on these themes.

The testing of Hypothesis 1 proceeded in four stages:

(1) An estimate was made of behaviour which suggested maladjustment or unsettledness displayed in school by sexually assaulted and control group children, and this was measured by the Bristol Social Adjustment Guides filled in by class teachers.

(2) A comparison of the children's underlying personality structure was made by an analysis of themes produced by the children in response to twelve T.A.T. pictures. An overall analysis was made of the needs, threats, emotions, actions and probable outcomes displayed in the stories, and also a specific analysis was completed of the themes relating to parent-child relationships.

(3) and (4) Stages one and two were repeated exactly one year later. This second testing was decided upon for two reasons. It was felt that a second testing might highlight any changes in development over a period of time in the two groups. Secondly, any conclusions based on consistencies of behaviour

or underlying personality needs observed at two testings so far apart would, it was felt, be more accurate than any similar conclusions based on only one testing. Two testings would highlight persistent needs or patterns of behaving, rather than transitory needs which were simply reactions to the environment.

Subjects

The sexually assaulted children—or subject children—were forty-one children whose names had been given to the police as having been involved in some kind of sexual offence. Thirty-six of these children later gave testimony resulting in Court proceedings against their attacker. In two cases there was insufficient evidence for proceedings to be undertaken by the police. In a further two cases the attacker was never traced, and in one case the attacker, an inmate of a Special Care Home, was returned before any legal action could be taken.

The subject children therefore form a specially selected group of sexually assaulted children. The majority of sexually assaulted children do not take part in Court Proceedings. Personality disturbance is thought to be greatest where such proceedings have been experienced. For this reason it is popularly supposed that the largest number of child sexual assaults are never reported by parents to the police, parents fearing that to obtain evidence, and then prosecute, often many months after the assault, would only increase the child's anxiety.

Control Children

The control children were chosen from the subjects' class on the basis of:
    (1) an equal I.Q. (within a few points)
    (2) equal class attainment
    (3) comparable age (a birthday within six months of the subject's)
    (4) the same sex
    (5) comparable religion (All the children in this study were Protestant.)

(6) the same ordinal position in the family and the same number of brothers and sisters (Whilst in every case there was not exact matching, overall the positions and number of brothers and sisters were almost exactly the same.)

(7) an identical socio-economic status.

Each subject child was allotted four controls.* It was felt that this would not only make an adequate control group, but would prevent the subject child from feeling 'picked upon'. It should be emphasised at this point that all the subjects believed that they were taking part in a study of personality development, which would extend over two years, and which would involve children of different ages and different intellectual abilities. They were only asked to make up stories about pictures shown to them. Their past history was never at any time discussed with them or with their teachers. (For notes on difficulties inherent in an investigation of this nature see Burton 1964.)

In only three cases was it impossible to obtain a full complement of controls for each subject child. In two cases the subject children were in a class from which another subject and four controls had already been chosen, and the class (a small one, composed of school leavers) did not boast any other comparable control children. In a further case the class (a small one in a Special School) did not have more than two comparable control children. The results for these children were discarded therefore from statistical analysis, but were retained in the text for general interest.

Personal details of subjects and controls

In order to allow for general comparisons between this subject group and the subjects of other studies already outlined, the personal details of the subjects, including those relating to the assault, have been broken down into fourteen categories. Where applicable, those of the controls are appended.

* One possible source of error must be acknowledged at the outset. Whilst all the subject children were known to have sexual experience with an adult, the control children were only presumed not to have had such experience. The parents of these children had at no time reported such an experience during the ten years before the first testing.

Personality Needs of the Children

(1) *Sex*

	Subjects	Controls
Male	6	24
Female	35	130
	41	154

(2) *Intelligence quotient*
(All subjects and controls were tested on Progressive Matrices, in addition to the results given by E.S.N. teachers on more appropriate tests.)

I.Q.	Subjects	Controls
80 or less	12	48
80–90	8	22
90–100	11	44
100–110	7	28
110–120	–	–
120–130	1	5
130 or above	2	7
	41	154

(3) *Time lapse since the assault*

Less than 1 year	8
1–2 years	8
2–3 years	7
3–4 years	7
4–5 years	3
5–6 years	4
6–7 years	3
More than 7 years	1
	41

(4) *Age of child at time of assault*

Less than 6 years	5
6–7 years	3
7–8 years	9
8–9 years	3
9–10 years	8
10–11 years	3
11–12 years	5
12–13 years	1
13–14 years	2
14–15 years	2
	41

(5) *Details of assault*

Rape or attempted rape	2
Indecent assault	11
Instruction in masturbation	2
Undressing of child	2
Homosexual	6
Fondling of child sexually	19
Exhibitionism	–
	—
	42 (One child had two
	— offences.)

(6) *Age of aggressor*

Under 20 years	12
20–30 years	7
30–40 years	5
40–50 years	3
50–60 years	4
60–70 years	4
70 and over	3
Unknown age	4
	—
	42
	—

(7) *Relationship of man to child*

Immediate family	2
Neighbour or friend	15
Person known to child but unknown to child's family	17
Complete stranger	8
	—
	42
	—

(8) *Place of assault*

Home or neighbour's house	13
Disused ground	6
Man's employment	6
Park	5
Entry/street	5
School	3
Car	3
Cinema	1
	—
	42
	—

(9) *Miscellaneous details of assault*

Assault perpetrated twice, or more frequently	6
Mention of reward offered	3
Mention of struggle on child's part	1

Personality Needs of the Children

(10) *State of subject and control child's home*

	Subjects	Controls
Mother dead	2	3
Father dead	1	5
Parents separated	2	2
	5	10*

(11) *Ordinal position of child in family*

	Subject	Control
First	14	45
Second	10	38
Third	6	26
Fourth	3	19
Fifth	3	12
Sixth	3	6
Seventh	1	3
Eighth	–	3
Ninth	1	1
Last child	9	54
Only child	2	4

(12) *Number of children altogether in the family*

	Subjects	Controls
One	2	4
Two	5	37
Three	10	38
Four	7	25
Five	7	13
Six	5	11
Seven	1	10
Eight	1	10
Nine	1	3
Ten	1	2
Eleven	–	–
Twelve	–	1
Thirteen	1	–
	41	154

* These details were acquired by the author in conversation with the child, the questions asked being 'What does your Mummy do?' 'What does your Daddy do?' Differences might be much greater if a direct enquiry to the home had been made. Children may compensate for parental absence by neglecting to add that the parent was not present in the home, whilst nevertheless supplying the required information. Several examples of this were noted. Because of the extreme caution with which the investigation was conducted, a more careful appraisal of the situation was not thought possible.

(13) *Employment of parents at time of testing*

Both parents unemployed	9	15
Father employed/mother home	18	72
Both parents employed	12	63
Mother employed (father unemployed, missing, dead)	2	4
	41	154

(14) *Age of subjects at time of first testing*

6–7 years	1
7–8 years	2
8–9 years	3
9–10 years	1
10–11 years	8
11–12 years	6
12–13 years	4
13–14 years	7
14 years and over	9

Testing

(1) Group testing was done in class using the Progressive Matrices as a timed test. Teachers of E.S.N. children were asked if they would furnish extra details of their pupils' I.Q. and educational attainments so that a more accurate estimation could be made of each child's overall ability. This testing was only carried out once as a means of discovering the subjects, and selecting suitable controls.

(2) The class teachers of all the children selected for study filled in B.S.A.G.s for the children and returned them by post to the author. Usually a different teacher was in charge of the group at the time of the second testing, but in some special schools, or in some of the special classes in the Intermediate Schools, the same teacher was present for the second testing, and completed the form two years running.

(3) All children were seen *individually* by the author in the school and asked to respond to twelve T.A.T. pictures. The showing of the pictures, the instructions given and the equipment involved were all exactly the same as described in Section 1 (page 41).

Before seeing these pictures, each child was asked:

(1) Do you have any brothers or sisters?
(2) What are they called?

(3) How old are they?
(4) Does your Daddy work? What does he do?
(5) Does your Mummy work? What does she do?

First Testing (1961–3)

The class teacher of each group of subject and control children were asked to complete a B.S.A.G. for each child. In only one instance was the Guide for the subject and those for the control children filled in by different teachers, thus avoiding a possible source of error in the ratings. In this instance, the child had been removed by the Court from the private school which she had attended, because she had committed a further sexual misdemeanour. Her extremely high intelligence and upper middle class background made it necessary to select a control group from the private school which she had attended at the time of the attack, and until shortly before the investigation. Her own Guide was completed by a teacher in the Training School.

Guides for 39 subjects and 136 controls were returned to the author and a statistical analysis of the difference between groups was made using a Friedmann Two Way Analysis of Variance ($K \pm 5$, d.f. $= 4$). The scores for each control subject were allotted arbitrarily to one of four columns, and the difference between subject group and all other groups was tested. The results for the two subjects without controls were excluded from statistical analysis, and control group results for the subject with only two controls were supplied by dividing the scores for subject and controls by five, allotting this obtained value to the other two places and ranking accordingly.

Only one syndrome indicative of maladjustment or unsettledness was found to yield a significant difference. This was the affection seeking syndrome, as predicted. ($X^2 = 11 \cdot 44$, $p = \cdot 05 > \cdot 02$.)

The sum of unsettledness scores obtained by the two groups suggested that the subject group was more unsettled. Statistical significance was not obtained however.

Similarly subject children appeared slightly more depressed, hostile to adults, affection seeking towards other children and displayed a few more nervous symptoms than control children.

None of the differences between groups for these syndromes was statistically significant however.

A separate analysis of the number of children in each group scoring any individual B.S.A.G. item suggested that the item which discriminated most significantly between the two groups came from the affection seeking syndrome; that is, subject children were most frequently described as sidling up to and hanging round the teacher.

Other B.S.A.G. items which related more frequently to subject than to control group members suggested that subject children chatted only when alone with the teacher, liked sympathy but were reluctant to ask for it, and asked for help only when they felt in the mood for it. They were obviously very much in need of adult approval and appeared very anxious to bring flowers or other objects to show their teacher, and in class they were always finding excuses for engaging the teacher. Similarly they were very anxious to attract the attention of their class-mates and were seen bragging to other children, wearing spivvish clothes or 'overdoing' their appearance, and trying hard to be accepted into the gang. Sometimes they appeared slightly hostile and would put on a resentful expression and mutter to themselves. At certain times they appeared unwilling to learn, and they gave up difficult school activities too easily. They also appeared somewhat nervous, tending to play games which were childish for their age, and they also bit their finger-nails badly.

Several short descriptions of subject children are now included, the descriptions being largely based on the B.S.A.G.s completed by the class teachers.

I shall call the first child Susan S. Susan was six years old at the time of the first testing. She was then attending a very overcrowded primary school in a slum area. Her home conditions were poor, and her parents were thought to be unsettled. Susan's mother was an intelligent woman who had qualified for a grammar school place, but was not able to take it because her father's desertion made it necessary for her to leave school at fourteen to work and help feed her six younger brothers and sisters. Mrs S. still continued to work in a cigarette factory after her marriage, and was only at home occasionally to look after

Susan and her four-year-old brother. She was somewhat disappointed in her husband, who was lacking both in intelligence and 'push'. He worked as a labourer in the dockyard. Susan was assaulted eight months before I first met her. She had been in the habit of visiting a twenty-six-year-old motor mechanic in the yard of his firm, which was quite near her own home. On one occasion he lifted her in his arms and at the same time put his hand between her legs.

Two months after the offence the case was heard at the Petty Sessions, and the man was fined and undertook to receive psychiatric treatment.

At the time of the first testing Susan displayed very considerable affection seeking tendencies. She was very anxious to do jobs for her teacher. She was for ever finding excuses for engaging the teacher, and frequently she sidled up and hung around her. In Susan's attempt to monopolise the teacher, she came to her frequently complaining of being hurt by others, or craving sympathy for minor scratches and bumps. She was always in need of petty correction. In addition, Susan seemed quite anxious to be 'in with the gang' and tried to pal up with newcomers to the school. She showed off to them by pulling silly faces. When they failed to take notice she became angry, trying to hurt them by hitting them or pushing them over.

Her behaviour suggested considerable restlessness: she could rarely attend or concentrate for long, and she was too restless either to work alone or to retain things for long. She was thought by her teacher to be very 'nervy', and would burst into tears if corrected. To avoid correction she would frequently lie, though at other times she was 'quite truthful'.

Susan's frequently professed worry was that she was not as pretty as the other girls, though in reality she was neat, clean and had a perky smiling expression.

By comparison, Alison P. seemed over-developed and 'mannish' in appearance. She had a gruff voice and, though clean and neat, did not appear very feminine. Alison was fourteen at the time of the first testing and had been placed in an E.S.N. class in an ordinary intermediate school. She was able to respond fluently to the T.A.T. pictures, but she endeavoured to draw attention to herself throughout the interview by exaggerating the difficulty of producing stories, rubbing her eyes and groaning.

Alison had an elder brother who had left home, and a younger sister. Her father was a machine inspector and her mother was not employed outside the home. Five years before I met her, Alison had been approached by a sixteen-year-old youth on a motor bike. He had asked her the way to a nearby village, and then suggested that she come and show him the way. He then took her on the motor bike to a lonely lane and assaulted her. Her parents were extremely annoyed and concerned about the offence, and three months later the youth was fined at a Juvenile Court.

In school, at the time of the testing, Alison showed considerable ambivalence between affection seeking and hostility. She was very friendly, anxious to greet and do jobs for her teacher, and she talked excessively to her. She liked to be the centre of attention in class and bragged and showed off to the other children. When her bids for attention were unsuccessful, she would squabble and make insulting remarks. If the teacher reprimanded her, she would mutter resentfully to herself, or would scowl, and look sullen. She always regarded punishment as unfair and would bear a grudge against the punisher. She was frequently moody, and her bad temper produced considerable fluctuations in her powers of concentration and willingness to work. When at games and team play, she was sometimes alert and sometimes lethargic.

In this variability of mood Alison was very similar to Mamie R., a twelve-year-old intermediate school girl with an I.Q. of 80. Neither of Mamie's parents was employed, and she was the second child in a family of four. She was not a very pretty child, and had to wear glasses because of her weak eyesight.

Four years before the test she had been indecently assaulted by a thirty-one-year-old labourer who had asked her to hold a stick in the ground for him, and then had gone behind her and touched her. Her parents were very indignant and the case came before the Petty Sessions and the man was fined.

At the time when I saw Mamie she was over talkative and over-eager to greet her teacher. She was very anxious to do jobs in school, and was always finding excuses for engaging the teacher. She constantly craved for sympathy and 'traded on' sympathy and interest. She needed frequent petty corrections, and was extremely put out if she did not gain attention. She liked to be the centre of her class-mates' attention also, and always wanted to be in with the gang. Despite this she was thought by her teacher to be always 'on the fringe' of the group. Her teacher described her as never holding friends for long and thought she was very much in danger of being shunned by others when eventually she worked. Mamie could not bear to be wrong and would never admit that she had made a mistake. She easily became impatient, and would frequently lose her temper if she could not do something. She tended to squabble and was a 'spoil sport' with the other children.

Mamie's mood varied considerably from day to day, sometimes she appeared very forward and sometimes she was very sulky. If corrected she would mutter resentfully and, like Alison, she regarded all punishment as unfair and bore a grudge against the punisher. If she lost at team games, she made a fuss about it, insisting that she was right.

Esme R. was nine at the time of the study, and a small, wild-looking, over-friendly, red-haired child, with an I.Q. of 74. She wore spectacles, had badly bitten nails, and her face and body were covered with sores, some of which were produced by her own incontinence, and consequent wet underclothing. Throughout our meeting she made bids for my attention and gradually moved her own chair closer to mine, until eventually she was sitting in my lap.

She attended an E.S.N. school and was thought by her teachers to be neglected at home, coming to school inadequately clothed, and with a dirty head and body. Her mother worked intermittently as a petrol pump attendant, and her father was sometimes employed as a dockyard labourer. She was the sixth child in a family of eight. Two years before I met her she had been taken into the ladies' toilet in a park near her home by a twenty-seven-year-old labourer who had interfered with her clothing. The man, who had previously been in a Special Care Home, was returned there before Court action was taken.

At the time of the first test Esme displayed very pronounced affection seeking tendencies in class. She was very anxious to do jobs, and tended to bring pictures and scraps of paper to her teacher at every available opportunity. She was always promising presents to her which never materialised, and she bragged about her probably non-existent possessions to both teacher and class-mates. By contrast, she spoke only rarely of her family. She appreciated praise, but was very put out if she did not get attention when she deserved it. At times she became sullen and resentful, and she could not be persuaded to do anything when she was in one of her moods. Generally she got on well with the other children in her class, and endeavoured to attract attention to herself whenever her teacher was out of the room. Sometimes however, if she felt she had been wronged or bettered, she would tell tales. Esme was always restless, forever fidgeting, and displayed only very limited powers of concentration, although she was anxious to learn. She was thought by her teachers to be making educational and social progress, although in these things she was very hampered, both by her limited ability and by her parents' neglect.

Margaret L. was thirteen when first seen by me. She was a very pale, thin, scruffy-looking child, with an I.Q. of 87. She was in the 'B' stream of a secondary intermediate school and lived in a small terraced house in a slum area of the city. She was the second child in a family of three girls, her mother was in employment and her father, a lorry driver, had left the family several years previously. On numerous occasions during the two years before I met her Margaret had been indecently assaulted by a twenty-nine-year-old labourer who was living with the family. The man had kissed her and run his hands over her body. At one point, Margaret had alleged that she was interfered with, but a medical examination had proved negative and there was insufficient evidence to bring the man to Court. He continued to live with the family.

Margaret, like the other subject children already described, showed very distinct affection seeking tendencies in school. She was over-eager to greet her teacher and very anxious to do jobs for her. Frequently she brought objects to show her teacher, and was always sidling up to her, or finding excuses for engaging her. Unlike the other subject children, Margaret made no bids for the attention of her class-mates, but was described as being an outsider, always on the fringe of the group. Margaret associated only with one other child and generally ignored the rest. She also displayed a lack of confidence in her relationship with her teacher and seemed frequently unable to meet her gaze or face up to her. She displayed none of the restlessness shown by the other subject children, already described.

Barbara was ten at the time of testing, an untidy, friendly child, whose poor eyesight made it necessary for her to wear spectacles. She was the third child in a family of four, and her mother kept house whilst her father worked as a prison officer. Barbara was a moderately intelligent child, but showed considerable anxiety over the impending eleven-plus examination. Two and half years before I met her, when she was just eight, she had been enticed into the home of a thirty-eight-year-old joiner, who had promised her chocolates. He took her into the bathroom and lowered his trousers, removed her knickers and made her feel his penis. Afterwards he gave her the promised chocolates and made her promise never to tell anyone. When Barbara was questioned about this offence, she admitted that she had already been to his house once before, when a similar offence had taken place. Her family were greatly shocked by this and the case was brought to Court, and the offender fined and bound over.

Barbara appeared somewhat depressed in school. She was very moody and showed an intermittent lack of interest in school work. She tended to day-dream and frequently wandered off on her own. Sometimes she appeared friendly, at other times she would avoid her teacher and the other children. Underlying her depression was a craving for sympathy from those around her, and she would frequently sidle up to her teacher, trying to secure her attention. She was very anxious to do jobs in class, and frequently brought flowers and objects for the nature table.

Finally, a brief description of Peter B. Peter was twelve at the time of testing, a very scruffy and dirty child, who had been ascertained as educationally subnormal and was being educated in the Special Class of a large, modern secondary intermediate school.

Peter was pale and looked anaemic. His teacher reported that he frequently complained of tummy aches and was sometimes sick in school. He had a twin sister and was the third child in a family of five. His mother worked in a linen mill, and his father had left the family six years previously to live in Canada. His mother cared for the family on her own.

Twenty months before I first met Peter, he had been indecently assaulted by a thirty-nine-year-old labourer who lived a few doors away from his home. Peter had been missing from home for six hours and when questioned about this admitted being in the man's house where he had been assaulted. The case came to Court and the offender received five years' imprisonment.

Peter was decidedly unsettled at the time of the first testing. His conversation was frequently rambling and incomprehensible; he was jumpy and his limbs twitched. He made aimless movements with his hand, and tended to slump and loll about. When corrected he would burst into tears, and though he longed for sympathy he was reluctant to ask for it. His persistence and interest varied greatly, and he would begin things well, but quickly flag and give up. His mood was variable too and sometimes he would appear friendly, but at other times sulky. He would only work if compelled, and generally appeared unconcerned about his work, which was frequently untidy and badly presented. Like the other subject children, despite this variability of mood and interest, he was nevertheless anxious for affection and attention, and was always anxious to greet his teacher and very keen to do class jobs. He tended to hang around the teacher and would also brag of his exploits. In the playground he frequently struck brave attitudes, though tended to funk actual violence. He showed off by pulling silly faces and would be a follower in any mischief that was going.

From these brief profiles and from the previous statistical analysis, it must be clear that the subject children, as compared with the controls, show behaviours indicative of slight unsettledness in school. As predicted by the first hypothesis, the most noticeable difference between subject and control children was in the amount of affection seeking behaviour engaged in by the subject children. This affection seeking behaviour was addressed both to other children and also to adults, and indicated a very real anxiety in the subject group about the maintenance of secure attachments.

As Stott (1964) has suggested: 'In many cases the child is patently seeking substitute attachments to compensate for the insecurity of his own family attachments.'

The existence of a slightly higher tendency to hostility to adults in the subject group (particularly the item relating to resentful mutterings and expressions) might also substantiate this. Hostile behaviour alternating with affection seeking behaviour very frequently indicates a lack of emotional security within the family. The child both struggles to gain affection and protests because it is unforthcoming.

The possibility cannot be ignored that the affection seeking behaviour observed in this study might also indicate an attempt on the part of the child to replace the adult with whom he had a sexual relationship. As many previous studies have suggested, children do not always view the sexual act as distasteful and many children may gain considerable comfort from thinking themselves loved and wanted by an adult. For this reason, the child's resentment of the figures of authority, observed in the classroom, may stem from his dislike of all those who might possibly have condemned his relationship with his 'friend'.

Alternatively, the child's affection seeking might express his need to cling to comrades and trusted adults following the sexual trauma. At the same time, the hostile behaviour seen in school might mirror his dislike of adults, whom he might consider, in the light of his recent experience to be hurtful and untrustworthy.

The presence of slight depression, and certain nervous symptoms might follow naturally from any of these emotions, or might indicate anxiety provoked by an inability on the child's part to obtain satisfaction for a strongly felt need for affection. It might also indicate the child's awareness that satisfaction of such a need would involve it in difficulties, possibly in relation to parents or the adult milieu.

Underlying personality structure. Hypothesis 1 predicted that the only observable significant difference between children in subject and control groups, when tested with the T.A.T., would be in the greater need for affiliation, fear of rejection, and awareness of personal guilt, displayed by the subject children On a separate analysis of themes relating to parent-child relationships, it was predicted that the subject children would tell more stories involving parental rejection and loss.

To test this section of Hypothesis 1 each child in the subject and control groups was individually shown twelve T.A.T pictures taken from Murray's standard set. Testing was done entirely in the child's school. No time limit was imposed on the child, and times for completing the twelve pictures varied from thirty minutes to nearly two hours per child. All children were seen in a room other than the classroom, and a sense of privacy was maintained throughout. In addition, I assured each child that the stories he made up would be shown to no one in the school, and that he must feel quite free to talk about whatever he pleased. In general, subject children showed a tendency to make up a longer story, and to occupy more of my time, no accurate details of these variables are included however. The supposition that they were actively trying to establish better relations with me would relate directly to their greater affection seeking behaviour, as seen by their teachers. It might also reflect a bias on my part, although every attempt was made by me to avoid it.

The order in which the subject children were seen was randomly varied within the group. In no instance had I any feeling that these children saw themselves as any more 'picked upon' than other members of the group. (It is worth noting here that in only two schools was the child's assault brought to my notice. This might reflect an unwillingness to disclose such a delicate matter to an outside investigator, but in view of the considerable co-operation given, and the many details supplied about the child, his home, and his personality, this lack of information was thought to be genuine.). All children co-operated happily, most reported that they had enjoyed the task, and no refusals were noted.

Scoring of the T.A.T. protocols was exactly similar in method to that outlined in Section One. The scores obtained for thirty-nine subjects and groups of controls were compared statistically using the Friedmann Two Way Analysis of Variance $(K = 5, d.f. = 4)$.

As predicted by Hypothesis 1, subjects told significantly more stories indicative of a need for affiliation ($X^2 = 42\cdot2$, $\rho = \cdot001$) and exhibited in their stories a significantly greater fear of rejection ($X^2 = 20$, $\rho = \cdot001$). Contrary to the initial assumption, there was no statistically significant difference between groups in the number of stories they told indicative of an awareness of personal guilt.

In addition, and contrary to the predictions made in Hypothesis 1, the subject group told significantly more stories showing a general fear of the external environment ($X^2 = 11\cdot4$, $\rho = \cdot05 > \cdot02$), and they more frequently expected their ventures to end in only modified success ($X^2 = 14\cdot7$, $\rho = \cdot01 > \cdot001$). The control group children on the other hand told significantly more stories indicative of a need for physical security—($X^2 = 14\cdot7$, $\rho = \cdot01 > \cdot001$).

Clearly therefore subject children are more preoccupied with satisfying a need for affiliation than are the control children. The stories they recounted exhibited both a fear of loss of association and also a positive striving for affection. They showed a greater fear of being repulsed, ostracized or rebuffed than control children and they were particularly fearful of being denied affiliations by lovers, friends and parents. In addition, they generally perceived their environment as being more threatening to them than did the control children, and they saw their attempts to meet their needs as having only modified success, that is, the need was met but the ending was asocial or unhappy.

Whilst not predicted, this general fear of the environment and the expectation of only modified success in their ventures may be explained in terms both of the T.A.T. themes themselves and the child's own awareness of the environment. Frequently the subject children told T.A.T. stories in which parents, friends or lovers died, became ill, or were enticed away by rivals. The number of these stories was not sufficient to reach statistical significance when the individual threats were examined separately. But when taken together, as a fear of the general environment, they reached statistical significance.

Similarly, in terms of the child's own experience, it does not seem too improbable to conclude that attempts to meet the strongly felt need for affiliation were frequently satisfied, but only in a transitory and insufficient way.

Parent-Child Relationships, as seen in T.A.T. Stories. A separate analysis was made of the number and type of themes relating to parent-child relationships in the T.A.T. and a statistical comparison was made of the subject and control group scores, using the Friedmann Two Way Analysis of Variance (N = 39, K = 5, d.f. = 4).

The prediction made in Hypothesis 1, that subject children would tell significantly more stories relating to parents' rejection and loss, was not substantiated. Control and subject groups did not differ in the number of stories relating to fear of their parents' separation or death, nor in the number of stories suggesting punishment by their parents. Subject children however told significantly more stories about parents than did the controls ($X^2 = 12\cdot0$, $\rho = 0\cdot02 > 0\cdot01$). This would suggest that as a group they were more preoccupied with their relationship with their parents than the control children. Obviously, however, in contrast to the prediction made in the hypothesis, they did not see their parents as utter failures or as being completely inadequate in meeting their needs.

Several complete T.A.T. protocols are now given. As will be seen, many of the stories relate to needs other than those for affiliation. Most subject children were not wholly preoccupied with the problems of gaining and retaining affection, but certainly a very substantial proportion of their themes concern such problems.

The first protocol is that of a twelve-year-old girl Jennifer, whose poor physical health made it necessary for her to attend a special open air school. She was a tall, thin, attractive child, the second in a family of six. Neither of her parents was employed, and home circumstances were considered by teaching staff to be poor. In school Jennifer appeared anxious for the attention of her class-mates, and rather restless and moody. She was inclined to be resentful of adults and would occasionally deface her work, rather than present it inadequately done.

One year before I first met her, she had been enticed by a postman, who visited her home, into going to see him at his house. She went on several occasions, and he was later accused of having 'unlawful carnal knowledge' and of indecently assaulting her. When the case came to the Custody Court four months later, both parents and child refused information concerning the offence.

A somewhat unusual theme appears in two of Jennifer's stories, that is, the theme of death following unrequited deep love. In these stories the mother, whose child leaves her, takes her own life as a consequence. No hint is given as to the significance of these suicides. We do not know whether they are to punish the child for her desertion, or simply a result of the mother's intense grief at this desertion.

(2) 'This girl is looking at someone thinking that she is taking her boyfriend from her and this man is ploughing with his horse.'

(3) 'She is crying—I think it is because she has to go away somewhere and she is going into her room—she's to go away because she's not working right, and she has to go away to a home for she has no Mother or Father. She's crying because she doesn't want to leave—there's a whole lot of friends she knows and she doesn't want to leave them. I think she'll just go.'

(4) 'He is going to go away somewhere to do a job—into the Army, I think—and this girl is saying "You must stay, you'll only get killed in the Army"—she's saying: "I love you so much—would you not stay", and he is saying "I must go because the war is on and it is my duty".'

(5) 'This lady must be looking for her wee girl or her wee boy—she is calling the name, and say it is a wee girl, she is saying "Jennifer, come to me—I want you to do something for me!" '

(6) 'This girl is saying "I love him, I don't want to leave him no matter what he has done..." Father is saying "He is a bad'un—you must not marry him." I think they will run away and get married and then she'll find out that her father was right that he is a bad'un and she'll leave him and come home again and get a divorce. I don't think her father will let her come in—he'll say "You should have took heed to me in the first place".'

(7) 'This little girl is sad or something—I think she'll have to go to a boarding school, that is why she is sad. Her Mother is saying "Sure, you will learn more" and she is saying "I don't want to go—I don't want to leave here" and she is saying "Sure, it will do you good." I think this little girl will run away because she'll have to go to Boarding School and go to her aunt's house and stay there till she is about 15 and can come home again. She ran away

because she didn't want to leave her friends and she'd be far away from home.'

(8) 'This girl has just finished all her work and she is saying "I wish I could live in a big, big, house with lovely clothes", and she says "but I will never be able to do that—I would have to marry someone very rich before I could live in a big house like that." I don't think she will ever live in a big house—she'll just stay in the one that she's in. She'll get married but not to a rich man, and live in a wee cottage but not in a big house.'

(9) 'This girl has been meeting someone like her boy-friend and she is running away because he said something to her and the girl in the tree is shouting down "What is the matter?" and the other girl is shouting "I don't love him, he's horrible"—and this other girl is saying "Why, what did he do?" and she's saying "He love's someone else," and this girl is saying "Sure, you can always get another boy-friend" and she's saying "Not as nice as the one I had" and I don't think she'll ever fall in love with him again.'

(10) 'I think this is his mother and this man here has to go to the Army and she is saying "Oh, don't go son—stay home" and he leaves and goes to the Army—she says "If you go to the Army I'll kill myself" and he goes to the Army and he comes home and finds her dead. And he blames it on himself.'

(14) 'Well, its night time and he is looking up to the stars and he is saying "Lord, I have to do it", and he thinks the Lord is saying "Why must you do it?" "Because I killed someone—so I will be punished this way by jumping out of the window".'

(16) 'This big house with a boy looking out of the window and a girl standing on the ground below—she is saying to herself: "Oh, isn't he a lovely boy!" and he is saying "Oh, isn't she a lovely girl!"—it has been snowing and there is snow on the window sill and he got a snow ball and threw it down. The girl took some snow and threw it up to him and she shouts up "Why are you in the room—are you not well", and he shouts down "I am not well —I've got 'flu." The girl was carrying a basket of plums and said "Would you like one?" He says "Yes" and she threw him up one and he caught it and ate it and shouts down "Oh, that was lovely." I think they'll fall in love with each other and get married and live happily ever after.'

(18) 'This is her Mother and she is trying to strangle her and saying "Why did you do it?", and the girl is saying "Do what?" and

the lady is saying "You married my son" and the other girl is saying "We were in love." This lady is saying "What, you in love with my son?"—She says "Yes", and then the other lady says "Did he love you?" This other girl is saying "Yes", and the lady lets her go and I think this lady will kill herself because of her son.'

Jennifer's elder sister, Angela, was also seen. She appeared an amazingly helpful, friendly and co-operative child, who was relaxed and enthusiastic during the testings. She was also very attractive though, like her sister, she suffered from chest trouble and was easily tired during the school day. Angela was thirteen at the time of the first test, and had been involved twelve months before with the postman who assaulted Jennifer. She visited him on numerous occasions, but not with her sister. Unlike Jennifer, Angela had had a previous assault, five years earlier, at the age of eight. She was invited by a sixty-two-year-old tractor driver to have a ride on his tractor, and when she was seated beside him, he put his hand up her clothes and explored her body. When the case came to Court, the jury disagreed twice as to the verdict, and the Crown entered a *Nolle Prosequi*. No order was made against the man. This previous case may in part explain the family's unwillingness to disclose information in Court concerning the later offence.

Angela appeared unforthcoming and hostile to her teacher in school. Her behaviour suggested a 'writing-off' of adults. She was thought to be a habitual, slick liar, and a sly and crafty child who was difficult to catch but nevertheless persisted in antisocial pursuits. When corrected, she became antagonistic and resentful, and was generally surly and suspicious. She rarely smiled. Her stories reveal her underlying need for affection however. She is very much involved with the problem of getting married or being married, and with the consequent burdens of child-bearing and housekeeping. There is also the suggestion in one of her stories that an honourable substitute for marriage is nursing. As an occupation this appeared first choice for many of the subject children; they frequently mentioned child care also as a proposed career. Both of these would appear to afford them ample opportunity to show pity and sympathy, and to be needed and wanted by less adequate individuals.

(2) 'I think he's ploughing the field—she's a schoolgirl and she

might come up with the teacher—she might wish to be married, have a family and live out in the country—she might like to do housework and that's why she's come up with the teacher.'

(3) 'She's crying because she's had an argument with somebody or she's fed up—or somebody's made her angry and she's in a bad temper—she's going into her house—she might make herself a cup of tea and try to settle herself down—or go to bed—or she might do some housework, and that's if she's married—it might come alright. Is that out in the country? She could have had a fight with someone over her children and she's sorry she's done it, and she's crying.'

(4) 'I think those two there are in love and she might be engaged and he's walking away from her, and she wants him to stay with her, and he wants to go. He looks angry. He could be fed up with her. I don't think she's fed up with him. She wants him—the way she looks in the picture. They might get married, and live in the town, and raise a family. They might not get on. She might become a nurse, and look after people in the hospital, and he might go out to war and have a battle, and come back, and she'll still be a nurse, and he'll want her, and they will marry. Or she might join up in the war, and look after the people who are injured or the young children. If she joined up as a nurse in the war—and he got wounded—she would have to look after him—and when he was alright he would become a doctor and they would be a doctor and nurse together, or else she'd get married.'

(5) 'She could be married and she might have two boys and she would mostly look to one of her boys and the one she took to—if the other was hitting him—she would always be hitting him, and the boy she would not want, would go away feeling he wasn't wanted—he would go with other friends—if he had any, and she would only have the one son, and she would worry about the other boy. And he might stay with his aunty and uncle and she would want him back home then, and she would be jealous of them—or the one she didn't want, would go as a sailor to sea, and she would take him back then—the two of them, and they would live all together then.'

(6gf) 'I think she's married to that man, and she might have a family, and she mightn't—or if they're not married, he'll be always coming to her, and giving her flowers and things to make her go out with him—and she'll be sick of the flowers, and have to go out with him, and they'll go in a car down to the seaside, and have a picnic with her, and she'll be lying in her bathing costume with the sun shining on her, and they'll have a swim, or a walk round the beach and have a meal, and then make their journey's way home—and then they'll probably get on and raise a family. She might have a son—her first baby—and he'll go into the Air Force, or join up as an Irish Guard, and then he'll go and leave his parents, or else he might stay at home with his parents and have a job in the town. Or maybe she had a wee girl, and she might be a swimmer and take cups, and they'd be proud of her. More proud of the little girl who was winning prizes—or a life-saver—or she might have a boyfriend and they'd go to his parents, and get engaged, and get married, and have children.'

(7gf) 'She's married and she has a young girl and the young girl doesn't look happy—and she wants to go away somewhere, and her mother won't let her—or she's reading her a story and the wee girl doesn't like that story. Maybe that little girl will come up famous—as a singer, and that is her only child, and they might go to Australia, and if she had no Daddy, she'd get married and have more wee brothers and sisters. Or they may stay where they are, and she'd still be a singer or a ballet dancer.'

(8gf) 'She might not be married, and she might be thinking of getting married, and she might not have a job, and she might be thinking of how she could get money to buy nice clothes and have a home—or she might have a job and meet a boy, and go to a dance, and dance with someone famous, with plenty of money and he would buy her things, and her mother something, and buy her a home, and she might become famous with him—a singer— and her mother would be always with her—and he might buy her a wee cottage house for her mummy and her to live in, and they'd go up into the hills and pick daisies—and her mummy and her boyfriend and she would go into a car, and go away down into the country, or to his relatives, and he would ask her to marry him, and they might have a family, and they might not, and go plenty of places, and they might go out in a boat or swimming, and she would be very happy. Her mother—she would probably bring her with her—and if she had more brothers and sisters, her mother would probably stay and look after them.'

(9gf) 'She's running away from a big palace, and that is her maid with her. Her mother and father could be locking her up in a room, so that no boys could come. Her mother and father didn't want her to get married—but she did, and she felt awfully lonely, and she ran away and her maid come too, and she'd see a big boat and get on it, and she'd meet other young girls and have fun with them and go to a dance. Probably she met a boy or a man, and he would ask her to dance, and then they'd go on the deck for fresh air and he would kiss her, and she'd slap him on the face and run away—or she might not—she might stay with him.'

(10) 'He could have been away out to sea, and this is his father or some friend of his, and he didn't know where to go, and that father or man—they'd be happy to see each other—and they'd stay. His father might clean him up, and give him something to eat and a drink and a hot bath, and put him up to bed, and he'd ask him why he went away, and he'd probably stay with him this time. That man there could be an old man, and he might get a printing machine and might print things—a printing money machine—and they'd probably come rich and they'd have a happy life.'

(14) 'I think he's a robber—probably robbed something out of that house, and is climbing out of the window, and the alarm is ringing, and the police are coming—and he'll jump onto the top of the van and get away—or he might be caught, and the police would take a statement off him, and he might come up to Court, and they'd ask questions and have witnesses—and if he was guilty, he'd be put in a cell, and he'd be crying, "Let me out, let me out", and they'd make him work—dig up ground or fix machines, and he'd be in prison for a long while, and then he'd go up, and he might be married and he'd want to go back and see his wife and children and lead a happy life then.'

(16) 'In a hospital, and probably somebody in an accident, and comes in on a stretcher for an x-ray and then goes through an operation—if he comes out alright puts him in a ward with other people, and the nurse comes and looks after him, and he's probably broken two legs and they're up in the air, and the nurse would give him an injection for his leg—and they'd give him exercises to strengthen them and give him swimming. He'd meet friends there and other people, and he'd probably meet girls, and the other girls might have polio, and they'd go out in their wheel chairs, and he'd get married, and he'd stand at his wedding, and he'd always be thinking of his legs, and always be shouting at his wife, and leave her and go into the hospital to watch T.V., and T.V. was over, he'd be in a bad temper with his wife, and go round in his wheel chair, and go to the doctor who would tell him to go back to his wife and they'd be happy.'

(18gf) 'A girl and this man, and that man waits to kiss her and she doesn't want it and he has her over the bannister and she tries to get free. Or it might be a lady—does that there look like a lady? He's busy fiddling round with her chair. Probably leave her alone and she'd run up afterwards and shout "Let me in" and batter at her door and she'd say "I don't want to see you again" and she would stay there until he went away. She would pack up her things, and go away to some other place and stay in a hotel, and meet plenty of friends there. She might not have liked that man."

Finally the protocol of an eleven-year-old schoolboy, Fred. Fred was the last of a family of three boys, both his brothers being considerably older than himself. His father was a boiler-man in the shipyard, and his mother worked the night shift in a spinning mill. Fred showed no signs of unsettledness in school, and was enthusiastic and helpful during testing. He looked pale, however, and small for his age, and his eyes were heavily ringed and his nails bitten well below the quick. He was thought to have a misplaced kidney and was frequently absent from school with kidney trouble.

One year before my first meeting with Fred, he and a friend had been assaulted by an older schoolboy. They were both in a gang hut when the boy came in and made them lie down on the floor. He opened their trousers and had imitation intercourse against their abdomens. Their parents were very indignant about the offence and reported it immediately to the police. A month later the boy was committed to a training school for an unspecified period.

Fred's stories do not suggest that he is starved of affection, but they do emphasise the importance of family relationships to him. Most of his stories centre on family life—his own in particular—and seem full of happiness and satisfaction.

(2) 'Once upon a time by the sea there was three people—two women and a man—and the man was ploughing with a horse and one of the women was standing by a tree and the other one was holding books and standing looking at her. There were huts all round the place and there was a house also. The woman beside the tree is looking up in the air and it's a very good day and the other man is looking at his horse and thinking about the two of them standing there and wondering what they're thinking about. He's thinking of asking them could he have dinner with one of them

and that's what the two women are thinking also. He's trying to get some courage to ask one of the women, and he's hoping one of the women will go away so he can ask the other one. But the two of them stood off there for an hour, and he hoped and hoped one of them would go away so he could ask the other. But one would not go. Then the one by the tree ran away and the man asked the woman which had books in her hand would she go out to dinner with him, and he told her that he would meet her in the same place at half five. So he departed and went home—so when half five came they met in the same spot and went out for dinner. They walked onto the road which led to town and they got into town inside the half hour and went to a place called Joe's Café. There in walked an ape, and the man asked the woman if she would like to go into the pictures for a while. When the picture had finished they started to walk home again. They cut off from the road, and went to the spot that they met, and they said "Good-bye" to each other and they departed. When the girl was walking home the man followed her and caught up with her and asked if she would have dinner with him tomorrow night, but she said she had to go out with her friend to her auntie's, so the man said "Would you be able to make it the following night," and she said "Yes". So they walked away from each other. Suddenly the rain came on and the woman ran as fast as she could, also the man, and as they ran they waved "goodbye" to each other, and the man shouted "I'll see you in two days!" '

(3) 'One day a man and woman was walking together in a country lane and they started arguing. The girl wanted to go to a show, and the fellow wanted to go to eat dinner, and the girl said "If we don't go to the show I will not see you again"—and he said "That's alright, well." And he ran away. The girl walked back down the country lane to her own home, and started to cry all the way. When she reached her home her mother asked her why was she crying but she said nothing and ran upstairs, and into her room. She stood at the cupboard and started to cry again—she cried and cried and cried all that night. When she woke up next morning she went out and walked into the country lane again. She met her boyfriend again and they both ran to each other and kissed each other and said "Do you want to go to a show tonight?" and she said "Yes". So they departed again and met that night in a country lane and went to the show.'

(4) 'After the war was over all the men came home again. They all came home by aeroplane from England. When they reached

Belfast Airport, there were taxis there waiting for them to take them home. One man got wounded during the war. When he came home his wife and his children were waiting for him. When they seen him wounded his wife cried and brought him into the house with the children too. So the father showed his children his presents which he had brought for them and the children went to bed and mother and father had tea by themselves and the mother asked her husband how he got wounded and many other things. The mother asked the father if he would go out, but he said no, he was tired, and he wanted to go to bed. He told her that he had to go to hospital next morning, to see about his arm—so they kissed and the husband went to bed—so did his wife. Next morning the wife got up to make the tea before he went to hospital. He had to go to hospital before half nine and it was already nine o'clock—so he got on his coat and went to the bus stop to get a bus and his wife waved at him saying "goodbye". He was at the hospital for three hours. When he came home his wife and his children was at dinner, so he joined them, and he said he was still very tired so he says he would go to bed again. He said "goodbye" to the children for they had to go to school, and told his wife to waken him about four o'clock, so he went up to bed and his wife put the children up to school, and went to get the messages in.'

(5) 'One morning my Gran came down the stairs looking for me. I was in the Library getting a book for myself. She called me and said my dinner was ready, so I chose my book and went up quickly. I ate my dinner quickly because I was late for school, so I ran round to the bus stop and got a bus—took the bus eight minutes to get up to school, and I just made it in time. It was just twenty to two.'

(6) 'One day my mother was looking in her jewellery box, when my father asked her what jewellery she wanted for Christmas, and she says "A necklace", and my father says "Alright, you will get one." So that evening when my father had finished work he went to buy my mother a necklace. It cost £7. When my father got home he had the necklace so that it would be a surprise for Christmas for mother. On Christmas morning, when I came down, my two brothers and my father, and my mother was up. I went over to play with my games and looked at the rest of my things. When mother went in to make tea, my father put the necklace on the table, and when my mother had finished tea and come in she said "Who's this necklace for?" and father said "You, " and she went over to father and kissed him. And my mother gave my

father a prize also—it was three books, and father kissed her for them. At two o'clock we had our dinner—we had turkey and all that day I played with my games, and I wasn't in bed too late that night nor was anyone in the family.'

(7) 'One day my cousin came up from Enniskillen with her mother to visit us. We all had tea together, and then my cousin and me played with the games I had got for Christmas—then my mother and me, my aunty and my cousin went out together. We went into the town and went into the pictures. It was a war picture. It lasted two hours. After it was over we went into a café and ordered some chips and fish. Then we went over to the bus stop to get a bus. The bus left us at the stop where we wanted to get off and we only had to walk round the corner to get home. We all took our coats off and went by the fire. I wanted to watch TV so turned it on. "Outlaws" was on. After "Outlaws" was over my aunty and my cousin had to go home. The last train was at half ten, so they left at ten o'clock. Me and my mother left them down to the station, and waved goodbye to them as the train went. It was just after half ten so me and my mother went home again. My father was in the house when we got home so we had tea and went to bed.'

(8) 'One day when I was at school my Mother was in the house thinking—she was thinking about my Grandda who was in the hospital with a bad heart. She thought he might die. Then she fell asleep and dreamt that she was up visiting him at the hospital. When she was walking home a man ran up to her, and said, "Do you call yourself Mrs Jones?" and she said "Yes." The man said "I have bad news for you," and my mother said "What is it," and the man said "Mr Jones has died." My mother and the man ran away back and saw my grandfather lying on the bed, with the clothes over his face. That moment she woke up again, and said "I must have dreamt it." That night when my father came home, and they were all at dinner, she told us what she had dreamt and my father said "That was a nasty dream!" '

(9) 'One day my aunt come to visit us. She come up from Bangor. After my mother had made some tea for her she said "Would you like me to draw a picture?" and we all said "Yes." So she drew a picture of a girl. It took her an hour to draw it and paint it. Just then my father came in and said "Who drew that picture?" and my aunty came from upstairs and said "It was me!" My father says "I didn't know that you were in Belfast," and she said "I have

just come two hours ago." My mother made some tea for my
father, and my father asked my aunt if she would draw a picture
of him, but she said she could not draw a picture of him, but we all
said she could, so she tried, and she did. It was getting late so my
aunty said she would have to go home now—so we all said goodbye
and she went home.'

(10) 'When my Grandfather was over in America working, my
Grandmother was worried about him, and she sent him a letter
to tell him she wanted him home again. So Grandfather decided
to come home. We were all at Grandmother's house that day
when Grandfather was supposed to come home. He reached the
house at nine o'clock in the morning. When he came in we all
kissed him, and my mother put on the tea, and we asked Grandfather many questions. That night when we all had gone home,
and there was only Grandfather and Grandmother in the house,
sitting watching TV, my Grandmother started to cry. My Grandfather asked her why was she crying and she said "Nothing."
Then Grandfather put his arms round Grandmother, and said "I
love you." Then they decided to go a walk so they put on their
coats and went a walk. They did not go far because it was cold
and they were soon back again. And both of them had tea and
they went to bed.'

(14) 'Last year I went down to my uncle's farm in the country
with my two brothers. We stayed there for two months. We
helped my uncle on his farm and threw straw from the window
down on to the ground. Every day we did that. We also milked
the cows and fed the chickens. He had horses on his farm. Every
day after we had dinner, my two brothers and I went a ride on
them. We rode all round the farm. After we did that, we went
into the town to sell his eggs and other things. Sometimes we sold
all the things, and sometimes we didn't, but most of the time we
did. When we came back from the town we always had tea, and
then washed and brushed the horses. After the two months were
up my two brothers and I had to come back again. My mother
was pleased to see us home again and so was my father.'

(16) 'One day I went down to Enniskillen to my Aunty's house.
My Aunty was surprised and made us tea and then we went a
walk down to the beach. I had my swimming pants with me, and
my cousin went in also. The water was cold and my cousin and I
kept on running out. Then we built a sand castle and then
knocked it down again. Then we decided to go out in a boat. We

143

were on the boat about an hour which cost us two shillings each. When we had come in again, it was getting on a bit late, so we decided to go up to Aunty's house and have tea before we went home again. Then Aunty made us a lovely cup of tea. My cousin give me some comics to read in the train. It took the train three quarters of an hour to get from Enniskillen to Belfast. When we reached Belfast station I had some money. I bought some sweets. Then my mother ordered a taxi to take us home. When we reached home my father had more tea waiting for us, so we took it and he asked us was it good. I said "Yes." That night before I went to bed there was sand all over my feet, so I cleaned it off and went to bed.'

(18gf) 'Last Christmas my cousin was in the house with my mother. My cousin was playing a game and my mother was sewing. My cousin went up the stairs to get a different game. When she got to the bottom of the stairs, my mother came out, and went over and put her arms round her neck and squeezed tight. She had killed my cousin. Suddenly my uncle came in and said "What have you done," and my Aunty said "I don't know." My uncle phoned for the doctor, but the doctor was too late—my cousin was dead—so he rang for the police. They asked my Aunty many questions—but she said she did not do it—so my Aunty had to go to Court and she was accused of killing the girl, and was sentenced to eight years.'

Second Testing (1962–4)

The second testing was undertaken in exactly the same way as the first, but without the preliminaries of widespread I.Q. testing, or questions relating to family structure. The children had been prepared for the second testing at the time of the first, and were reassured by me about the nature of the study. They were told that I was interested to see how their stories had changed now that they were a year older. Teachers were told that a repetition of the Bristol Social Adjustment Guide testing would enable me to make comparisons in the behavioural aspects of the child's personality, occurring as a result of time.

Unsettledness and maladjustment seen in school. Of the thirty-nine subjects whose scores were used in the first testing, twenty-three subjects and controls had left school, and sixteen control groups

144

were insufficient usually as a result of one group member's removal to another district. Two sets of Bristol Social Adjustment Guides were not returned by class teachers.

Statistical analysis of the B.S.A.G. scores was therefore only possible on eighteen complete sets of subject and control scores, and the remaining scores could only be compared non-statistically. Each Bristol Social Adjustment Guide syndrome was subjected to statistical analysis using the Friedmann Two Way Analysis of Variance ($N = 18$, $K = 5$, d.f. $= 4$).

Hypothesis 1 had predicted that a statistically significant difference would be found in the affection seeking behaviour displayed by the two groups of children. This prediction was not substantiated. No statistical differences were found for any of the sixteen items. However, a non-statistical comparison of the two entire groups suggested that, as in the first testing, the greatest difference between groups lay in the affection seeking syndrome. Whilst no longer statistically significant, affection seeking remained a prominent feature in the response repertoire of the subject child. Also noticeable, and possibly due to increasing age, was a slight increase in the amount of restlessness shown by the subject children. No other differences were noted between groups, and the tendency for the subject group to be more unsettled than the control group seemed no longer apparent.

The number of children in each group scoring separate Bristol Social Adjustment Guide items was analysed, and several items seemed characteristic of the subject children on this second testing. They were described as sometimes lacking interest, and frequently wandering off alone. Their affection seeking tended to take the form of frequently bringing items to show the teacher, and also craving for sympathy from him. Towards their classmates, subject children were frequently over-brave, taking unnecessary risks, and they liked to be the centre of attention. They were still somewhat hostile and still maintained a resentful expression and muttered indignantly from time to time.

In comparison to the year before, many of the more noticeable affection seeking responses had been discarded. The child no longer appeared so anxious to engage the teacher on the slightest pretext, nor tended to brag so openly to other children, or dress spivvishly. Instead, affection seeking tended to be more frequently displayed in a craving for sympathy. Similarly, several items indicating nervous tension, for example excessive nail biting, playing with younger children, and the tendency to give up easily, were no longer present. Instead, depressive tendencies were more apparent, for example, the lack of interest in school activities, and the tendency to wander off alone.

On such slender evidence as a non-statistical analysis of these items it would be impossible to state with certainty that there had been a change of direction in the child's affection seeking behaviour. But there exists the possibility that the year's time lapse brought about a lessening in overt adult-child affection seeking, accompanied by a degree of depression, and an increasing interest in the child's own body. No data exists to give us a norm by which to assess accurately the degree to which this may be a characteristic of general development, and not restricted solely to our group.

Underlying personality needs and threats. Testing proceeded in a manner similar to that of the first year. Thirty-seven subjects were seen by the author (four having left school) and 129 control children. (The remaining twenty-five control children had either left school or were unable to be traced because of removal.) For the purposes of statistical analysis therefore twenty-seven sets of subject and control scores were intact and were investigated using the Friedmann Two Way Analysis of Variance ($N = 27$, $K = 5$, d.f. $= 4$).

As predicted, and as seen at the time of the first testing, subject children told significantly more stories indicative of a need for affiliation ($X^2 = 20$, $\rho = 0 \cdot 001$) and significantly more stories indicative of a fear of rejection ($X^2 = 17 \cdot 5$, $\rho = 0 \cdot 01 > 0 \cdot 001$).

In addition, and contrary to the initial prediction, the subject children told significantly more stories indicative of a fear of personal inadequacy ($X^2 = 16$, $\rho = 0 \cdot 01 > 0 \cdot 001$). They were frightened of their own guilt, and their physical, mental and motivational inadequacy, which together prevented satisfaction of their needs. The subject children also told significantly more stories indicative of a fear of death ($X^2 = 18 \cdot 2$, $\rho = 0 \cdot 01 > 0 \cdot 001$). They were frightened not only that the death of a loved one would prevent satisfaction of their needs, but also that their own death would result in this deprivation.

As in the first meeting, and contrary to prediction, the control children told significantly more stories indicative of a need for security ($X^2 = 18\cdot2$, $\rho = 0\cdot01 > 0\cdot001$)

In contrast to the first testing, the subject group at the time of the second testing showed no greater fear of the environment than did the control group. Neither did they display a greater tendency to end their stories in modified success. As predicted, no differences were apparent in the general emotional tone of the stories, in the action patterns, and in the expected outcomes.

Fear of personal guilt, which the first Hypothesis predicted as appearing significantly more often in the T.A.T. protocols of the subject children, was more apparent in the themes of this group on the second testing.

In essence, the results of the second T.A.T. testing confirm those of the first year. As predicted, the subject group show an inordinate need for affection, coupled with a fear of rejection. Increasingly they see themselves as inadequate, and in the second testing show an increased fear of personal guilt, and a real fear of death.

By contrast, and not as predicted, the control group show a need for security, and with increasing age become more preoccupied with the need for achievement.

Parent-Child Relationships, as seen in the children's T.A.T. stories. Finally, an analysis of the themes relating to parent-child relationships was made and a statistical analysis of the differences between groups was made using the Friedmann Two Way Analysis of Variance ($N = 27$, $K = 5$, d.f. $= 4$).. Hypothesis 1 had predicted that subject children would see their parents as significantly more rejecting, and more frequently dead, or absent than would the controls, but no significant difference existed between groups for these categories on the second testing. The sum of stories relating to parent themes was still greater for the subject group than for the controls, but this difference was no longer statistically significant. Subject children were seen to be more involved than control children in parent-child relationships and problems, but less obviously so than at the time of the first testing.

The three essential features of Hypothesis 1 were:

(1) That sexually assaulted children would appear more affection seeking in school than a carefully matched group of control children.

(2) That sexually assaulted children would display a need for affection, a fear of parental loss or rejection, and an awareness of personal guilt, on a test measuring personality structure.

(3) That in other forms of behaviour, and in other personality needs and fears the two groups should not differ significantly.

In essence Hypothesis 1 appears to be substantiated by this study. Sexually assaulted children do show a need for affection and a fear of rejection which remain constant. Their behaviour is overtly affection seeking, although less significantly so at the time of the second testing. Several factors do not substantiate the initial prediction and need further explanation however.

(1) *Absence of guilt in the subject group.* This is particularly striking in view of the select nature of this group (the majority of them having undergone Court proceedings). Clearly guilt does not arise automatically either from association with a guilty adult, or from perceiving their parents' distress at the assault. In this study, guilt is seen to become more apparent with time, and the suggestion is made that it may represent an awareness of personal inadequacy, that is, an inability to gain love, rather than an awareness of moral shortcoming. This suggestion might explain the significance of the awareness of personal inadequacy score on the second T.A.T. testing, and the increasing restlessness and depression of the group, as seen in class. A further possibility, but perhaps a less likely one, is that as awareness of moral guilt might be so repressed following the event that a considerable time is needed before the child permits itself to perceive it. (Of particular interest is the story of subject 12, contained later on page 158). Here the child was unable to tell her parents about the assault, until she was officially exonerated from any suggestion of 'allowing herself to be captured'.

(2) *Perception of the environment as threatening.* In the first test fear of the external environment was particularly apparent, but at the time of the second testing it was almost non-existent, being

replaced by a fear of death. It is suggested that this may reflect nothing more than change of emphasis in the subject's objects of fear. At first, from the T.A.T. themes, it was apparent that subject children feared rivalry, illness and death as threats to the satisfaction of their need for affection. Individually, none of these fears was paramount. At the time of the second testing, fear had crystallised into a specific fear of death. This might reflect either the child's increasing fear that there would be no solution to his needs (parents would die, rather than return or get better) or his increasing fear that he would never be adequate enough to win affection. (The ultimate personal inadequacy would be death.) It is interesting to note that on neither testing did the subject group show any greater fear of violence than the control children. Clearly, their experience did not leave them with the feeling that the environment was a particularly violent or dangerous one.

(3) *Lack of awareness of parental rejection or loss.* In the circumstances, the lack of awareness of their parents' rejection or loss, postulated in Hypothesis 1, appears surprising. The subject children are more aware of parent figures and their relationships with them, than are the control children, but they do not especially see the parent figures as threatening, rejecting, or otherwise lacking. This may represent an extreme defensiveness on the part of these children, but more probably it represents a realistic assessment of the parents' adequacy. These children do not seem to have sustained excessive rejection. If they had, their behaviour would most certainly reflect considerably more hostility, or less concern for adult approval. Nor do the subject children seem to view the chances of obtaining affection with less than optimism. If they did, depression would be far more in evidence. Many of their stories portray parent figures as helpful, and the children see themselves as helping their parents. It would seem probable therefore that as a group subject children have an innately greater need for affection than do the control children. Consequently the parents, while objectively satisfactory, and possibly satisfying the needs of their other children quite adequately, cannot fully meet the subject child's possibly excessive need.

To further exemplify this suggestion, several examples of T.A.T. themes relating to parents, and told by subject children, are included here. A very real need for affection is apparent in all of them, and generally this need is eventually satisfied. At first parent figures appear to be unsatisfactory, not fully aware of their child's needs, but when the child is able to communicate these, either in words, or through his behaviour, all is well. The stories usually end in some degree of happiness, with the parents involved at last with the child.

(S.13) 'A little girl called Ann, and Ann's father and mother were very rich and had really no time for Ann. When it was Ann's ninth birthday, her mother and father were away on a business trip, and her nurse Sheila was the only one who stayed with her, when her mother and father were away. Ann loved her nurse but would rather have had her mother and father at her birthday party. Ann had lots of friends but rarely saw her mother and father for they were always out and never stayed with her or took her with them. One day Ann was very ill and the doctor could find nothing wrong with her, and the doctor said she had something on her mind and he took her into hospital, and when she was there her father and mother came to visit her and she got better—and the doctor told them if they wanted to make her well they would have to be with her and after that they were always at home.'

(S.16) 'Mary is a wealthy child but a sad one at that. Her mother and father leave her in the care of a maid, very often, while they go on big trips and do much business. Her mother is at home this week and reads her a story, but Mary does not listen. "Why can't I be like other children?" she says to herself, "whose mothers don't go on big cruises!" Mary thought hard about it all day, and that night she ran away, but the servant boy followed her, and the next day Mary was found not in her bedroom, not anywhere in the house. Where could Mary be? Nobody knew. Her mother was in an awful state and sent for her father. Mary returned home two days later and her mother was glad to see her—ran and hugged her child—"Oh, where have you got to," she said, "I've been worried about you." Mary replied in a low voice. "Why can't I be like the other children and have my mummy and daddy at home." The mother and father realised their stupidity and if not her mother stayed with her, her father did, and Mary became a happy and playful girl.'

(S.19) 'Once there was a woman who had a little girl of nine years of age. The woman lived in America, and the girl in England, and they never saw each other. The girl lived with her aunt and uncle, and they had two housekeepers, a man and a woman, and every day the housekeeper read to her a story, sitting beside her on a long settee, and the housekeeper leant on a little table, and the little girl was looking away from her. Then she started to cry, and she was thinking of her mother and why she could not see her, and the housekeeper told her her mother had an important job and could not come to see her. Then her uncle came in and the housekeeper told him, and her uncle said her mother would be back in two months to see her, and the little girl was so pleased. But then a letter came saying her mother had an important appointment and could not break it, so she could not come. The housekeeper said she could not read it for it would break her heart. The little girl burst out crying and said she would run away and never come back and the housekeeper said "Don't do that, your mother says if she cannot come next month, you will go and live with her. ' And she did that and lived with her forever.'

(S.22) 'A picnic on it and about five people in it—the place is all laid out, so it is, and there's three boys and two girls and they are all very young people, and there's a boy, and he looks very ugly and he's very sad. And the rest of them are drinking lemonade and there's sandwiches and all on the ground. And the boy who is ugly is over by the tree and he's crying—sad—and the rest are talking, laughing ,and he looks at them and feels like killing them. But just then another girl comes in, and she's not ugly, she's all right. She goes over to the man by the tree, and she says "What's the matter?" He says "Nothing." And turns his face, and then a couple of minutes later they are sitting together by the river and everyone is happy now. He most wanted a girl but no other girl wanted him for he was ugly, and this girl came along and comforted him.'

(S.31) 'About a young girl who hadn't a very happy life. Her mother and father are always arguing and fighting with each other and she had to take care of herself and take a job after school. Her mother and father split up and the girl is sent to boarding school where she lives and prefers it very much to her own home life. She makes a whole lot of friends at school and enjoys it very much indeed, but after a few years at the school her mother and father try to patch it up and send for her. At first she doesn't like the idea and thinks she will just have to go through what she went through before. But she decides to give it a try and the family is together again and find out they can live together far better as a family. She finds that everyone needs someone to belong to.'

(S.31) 'About a young boy. His mother and father had a lot of money and he was very well looked after but he rarely saw his mother and father. It was always other people that was left to look after him. So one night when he was lying in bed he thought he would try to draw attention to himself and get his mother and father to pay attention to him, so he decided to run away. He opened the window and climbed out. At first he thought he would get far away with what money he had. But then he thought he would go only a little way and deliberately get himself brought back to try and draw attention to himself. By morning he reached a town and thought he would get some sleep, so he climbed into a field and lay under the shelter of the hedges. He decided the longer he would stay away the more anxious his parents would become—so he slept in fields and bought from the shops in the day. He stayed at large for a few days until he was spotted by a farmer who had heard about a young boy missing. He went off and sent a message to the young boy's parents to tell them where he was. The young boy had seen the farmer but did not want to get away very far as he'd had enough of living outside. He moved further down to the next few fields and hid there for a while. He saw a police car draw up and the policeman come and search for him. At the first sight of the police he thought he must get away from there, but then he got a grip on himself, and decided to stay there. Finally the police came running over to where he was. They took him back to the car and before long he was back home. The mother and father were now quite worried and realised how foolish they had been to neglect their son. When they saw the car coming up to the house they ran out overjoyed to meet their son. As the young boy went in to his mother and father he smiled knowing he would now have more attention and a much happier life.'

(S.30) 'This little girl's mother has just had a wee baby but the wee girl is jealous, because before the baby came she had everything she wanted and her mother and father had spoilt her. Now she'll have to share everything with the baby. Her mother is telling her how nice the baby is, and she will soon get to like it, but the wee girl doesn't listen. She doesn't even want to look at the baby.'

(S.32) 'Three boys in the picture. One is a rough kind of person who is always getting into trouble and is always looking for it. The

152

second is the kind who would always follow the first—not being very intelligent would always follow the first to please him. The third is quite different—not like the others at all—but afraid of separating himself from the group in case he would be the outcast of the district. The three are now planning something which in the course of doing it will be breaking the law. The first will not care about being caught neither will the second, but the third will be the most nervous of the three and he will have to be urged on by the other two.'

CHAPTER XIV

Unsettledness in Relation to the
Time Lapse from the Assault

Hypothesis 2 predicted that no greater unsettledness would be apparent in the behaviour of children whose assault had occurred only a short time before the personality assessment was made, compared with the children whose assault had occurred at a much earlier time. This hypothesis therefore tested the assumption that sexual assault by adults does not have an unsettling effect on the child's general personality development.

Two groups of subjects were formed, and a statistical analysis was made of the difference in the B.S.A.G. syndrome scores of the two groups. The first group (N = 15) comprised children whose assault had taken place anything between four months and one year ten months before the personality testing was made. The mean time lapse from the assault to the testing was one year one month. The second group of children (N = 24) had been assaulted at some time between two years one month and seven and a half years before the personality testing took place. The mean time lapse between the sexual incident and the testing was four years and three months.

A statistical comparison was made of the unsettledness scores using the Mann Whitney Test. (Because n_2 exceeded 20, Z values were computed, and the probability was derived from the normal distribution table.) Contrary to expectations one syndrome—that of unforthcomingness—was seen more often in the scores of the children in Group 1 (Z = 2·485, p = 0·0064) suggesting that in this sample children whose sexual assault had occurred on average only one year before testing, were more unforthcoming, *possibly* as a result of the experience, than children whose assault took place on average more than four years before the testing.

Unforthcomingness, as a symptom of unsettledness, expresses a lack of confidence in strange people and new experiences, and a defensiveness against them. It does not indicate a lack of interest in affection (Stott 1964), nor does it appear as a characteristic of the subject group as a whole. On the contrary, Hypothesis 1 suggests that subject children at both times of testing are actively making contact with adults and other children. It must be concluded therefore that there occurs an impairment of natural assertiveness, probably as a result of the assault, or the subsequent family upset and Court proceedings. It is reassuring to note that this remains a temporary characteristic, passing presumably with time and increasing confidence.

Clearly, with the exception of this tendency to unforthcomingness in the group whose sexual assault was most recent, Hypothesis 2 must be accepted. The sexual assault does not appear to have an excessively unsettling effect on the child's personality development, as seen in his behaviour.

This finding is substantiated by an analysis of the T.A.T. themes produced by the subject children, at the time of both the first and the second testings. Only one story indicative of distress following the event was told to me, in the first testing. Several further stories of a similar nature were recounted on the second testing, suggesting that unfamiliarity with me and the test situation may have made the children more cautious in the first year. (This supposition is further substantiated by the fact that the first year's story was told to me by a very mentally retarded child. Her intellectual impairment may have made it difficult for her to distinguish situations in which she should show caution, and she evinced considerable pleasure in telling her 'distress' story to me.)

The following stories are the only stories suggesting distress occasioned by the assault to be found in the 984 themes produced by the subject children in the first and second testings. It will be apparent from the small number of these stories that no really extensive anxieties concerning the sexual trauma are present in the subject group. It is possible that anxiety of this sort might be considerably repressed, but some behaviour indicating tensions and anxiety would then be expected, and this was not apparent in the subject group as observed in school. One is forced to the conclusion therefore that subject children have suffered little real lasting fear or anxiety as a result of their sexual experience.

(S.31) 'Three people in the picture—one, the man who is the victim of a criminal assault, and the two people grabbing him trying to rob him. He seems already to have taken a beating and has given in to the two men who are robbing him. He doesn't seem to be the bravest kind of person, just an ordinary man with children and married, and he can't realise that he is being subjected to this type of assault. The two who picked him didn't seem to care who it was, just someone who wouldn't make a fuss.'

(S.30) 'The two girls in the picture are being chased by someone. They are trying to get home before the person catches them. They are out of breath and cannot run much further—they are thinking they will be caught, but just as the man catches one of the girls a man in a car comes round the corner—it is the girl's father. He stops the car and the other man runs. Her father chases after him but he cannot catch him. He returns and takes the girls home safely in his car.'

(S.5) 'Two sisters and they're on this small island and a man brought them over on a boat and the lady says "We'll go in for a swim," and the lady says "We'll have our picnic after." And when she goes for the picnic she sees a man and they ran and ran, and she says to her sister "It's that man and he's looking at us, and he's coming after us," and they got to the boat and there's no man there and so they say they'd better swim and the man catches up with them and he says "It's all right I was only seeing if there was anyone there," and they say "That's all right. I'm going to the park, there's more people there and it's all right— there's more people watching there and no one can touch you," and they wrap her up in a shawl and get a taxi home and get dressed for a picnic, and the man comes and says "Is there where you live?" And she says "Yes". And when they go to the park the man follows them, and when they are feeding the swans the man comes up behind them and the woman screams, and the Park Keeper comes and says "Leave that lady alone" and he says he is her father and he can do what he likes with her, and she says no he isn't and she doesn't want him to touch her—and they go home and bolt all the doors and in the night the one who screamed feels sick, and they go to the bathroom and then there's a tap and there's a big man there, and they scream, and the butler and the two maids come and lift him and put him outside. And they tell him never to come near again or they'll tell the police, and next morning they find a letter from the man saying he'd get them today, and the butler goes with them and he scares the man and he runs away and never comes again and the girls are very glad they had their butlers.'

The same child also recounted this story:

'The little girl and she's walking down the street and she sees this man on the other side and he's a mask on his face, and she sees a car with an engine running and he says "Come with me," and she says she's not allowed to go with strange men, and she's eight, and he says "Well, run along or you'll have to come with me" and he gives her three shillings, and she runs home and tells her mother, and she tells her husband who takes the girl back to the bank, and they see the masked man, and he says, "If you don't go away, you'll be killed" and they go away, and a man runs down to the police station and tells the police men, and six comes out, and there's no more in the Barracks except the Sergeant and the constable, and they phone through to the next town to say they need more men, and would they send some over. And there's only two there, and in half an hour's time they sent over six men and disguised themselves as ordinary citizens and go down to the bank and one of them is captured. They tell the others to drop their guns and they do, and the little girl gets two and six from her daddy for telling him about it.'

(S.12) 'One day Mary was coming home from school and her father was ploughing the fields and looking over the horizon. Her mother was standing and looking at the sky. Mary was looking very worried and carrying her books. Mary's mother asked her what worried her but she didn't want to tell her so she turned away and then she went home and lay down on the settee and started to cry. Her mother came back and kept on asking her but she still wouldn't tell. It was six o'clock and her father came in and asked her but she still wouldn't tell. That night Mary was very worried and burst into tears in the middle of the night. She didn't want to go to school and her mother kept her off, for she had made herself sick with crying. She helped her mother in the house and weeks passed and still Mary didn't go to school. Mary kept on doing housework for her mother, but still wouldn't tell her what had passed. Then she kept on crying but she still wouldn't tell her mother. It was on her fifteenth birthday when she ran out into her bedroom despite her visitors, and wept and wept. Her mother was a little angry for doing that in front of her guests. Mary was fifteen years old now and was leaving school at the end of the term so she went to school and the teacher was very angry and caned her hard, but still she wouldn't tell. It was a year after and Mary was in a good job and Mary was giving her mother some money to buy things to make the house look nicer. On a Wednesday it was Mary's day off, and she decided to go for a walk in the woods and went in and walked towards the woods. Then suddenly a great ... [Here the child stopped for a few seconds] ... black figure jumped out from behind a tree in the woods and said "Now I've got you, what are you going to do now?" Mary ran and ran but she couldn't escape, and the figure grabbed her and pulled her into the hut in the middle of the woods. Weeks passed and she still wasn't home and her parents were worried, but they were too far out in the country to call the police. She was being fed and given water, but the figure never let her out. Her mother said "She's run away from home, the little monkey!" But her father said "Our Mary wouldn't do a thing like that." Six years passed and Mary came back. Her parents didn't know her, and she couldn't speak or hear and was blind, and she'd felt her way along. Mary's mother decided to go and fetch the police and harnessed the cart and set off. It took a day and a half to get there and she told what had happened to Mary, and the Officer sent four policemen and Mary led them to the little house. The big black figure sat on a chair in front of the fire. She cried. Mary had now learnt how to learn her fingers in the dumb language. The police went over and grabbed it and took off the black coat the figure had over its head, and a great fearsome mask, and they said "Look, who it is, we've been after him for years. Mary has done us a good turn *by allowing herself to be captured*." Mary began to smile, and from that day forth she was never worried again.'

The same child also recounted the following story:

'One day Jane came in holding her head as if she'd fallen down. She was very worried. She was living by herself. Her mother and father were dead and there was no one to help her. She was in the middle of a big town and she realised someone had pushed her and she couldn't find out who it was. They went to the police and they said another four girls had been pushed by him, and been killed. The police said "You're lucky, the other girls were killed by the Monster as we call him." They found a footprint and traced it to a clown in the circus called Funny Joe, and he was hung and he had to pay £1,000 damages to Mary, who lived happily ever after, with her cat and her dog, and no girl was afraid to walk there again.'

CHAPTER XV

The Relationship between Intellectual
Retardation and Affection Seeking

The third hypothesis predicted that intellectually retarded children would display significantly more affection seeking behaviour than intellectually average children, despite the fact that both groups of children would display a considerable underlying need for affection.

This hypothesis assumes that children of low intelligence will find greater difficulty in hiding or controlling their need for affection than will more able children. The need to inhibit affection seeking behaviour is thought to arise from the demands of society, and particularly from the child's awareness of his parents and the society's disapproval or disgust at the sexual episode.

The testing of this hypothesis relied upon a statistical comparison of the affection seeking tendencies, as seen in school and measured on the B.S.A.G., and the underlying need for affiliation scores, measured by the T.A.T. of children with below and above average I.Q.

Of the twenty children in the subject group who had I.Q.s of less than 80, nineteen were found to be in Special Schools, or in Special Classes for E.S.N. children in normal secondary intermediate schools. (These E.S.N. children therefore represented over 45 per cent of the total subject group.) These children were taken to be the First Group, the group of intellectually less able children.

The second group consisted of children whose I.Q.s ranged from 80 to 134, the intellectually more able group. Hypothesis 3 predicted that the first group would show significantly more affection seeking behaviour, as measured by the B.S.A.G., than the second group. No difference would exist however on underlying need for affection.

A statistical analysis was made of the difference between the two groups, using the Mann Whitney Test. Because of the large samples, the Z value had to be computed, and the probabilities derived from the normal distribution table. A comparison was made of the affection seeking and underlying need for affiliation scores displayed on both the first and second testings.

From the results obtained, Hypothesis 3 would seem to be substantiated. The educationally subnormal subject children displayed significantly more affection seeking behaviour at the time of the first testing, than did the intellectually more able subject children ($N_1 = 17$, $N_2 = 22$. $Z = 1·66$, $p = 0·0485$).

This difference between groups was still apparent at the time of the second testing, although it was no longer statistically significant. There was no difference between the groups on the need for affiliation scores, on either testing.

One must conclude that intellectually average children are more able to perceive the danger to themselves of displaying their most basic needs. Perhaps also they are better able to co-ordinate and control their impulses. By contrast, the E.S.N. children who formed so large a part of this, and other sexually assaulted groups studied (e.g. Moses 1932, Bender and Blau 1937) showed significantly less ability to do so. It may be this inability to control socially dangerous impulses which has made so many E.S.N. children easy victims for adults with sexual intentions.

CHAPTER XVI

Discussion of Present Findings

Two crucial questions have been raised by previous studies of the child victims of sexual assaults. They are the questions of child participation, and subsequent trauma. Generally, the results suggest that a considerable minority of such children have participated in the sexual experience, often to satisfy unconscious personality needs. Trauma is found only infrequently following the attack, and almost always in children who showed serious personality disturbance before the offence.

This study was concerned with evaluating the subsequent personality development of a school-age group of sexual assault victims. No assessment was possible of the exact degree of participation involved—this would have necessitated a more direct questioning of the child immediately following the assault—nor was it possible to assess the extent to which the parents' circumstances and attitudes, for example, superego lacunae, might have predisposed the children to a pattern of sexual acting-out.

The results however indicate that the underlying personality needs of the children were such that relationships with adults would have been acceptable, rather than frightening, and no considerable degree of trauma was sustained. As a group, these children showed a significantly greater need for affection, both in phantasy and behaviour, than a comparable group of control children. This sort of behaviour has been described by Stott (1964) as an attempt to seek out substitute attachments to compensate for insecurity in the family setting:

The quest for surrogate parents may induce the child to help the milkman or other tradesmen on their rounds, or a shopkeeper in his shop. He may attach himself to a gang of roadmen or to an allotment-gardener. Sometimes the affection hungry child will take up with an individual on the look out for a victim of sexual malpractices.

A retrospective study, such as this, in which subjects were seen on average three years after the assault, permits no accurate assessment to be made of the part played by the child's personality in the course of the offence. However, the permanence of the affiliative need—observed on two testings, a year apart—might suggest that a relationship did exist between the child's need and his sexual involvement. To establish this point accurately, however, a developmental study would be necessary.

A further explanation for the significantly greater affection seeking to be observed in the phantasy and behaviour of the subject group, cannot be ignored. The assault may have afforded some emotional satisfaction to the child, and awakened a need for affection, which when the physical satisfaction had to be relinquished, became a permanent feature in the child's response repertoire. This preoccupation would be particularly noticeable in children who were suffering some emotional frustration before the offence.

This suggestion is best summarised by Halleck (1962): 'If a child was experiencing emotional deprivation and parental neglect at the time of the act (sexual offence) it tended to take on an aura of comfort and satisfaction. It was therefore difficult to relinquish in later life.'

Such pathological fixation is thought by us to underlie the observation of Rabinovitch (1953) that sexual psychopaths were almost invariably seduced as children by adults. He believes that such seductions activated a 'compulsive need to re-experience gratification at the genital level'.

'The need is often inordinate once the pattern has been established and serves as a dynamic force motivating delinquent behaviour. In most cases . . . genital contact had occurred many times over a period—one isolated event does not tend to establish a compulsive need for repetition.'

Only six of the forty-one children observed in this study were definitely known to have experienced more than one sexual contact with an adult, hardly making for an empirically verifiable tendency to fixation!

Freud was the first to recognise the child's need for a positive relationship with loving parent figures. Where such a relationship was deficient, due to loss of a parent, their inadequacy or rejection, he noted that serious disorientation of personality would result. In 1931 he described one type of libidinally deprived personality. He labelled it the erotic type.

> The erotic type is easily characterised. Erotics are persons whose main interest . . . is focused on love. Loving, but above all being loved, is for them the most important thing in life. They are governed by the dread of loss of love, and this makes them peculiarly dependent on those who may withhold their love from them.

Goldfarb (1945) enlarging on this type of deprived child, suggests that the personality becomes congealed at a level of extreme immaturity. 'The affective need is never met and therefore the child needs constant demonstration of love, but his affection is indiscriminate and he will go off with strangers.'

This dependent, affection seeking personality appears to characterise this group of sexually assaulted children, suggesting a real deprivation of parental affection, probably in the pre-oedipal stage.

No independent assessment was made of the parents' attitude, but the questions relating to parents' occupation answered by each child, did not suggest an excess of separation or death in the subject group. These answers however did not afford any indication of the 'partial rejection' considered to be the cause of the most acute anxiety, and the excessive need for love.

In their T.A.T. themes, sexually assaulted children showed a significantly greater fear of rejection on both testings than did the controls. They also showed a significantly greater preoccupation with themes relating to parent figures, suggesting excessive dependency.

In contrast to many previous studies (in particular, that of Young 1956) the parent figures were viewed as good and helpful.

This surprising characterisation is not unlike a masochistic response, noted in some affectionally deprived children by Menaker (1953). The child's inability to secure affection is accompanied by an increasing awareness of personal unworthiness or inadequacy. The children, lacking the strength to break away from the unsatisfactory parent figure, explain their un-lovedness in terms of their own unworthiness, and by contrast, and to allay anxiety, over-emphasise the excellence of the parent figure.

To quote Menaker:

> The normal development of the ego is as directly dependent on getting love from the mother at the earliest infantile level, as is the physical development on getting milk. If mother love on the oral level is absent or insufficient, the individual suffers a psychic trauma which must eventuate in a malformation and malfunction of the ego. The masochistic reaction is one form of attempt on the part of the ego to deal with the trauma. It sacrifices itself, that is its own independent development, and the sense of its own worth, to sustain the illusion of mother love—an idealised mother image —without which life is impossible. Actually the ego in its weakness, has little choice and perhaps no alternative reaction.'

This suggestion explains the personality changes wrought by analysis on a sixteen-year-old sexually delinquent girl, seen by Eisner (1945). At first, the girl supported her mother un-questioningly, maintaining she was right in everything she did or said. With increasing security, she was able to reject this idealised image, and replace it with a more realistic one.

Whilst present in the subject children to an excessive degree, this idealisation of the mother image seems common to all children. It undoubtedly arises from repeated physical satisfac-tions obtained from her in infancy, and perhaps is used as an anxiety allaying device when the child is so physically vulner-able. With maturity and increasing self-confidence, it is normally discarded, and a more realistic appraisal of the mother made. Symonds (1945) noted the increasing disillusionment with parent figures as the normal child reaches adolescence.

Where parents reject their children or where their love is less constant, greater insecurity will exist; consequently the child may never be able to discard the ideal image, and the unreality may be perpetuated.

Dependency of this sort is seen not only in the significantly greater number of stories referring to parent figures, but also in the sexually assaulted children's behaviour. As a group, they tended to play with younger children, and to crave for adult sympathy. The increase in this latter behaviour, accompanied as it was by an increasing fear of death at the time of the second testing, may perhaps be explained by the thesis advanced by Anna Freud (1948). She maintained that in the first year the all important step from primary narcissism to object love takes place, the child's attention being lured away from exclusive concentration on the happenings of his own body and directed towards persons in the outside world.

> In those cases where the mother is either absent or neglectful, or emotionally unstable and ambivalent, and therefore fails to be a steady source of satisfaction, or in the cases where the care of the infant is insufficient or impersonal or given by changing figures, the transformation of narcissistic libido into object libido is carried out inadequately. There remains a stronger tendency in all future life to withdraw libido from the love objects to the self whenever the object world proves disappointing.

Bridges (1927) was one of the first to note the inordinate number of physical symptoms reported by delinquent girls, in whose early love life there was presumably some deficit. Similarly, this falling back on the body for satisfaction, following a further disappointment might account for the increased autoerotic behaviour following assault, found in a number of studies (Bender and Blau 1937).

A further result of this postulated insufficiency of maternal affection is usually an increase in parent directed hostility. Klein (1932) and Anna Freud (1948) see the genesis of such hostility in the first years of life. Certainly, it may result from an early disappointment, or it may be a reaction to a dis-illusionment at a later stage. It may manifest itself in sporadic outbursts—of which, the sexual assault in certain children, may be one (Klein 1937). This in turn may activate the sort of dependency seen in this group, the child endeavouring to make up for its hostile acts. The hostility may be more generalised however, and lead to an overall rejection of parent commands. Consequently, no efficient conscience is formed and the child never feels any need to inhibit any form of impulsive behaviour, or any guilt at transgressing moral codes.

Clothier (1955) noted the absence of conscience and guilt in the majority of the teen-age unmarried mothers that she studied.

Because of an early deprivation of her parents' love, the child never acquires a sense of responsibility:

> Her relations to people are clamorous efforts to squeeze from them some satisfaction for her still impelling need for gratification of a dependent sort. She wants, at any cost, attention and approval and material evidences of acceptance.
>
> . . . this personality crippled and vulnerable adolescent remains naïvely hopeful that through her sexual powers she will find a man who will compensate her for her deprivations, and who will give her self-assurance. She submits gratefully to any man who is friendly and gives her a good time, or even to anyone who excites her—and because of her unhappiness, and weak ego and super-ego development she is easily excited.

As a group, these sexually assaulted children certainly showed every evidence of needing affection of this sort, and similarly they showed no inordinate amount of guilt or anxiety following the affair. This seemed especially surprising in view of the fact that almost all of these children had undergone the sort of Court proceedings most often thought to cause guilt in children.

Lack of guilt might however arise from an inability on the part of these children to see the sexual activity as undesirable. Where a child is unaware of the mores of society, either because of intellectual impairment or lack of self control, and is responding to deep rooted primitive instincts, no inordinate amount of guilt would be expected.

In this study a real relationship was seen to exist between overt expression of affection seeking tendencies, and intellectual retardation. Children in Special Classes, or Special Schools (who represented 45 per cent of the group) were seen to exhibit significantly more affection seeking behaviour than more intellectually able children, although there was no difference in the strength of the underlying need. This relationship would seem to indicate either an inability to perceive the conventions of society, or an inability to control impulses, the child appearing an 'impulse ridden character' (Gerard 1953).

Freud was the first to emphasise the existence of sexual urges throughout childhood, a position continually substantiated by anthropologists, for example, Malinowski noted frequent intercourse in girls of six years and over in Melanesia. Even within our culture, the disparity in ages at which a child may be considered a legitimate sexual object has been stressed frequently (Rabinovitch 1953, Halleck 1962). Not only will all children differ in the age at which they are ready for sexual intercourse (Kinsey 1953, Frank 1951), but from one socio-economic group to another differences will exist in degree of expression permitted. There is no wonder therefore that children with less ability to perceive and respond to these inhibitions of society, will respond most frequently to more deep-rooted primitive urges.

Certain children may indeed have stronger urges and a greater inability to control them. Bender and Cramer (1948) have noted greater emotional needs in brain-damaged children, and Ophuisen (1945) the greater difficulty of these children in controlling them. Several studies (Bender and Blau 1937; Weiss, Rogers and others 1955) have noted the restlessness, hyperactivity, and nervous mannerisms of sexually assaulted children, suggestive of a degree of neural impairment. The finds of this study would not contradict this. As a group these children displayed several minor nervous characteristics, and their inordinate craving for affection might well reflect an excessive need for stimulation caused by some form of minimal brain damage.

An alternative explanation for the large number of mentally retarded children who become sexual assault victims, may be that the emotional disturbance, symbolised in the sexual acting-out, causes the intellectual retardation. Many children with emotional problems are not only held back in school performance, but also respond very inadequately to intelligence testing. These children classed as E.S.N. may in fact have higher intelligence quotients but their intense affection seeking preoccupations, may have impaired their functioning.

It is interesting to note that the majority of subjects tested in this study were in the latency period—both at the time of the assault, and at the time of the testing. Whilst Freud always insisted that true latency was a theoretical extreme (1905) he nevertheless stressed that children whose sexual preoccupations persisted in this physiologically latent stage would suffer intellectually. Whilst he himself (1907) and several other analysts (Klein 1932; Bender and Kramer 1948), have observed cases where sexual acting-out was accompanied by no intellectual retardation, such cases are usually regarded as exceptional, and sexual preoccupations during latency would normally be expected to be accompanied by some diminution of intellectual ability. Bender and Blau (1937) in their study of children involved in sexual activity with adults noted:

> the infantile stage is prolonged and reverted to in the younger child, and the so-called latent stage with its normal intellectual and social interests is sacrificed. There appears to be mental retardation in some cases, and school accomplishments are thwarted.

Finally, the problem of subsequent trauma must be considered. Most follow-up studies of child sex assault victims agree in viewing the sexual trauma as incidental to the development of any deviant personality characteristics observed later (Rasmussen 1934, Bender and Grugett 1952).

Most children so involved make an adequate personality adjustment: only a few of the more disturbed children, for whom the sexual acting-out was undoubtedly symptomatic of a general disintegration of personality, make a poor adjustment.

This study substantiates this viewpoint. There was no evidence in the T.A.T. themes of an excessive anxiety or fear of violence or injury. Only one tendency, to unsettledness and unforthcomingness, appeared more frequently in children whose assault had taken place only a short while before the test. This syndrome expressing as it does the child's defensiveness against new situations and strange people is completely understandable in the circumstances. It might be accounted for by the shock of the offence, or by the more general environmental disturbance resulting from its discovery. As a characteristic of the group it appears to wane with time. Except for the significant difference to be observed in affection seeking behaviour, as a group sexually assaulted children did not differ in degree or type of unsettledness from a carefully matched control group, when tested on average three years after the assault.

Some evidence exists to suggest that even this affection seeking behaviour may wane with time. Bender and Blau (1937) observed: 'The children were able to abandon their sexual preoccupations and practices when improved opportunities allowed fulfilment of their individual capacities and drives towards identification and constructive behaviour.'

Perhaps this may have accounted fot the non-significance of the affection seeking syndrome in the behaviour of the sexually assaulted children at the time of the second testing.

A not infrequent result of the B.S.A.G. testing is that the teacher becomes more aware of the needs of the pupil and makes some attempt to meet them (Stott, personal communication). In this study the significance of the affection seeking syndrome must surely have been apparent to the teachers rating the Guides, on the first testing, and as so many of them were specially trained to deal with children in Special classes, they may have taken extra effort to meet their pupils' needs. Anxiety relating to affection seeking in school would have been reduced, and despite the child's underlying preoccupation with the need for affiliation, affection seeking behaviour, as seen in school, would not have been so apparent in the second year.

The suggestion is therefore made that sexual assault of children by adults does not have particularly detrimental effects on the child's subsequent personality development. Given greater affection—by parents, following the event, or by others in the child's environment—the need for affection, which may well have predisposed the child to this form of sexual acting-out, will be outgrown, and affection seeking preoccupations assume a more normal part in the economy of the child's personality.

Part Three

ASTHMATIC CHILDREN

CHAPTER XVII

Introduction to the Problem

Since the pioneer study of Rogerson, Hardcastle and Duguid thirty years ago, numerous attempts have been made to explain the part played by personality factors in the aetiology of childhood asthma.* This first study stressed the importance of a faulty mother-child relationship in the causation of the disease. Specifically, it suggested that the child was expressing physically the problem of an unresolved dependency, produced or aggravated by an awareness of his mother's rejection.

Subsequent studies have laid equal stress on asthma as an expression of deviant personality development. They have given quite contradictory explanations however of the causative factors involved. For example, some studies have emphasised the affection seeking aspects of the asthmatic attack, viewing it as an attempt to wrest affection from an uncaring mother, whilst other writers have suggested that asthma represented nothing so much as the child's cry for help in the face of an engulfing over-possessive mother.

Similarly, some analysts have attempted to relate the development of asthma to the existence of a specific personality type whilst other psychiatrists, like Alexander (1948) have observed:

> The nuclear psychodynamic factor is a conflict centring on an excessive unresolved dependence upon the mother. As a defence against this infantile fixation all kinds of personality traits may

* As our working definition of asthma, we use that of Alcock (1960): 'Asthma is a disease entity involving attacks of bronchospasm, predominantly expiratory in nature, without primary organic disease of the chest.' A distinction is usually made between spasmodic and bronchitic asthma (for an adequate medical distinction, see Sheldon 1951). The asthmatics in this study were all *spasmodic* asthmatics. We presume from clinical and empirical literature—although this is rarely stated—that most other studies of child asthmatics involved children with a similar type of disease.

develop. Accordingly, we find among persons suffering from asthma many types of personalities—aggressive, ambitious, argumentative persons, dare-devils and also hypersensitive types.

Equally, some theorists emphasise trauma sustained in specific training situations—such as over rigorous potting, or the suppression of infant crying—as fundamental to the emergence of an asthmatic pattern, whilst others postulate that an over-all harshness of maternal attitude rather than a specific stress is the causative factor.

Faced with such controversy, it seems little wonder that many allergists tend to discount the psychiatric suggestion that an asthmatogenic personality invariably antedates or accompanies the illness. The criticism is levelled that the nature of this asthmatogenic personality is dependent upon the persuasion of the individual psychiatrist, rather than upon the exact nature of the symptoms observed. However, for two reasons, a purely allergic explanation of the cause of asthma seems equally inadequate. Firstly, no substance has been isolated as the specific cause of asthma, and not the cause of other allergic manifestations. Secondly, despite exposure to substances normally capable of producing allergic reactions, many asthmatic patients in hospital—that is, away from the possibly threatening home environment—produce no asthma or evince no allergic hypersensitivity.

At the present time, most medical studies agree in attributing some degree of causation to each of three separate factors—allergic, infective and psychological. From individual to individual, and even perhaps within the same individual from time to time, the predominance of any one of these factors will vary. Attacks in most children will probably result from a combination of allergic, psychological and infective stimuli, rather than from the exclusive action of only one type of stimulus.

The problem therefore exists as to how much emphasis can be placed on personality factors in the aetiology of childhood asthma. The psychiatric conclusions were in the main based on the analyses of small highly selected groups of children and any generalisation of results might be inaccurate. In some children —those whose emotional development was not distorted enough to warrant psychiatric attention—psychic conflicts of the sort noted by the analysts might not exist. In other children, such conflicts might have acted as catalysts, their presence at the outset unleashing the disorder which was perpetuated by allergic or infective factors.

It was decided therefore to study the personality structure of an unselected group of child asthmatics, in an attempt to check the clinical specifications of personality type, and the conflicts underlying them. At the same time, an investigation of the personality needs, and their attitudes towards child upbringing of mothers of asthmatic children was undertaken to ascertain whether theories of rejection and early parent-child conflict could be substantiated. Both groups were compared with a carefully matched control group of mothers and children in order to specify more accurately any underlying personality needs or behaviours observed.

A variety of approaches to the problem was used* in order to obtain information about possibly different areas of personality functioning. The behavioural aspects of personality were studied and also the underlying needs, both of mothers and children.

The study therefore includes:

(1) a summary of the relevant psychoanalytic literature;

(2) a formulation of hypotheses based on these clinical speculations;

(3) an account of the empirical work already undertaken on the personality structure of the asthmatic child;

(4) an account of the present experimental study;

(5) a discussion of the results.

* Weblin (1963) commenting upon the variety of psychological explanations for childhood asthma, observed: 'The many different "opinions" are often based on research or testing methods dissimilar in scope, "depth", and certainty of interpretation.'

It is also more than probable that they show up real diversity in underlying conflicts. As Knapp and Nemetz (1957a) have so aptly commented, there may be 'no simple psychic Bacillus asthmaticus' just as there is no simple allergic substance.

CHAPTER XVIII

Clinical Description and Formulation of Basic Hypotheses

To careful clinical observers, the child asthmatic has long appeared to be caught in the vice of a neurotic conflict. His illness is interpreted as the masochistic symbol of his struggle for independence from over-possessive parents, waged in the perpetual fear of loss of mother love. His personality seems therefore to differ little from that of any other neurotic child in conflict. He is described as over-anxious and fearful (Rogerson, Hardcastle and Duguid 1935; McDermott and Cobb 1939; Bostock 1956); aggressive (Dunbar 1938; Bacon 1956; Alcock 1960); yet unable to express this aggression openly and therefore frustrated (Bostock 1956); guilty (Knapp and Nemetz 1957a); over-dependent (Rogerson, Hardcastle and Duguid 1935; French and Alexander 1941; Gerard 1946; Sperling 1959) and deeply and pervasively depressed (Knapp and Nemetz 1957a; Alcock 1960).

The degree of importance attributed to these characteristics seems to depend on the theoretical standpoint of the individual clinician. Rogerson, Hardcastle and Duguid (1935), whose pioneer evaluation was based on the therapeutic interviewing of twenty-three child asthmatics and their mothers, believed that fear of separation from the mother accounted for the extreme dependency and over-anxiety that they observed in these children.

They noted the great anxiety that the children showed when alone in the room with the examiner, the younger ones frequently refusing to be separated from their mothers. In a play group these children made repeated excursions from the room to reassure themselves that their mothers were just outside the door. They appeared quieter and more repressed than the majority of other children, and preferred to say nothing in answer to a question, rather than risk making a mistake.

Further features of the anxious personality—excessive cleanliness, punctuality and meticulousness—were noted by McDermott and Cobb (1939) in the twenty-nine asthmatic children that they examined psychiatrically. Bostock (1956) suggested that the apparent over-anxiety might spring from a mixture of fear and frustration. After examining thirty-six asthmatic children with the T.A.T., he concluded:

> Such children are deprived of a normal thrusting outlook. Instead of learning to swim with and against the tide of life, they are submerged by over-possessive parents. Caught within the net of over-protection, their wishes are thwarted and nature urges them to escape. Watched incessantly, they feel bewildered.

That parental over-possessiveness produced and fostered dependency was noted by Rogerson, Hardcastle and Duguid (1935) who observed a lack of maturity and self-confidence in their cases. Sperling (1949) attributed the dependency solely to an acting-out of maternal wishes and commented: 'The mothers ... had an unconscious need to keep the child in a helpless and dependent state to a degree which I have encountered only in the mothers of psychotic children'.

That the dependency might appear in phantasy forms was noted by Saul and Lyons (1951) who believed that it represented a wish to return to the womb, and could be seen in the frequent appearance of intra-uterine symbols, especially water, in the dreams of asthmatics.

That dependency might mask or alternate with hostility was noted first by Dunbar (1938). She remarked on the intense aggressiveness of asthmatic patients, and on their tendency to act out aggressive impulses.

Three reasons have been put forward to account for the prominence of aggression in the asthmatic personality. Bacon (1956), basing her conclusions on the analyses of only six asthmatic patients, links it with excretory phantasies:

> Each attack of asthma was preceded by excretory defiance directed against one or other parent or parental image, when the patient was unsuccessfully but aggressively fighting parental domination. By excretory defiance is meant anal, urethral, or excretory impulses hostile to the parent.

Similarly, Bostock (1956) attributes it to a reaction against parental correction. He postulates that maternal rejection leads to insecurity in the children, which begets frustration, fear, irritability and hostility. This produces, in its turn, correction with or without punishment on the part of the mother. 'Correction and punishment engenders more aggression and still more aggression.'

That it might be a defensive rather than a reactive mechanism is suggested by French and Alexander (1941). The child may actively provoke the parent by his aggressive behaviour, in an effort to see to what extent he is secure. If, despite his aggressive behaviour, he is accepted and tolerated by the parent then he feels that he is in no danger of rejection.

A final possible interpretation of the aggressive behaviour is emphasised by Coolidge (1956) and Alcock (1960). Believing that the illness itself is essentially aggressive, they see it as a means of controlling and punishing the guilty parent. That the attack might also represent a masochistic attack on the self was recognised by both Brown and Goiten (1943) and Knapp and Nemetz (1937), this need for self-punishment being produced by the guilt which the child experiences in his conflicts against domination.* Knapp and Nemetz introduced, in their study of forty adult asthmatics, many of whom had developed their asthma in childhood, the concept of asthmatic depression. Noting how this pervasive depression is at variance with the child's ostensibly cheerful acceptance of his disability, Alcock (1960) suggests that it may be associated with a conflict on the pre-genital level.

The neurotic conflict underlying the asthmatic personality

To understand the asthmatic child, one must first understand his mother. It is *her* neurosis that is considered by clinicians as primarily producing and perpetuating his illness. She is described as being unable to accept the role of motherhood, simultaneously rejecting and, in compensation, over-possessing her child. He in turn, both resents and fears the rejection, and oscillates between the attempt on the one hand to escape her

* For an exposé of the dynamics underlying self attack, see Menninger, Section 1, page 19.

domination and on the other, to placate and be subservient to her, lest he lose all love.

Hostility, masked by over-solicitousness, was first remarked in mothers of asthmatic children by Rogerson, Hardcastle and Duguid (1935). Noting an almost pathological over-protection on the part of seventeen of the twenty-three mothers they observed, they attributed this, not to solicitousness in the face of sickness, but to an attempt to overcome guilt feelings aroused by their own deep hostility to the children. It was the child's perception of this hostility, masked as it was by over-protection, that in their view accounted for his fear of separation from his mother.

Bostock (1956) detecting complete rejection on the part of twenty-two and partial rejection on the part of eight of the thirty-eight mothers of asthmatic children he observed, extended the argument:

> . . . the mother's rejection and guilt lies in the unconscious. Guilt exists because reproduction is a basic urge, and its rejection is negation of a life force. The mothers, ignorant of the process, often exhibit patient and kindly self-control in the face of difficulties.
>
> However, in spite of skill in dealing with their problems, the conduct does not deceive the child who picks up double entendres, hidden sarcasms, and slips of tongue. More important, it senses a lack of emotional warmth which is almost impossible to disguise.

The psychoanalytic explanation for maternal rejection, best summarised by Benedek (1956), suggests that where a mother was unable to identify satisfactorily with her own mother— that is, to love and be loved by her, thus taking on something of the mother's personality—she is unable to mother her own child adequately. The child's needs remind her of her own unsatisfied needs, and her rejection of her infant is exactly similar to that of her own mother's rejection of her.

Both Jessner (1956) and Coolidge (1956) have noted conflicts in relation to their own mothers, on the part of mothers of asthmatic children. Jessner (1956) notes the way in which the child becomes a symbolic self-representation for these mothers. Through the child they act out their own still active conflicts between dependence and independence.

They hold on to him and push him away at the same time. The

child responds in kind. He feels the wish for closeness and protection, and at the same time the drive towards independence and growth—he feels enveloped and choked by his mother's needs to keep him close.'

Jessner, in direct contrast to Bostock and Benedek, stresses the opportunity that pregnancy affords these immature mothers for this complete identification. Consequently, he stresses the mother's complete enjoyment of pregnancy, and notes her frequent difficulty in parting with her children in labour. Coolidge (1956) in discussing three cases of asthmatic mothers of asthmatic children also emphasises this suggestion. During the pregnancy of one of the asthmatic women he studied, he noted:

> There was a powerful feeling of possessiveness towards her unborn baby for whom she could breathe, and whom she could nourish, protect and develop, without her mother's intervention. Simultaneously she identified passively with the fetus. Feeling fused with it, her own regressive longing could be fulfilled. For the first time in her life the mother felt satisfied—she was both mother and child.

To maintain this complete identification, so vital to the mother's own emotional health, the child of this asthmatic mother had to develop asthma. Only then could the mother feel: 'We are the same and therefore magically unseparated'.

She focused on the child's respiratory tract and hovered with anxious concern over maladies in this area.

> Early in life the child fell into resonance with the mother's need and also developed a special need for a clinging possessiveness toward her. It learned that intense feelings of sameness could be realised via disturbances in respiration. The respiratory functions for the child became libidinised and a source of fear and concern.

Coolidge made the point that the mother seemed to have less asthma herself by vicarious use of the child's symbol as her own.

Upon improvement of the child's asthma he noticed that the mother became depressed, developed more asthma herself, and said that she was thinking of having another baby to 'cure' her of the asthma.

Too close an identification with such an over-possessive

mother might stunt the child's subsequent personality growth. Several writers (Deutsch 1955; Coolidge 1956; Monsour 1960) agree in attributing to the child some awareness of this danger.

> The 'wish' on the child's part is for shelter and protection, for the intra-uterine position where all needs even breathing, are automatically met. But the claustrum is as much frightening as desired, as much reflecting helplessness, frustration and death as gratification and safety. (Deutsch 1955)

Coolidge (1956) commented on one asthmatic child,

> As the child grew older it craved increasingly to break away from this asthmatic way of life and grow up independently like its siblings and other children. It recognised that the asthmatic bond was a dead-end road but was held in a vice. Its fears of abandonment, retribution and death were constantly fired by the murderous resentment felt toward the mother for being moulded and kept in such a dependent and infantile status, as well as from the frustration of not having the promised but impossible wishes fulfilled.

Monsour (1960) believes that the asthmatic attack is an effort at self-preservation in the face of an engulfing object. He believes that the mother communicates her own fear of ego extinction (dying) to the child and, just as those who are dying experience difficulty in breathing, so the child, symbolising the mother's and its own death-fear, starts to wheeze.

A necessary concomitant of ego integration is the achievement of personal independence. That any step towards this independence might precipitate fear in the asthmatic child was recognised as early as 1941 by French and Alexander.

They suggested that the child feared parental opposition whenever he so much as wished for personal freedom. He therefore felt that he had to placate his mother for his guilty wishes. By being ill, by confiding his wishes directly to his mother and seeking her forgiveness, or by provoking her anger and then seeking reparation, he continually assured himself that despite his supposed guilt, his mother still cared. When, however, such wishes persisted, and the necessary absolution was not obtained, an asthmatic attack occurred. It therefore represented the most extreme method of protecting the individual from his own guilty desires.

That the symbiotic relationship established between mother and the individual asthmatic child is specific to them and does not spread to other members of the family has been recognised (Sperling 1949).

As early as 1939 McDermott and Cobb made the observation that asthmatics were frequently the oldest children. Nineteen of the twenty-nine children they examined psychiatrically were the eldest or only children. It can be argued that having established this symbiotic relationship with one child, the mother achieves sufficient freedom from her own emotional conflicts to allow her remaining children to develop satisfactorily.

The symbolic nature of the asthmatic symptom

An awareness exists in the clinical literature of the non-specific nature of the neurotic conflict underlying asthma. Asthmatics frequently show evidence of other psychosomatic symptoms (Ibor 1956; Jessner 1956; Buffum 1957). Knapp and Nemetz (1957b) suggest: 'The triad of dependency, orality and masochism [which they consider as basic to the asthmatic conflict] have been mentioned in many psychosomatic syndromes. The fact that it may exist does not indicate how "primary" a part it plays, nor explain the choice of asthma over any other syndrome.'

Arising from the clinical formulation of the asthmatic conflict, as a conflict between the child's need for closeness and desire for separation, two explanations for the symbolism of the illness have been advanced.

The first, derived from the hypothesised fear of asthmatics of losing the mother, seeks to explain the asthmatic attack as a primitive cry for maternal help. Describing an adult male patient who was under analytic treatment, Weiss (1922) wrote: 'The attack resembled nothing so much as the behaviour of a shrieking helplessly sprawling, new born child with blood red, swollen face'.

Bostock (1956) extended this notion by suggesting that the asthmatic attack closely resembled 'the frozen pattern of an infantile cry', that is crying, accompanied by generalised activity, but no tears, a crying pattern found in infants of under three months. He noted that some asthmatics evince considerable difficulty in shedding tears.

Knapp and Nemetz (1957b) offer a clear expos of the dynamics of the suppression of tears. Quoting the case of Mrs H, they write:

> Her constant crying as a colicky infant was family legend. In childhood her frequent weeping was severely suppressed by her parents, who impatient with her, sent her to her room whenever she cried. In time, she suppressed the tears herself and rarely cried, feeling foolish and childish whenever she did. The crying of her children was especially distressing to her, arousing a panicky helplessness and rage. She felt trapped by the cry which 'walled her in'. Later she found that feelings and sensations of wanting to weep preceded episodes of nasal obstruction and of asthma.

Numerous descriptions are given of the asthmatic's inability to cry (French and Alexander 1941; Abramson 1951). Monsour (1960) and French and Alexander consider that the beginning of a normal crying pattern in the asthmatic is a sign of a satisfactory prognosis.

That any cry to the over-possessive mother might represent a threat to the child's imperfectly integrated ego has already been commented upon. In addition to representing a cry for help, the asthma may also symbolise this. First, as Bostock notes (1956), the generalised activity which accompanies every attack is not unlike the fright appearance of all small infants and animals. They attempt through their bodily contortions to put on as fearful a front to danger as possible. This may represent an attempt to keep the feared mother away.

Secondly, as Bostock notes, breath-holding may occur in certain individuals during attacks. This he suggests results from an attempt to arrest the crying pattern, lest the feared mother hears and further encroaches on the individual's independence.

Breath-holding is then a symptom of the inhibition of intense emotion.

That this explanation concurs with those of all allergists and psychiatrists seeking a more physiological explanation for asthma should be noted.

Wittkower and O'Reill (1935) consider that asthma is precipitated 'when the respiratory system is subject to contradictory and unco-ordinated stimuli such as might result from abrupt inhibition of strong emotion'.

Holmes (1950) has found that interruption of the sympathetic nerve supply to the nose is followed by dyperaemia and swelling of the nasal mucosa, together with hyper-secretion. Similar changes occurred with emotional conflicts and with feelings of humiliation, frustration and resentment.

Summarising the literature, Rees (1956) maintained that: 'emotional tension stimulating increased parasympathetic activity can cause the specific nasal changes found in vasomotor rhinitis and the bronchial changes found in asthma'.

While most clinicians would postulate that the specific conflict underlying the intense emotion, producing the attack, was a mother-separation conflict, Metcalfe (1956) pointed out that any intense emotion might well produce the same effect.

Adding further emphasis to the idea that the asthmatic sees the world as threatening is the argument which suggests that the asthmatic attack represents 'an attempt on the part of the organism to shut out noxious agents, either actually or symbolically' . . . (Rees 1956).

Flanders Dunbar (1938) was the first to note the great importance attributed to the sense of smell in asthmatics. Her observations have been substantiated by Stein and Ottenberg (1958) who found that twenty-two of the twenty-five asthmatic patients they interviewed believed that odours precipitated their attacks. An analysis of the character of the odours revealed that they were for the most part anal derivatives.

Ibor (1956) suggests that it is the asthmatic's perception of the world as threatening that results in attacks. Consequently the asthmatic patient is thought, through his asthma, to be vainly trying to exclude the threatening world from entering into his body.

Miller and Baruch (1950) draw an analogy between the psychological dynamics of the allergic and physiological dynamics of the somatic symptoms.

Bronchial asthma, a common allergic syndrome, may be considered an abnormal physiological mechanism called forth in certain individuals to fight anything that threatens the respiratory mechanisms. The threatening agents may be physical, as ragweed pollen, or psychological, as maternal rejection. In either case definite physiological responses result.

(1) Bronchospasm to keep the noxious agent out. This could be said to parallel keeping the awareness of a person's hostility out. (Hostility produced in reponse to maternal rejection and over-protection.)

(2) Outpouring of mucus to dilute the noxious agent, just as displacement and indirection dilute hostility.

Cough in an attempt to get rid of the noxious agent which may be likened to trying to get hostility out. These effects however come into conflict with the necessity to breathe—to draw oxygen into the lung, and get rid of carbon dioxide. A physiological conflict is then set up which parallels the psychological conflict. The blocking of the bronchi by spasm and mucus obstructs the easy entrance and exit of air, just as the psychological blocking guards against the impact of conscious admission and the easy expression of hostility.

This position was essentially that of Bacon who, following the analysis of six asthmatic patients, advanced the thesis that: 'Just as the allergic asthmatic attack is a response to physio-logical irritation of the respiratory tract—neurotically deter-mined asthma is a response to unconscious fears of assault upon the respiratory apparatus, and the physiological changes that accompany it are attempts to ward off that assault'.

The origin of these respiratory irritations she believes to be 'excretory defiance', anal, urethral, or sexual excretory impulses hostile to the parent, and provoked by parental domination.

She contends that one or both parents of the asthmatic child have made him, by coercive toilet training, feel guilty for 'defiant' excretory acts of soiling. To the child these acts may symbolise the only means of hitting back at the over dominant parents; and yet because he fears the loss of their love, he also fears his own self-assertiveness, symbolised in soiling. 'Since the child wishes to soil, it fears being soiled.' It therefore endeavours to block out all odours or smells which might symbolise anal assertiveness.

Formulation of basic hypotheses

In summary, we may say that the clinical literature on the personality structure of the asthmatic child has suggested that basically he is a neurotic child, with the fear of loss of or separation from his mother at the root of his neurosis. He has been consistently described as over-anxious, fearful, dependent, aggressive, frustrated, guilty and depressed.

His personality reflects his need to cling to a rejecting and over-possessing mother, and his fear that this dependency will overwhelm him. His feeble struggles for self-assertion increase his guilt and depression, and do nothing to relieve the aggression, occasioned by this awareness of rejection. His illness both symbolises and permits discharge of the emotional tension which he experiences.

From the clinical impressions it would seem possible to abstract several simple hypotheses, capable of empirical investigation, and open to clear refutation or confirmation.

Hypothesis 1. Asthmatic children are more unsettled than otherwise comparable, but non-asthmatic, control children.

This unsettledness will show up in their behaviour. At school, they will tend to show significantly higher scores on scales measuring maladjustment and unsettledness. At home, their mothers will notice more jealousy, moodiness and depression, more fears and night terrors, and more problem behaviour, than will the mothers of the controls.*

In their phantasy productions, asthmatic children will tend to tell more stories of an unhappy or conflictful kind and fewer with successful outcomes. Their phantasy heroes will tend to have more affection seeking and assertive needs than will those of the controls, and will perceive the environment (both intra- and extra-psychic) as more threatening to the fulfilment of these needs. Asthmatic children will tend to take less positive or adaptive action to overcome these threats.

In accordance with the clinical studies already discussed it is predicted that when themes relating to parent-child relationships are analysed separately, asthmatic children will see their

---

* At the outset it must be stressed that both mothers and teachers may be biased in the degree of unsettledness which they attribute to the asthmatic child. Because they are aware of the illness, and the limitations it imposes on his behaviour they may tend to exaggerate his anxieties, fears and depression. Equally, because of their own frustrations in the situation they may tend to exaggerate the more problematic aspects of his behaviour.

parents as more threatening than will control children, and will display a greater need to escape from the conflictful parent situation, and more fears of parental separation or death.

Hypothesis 2. This relates to the degree of unsettledness to be found within a group of asthmatics.

Dunbar (1946), Miller and Baruch (1948) and Rees (1956) have suggested that the asthmatogenic personality antedates the illness, and is a causative factor in its aetiology. Whilst severity and length of illness might accentuate this personality conflict, they do not give rise to it.

Their view is opposed to that of Langeveld (1954), Rappaport (1957, p. 812) and Neuhaus (1958), who consider that the personality characteristics of the asthmatic child—like those of any chronically ill child—are solely a reaction to restrictions of the illness. They do not exist before the illness and intensify as the illness is prolonged.

From the clinical speculations already discussed it appears to us that some degree of emotional conflict may have existed before the onset of the illness, but understandably this may be increased by the frustrations inherent in the illness situation.

It is this suggestion which is tested in the second hypothesis. It is postulated that:

Within a group of asthmatic children differences in the degree of unsettledness will exist dependent on the length of the illness.

Three possible results may be anticipated:

(1) Unsettledness increases with the length of illness—the frustrations of the asthma increasing the unsettledness.

(2) Unsettledness decreases with the length of the illness—the possibility for dramatic acting-out permitting expression of anxiety, and therefore lowering the subject's general level of unsettledness.

(3) No difference appears in the degree of unsettledness as a function of length of illness.

Hypothesis 3. This relates to the supposed rejection of asthmatic mothers:

In accordance with the clinical observations already discussed, it is postulated that *the mothers of asthmatic children will be more rejecting in their attitude to their children than the mothers of the control children.*

Blau (1957) summarises the controversial aspects of this issue:

> It can be argued that the illness in the child calls forth certain reactions in the mother. Undoubtedly, there is a reciprocal process with mutual feedback effects, but the basic aetiology must be sought in the original maternal neurosis.

That the rejection is primary, that is, existed either before the child's birth or the onset of its illness is stressed by French and Alexander (1941); Gerard (1946), Sperling (1949); Coolidge (1950); Miller and Baruch (1950); Bostock (1956); Jessner and others (1956) and Rees (1956).

The reverse position—that the rejection was produced secondarily, and as a response to frustration and disappointment on the mother's part—has been taken by Rogerson, Hardcastle and Duguid (1938) and Abramson (1954).

Accordingly, *this study will attempt to estimate at what point in time maternal rejection, if present, was engendered,* that is, whether it is primary, or secondary to the commencement of the child's illness.

Indices of primal rejection are taken to be:

(1) expressed maternal dislike of or indifference to conception;
(2) excessive pregnancy sickness, hypertension, etc;
(3) reported emotional upset during pregnancy;
(4) reported difficult, instrumental or protracted births;
(5) reported non-establishment of breast-feeding or reported antipathy to breast-feeding where it has been established;
(6) immediate infant feeding and behaviour problem—colic, withdrawal, excessive crying and gastro-intestinal disorders.

Justification for the adoption of these criteria as indices of primal rejection is found in Appendix 1.

Hypothesis 3 predicts that the mothers of asthmatic children will more frequently report difficulty about these points than the mothers of controls.

The mothers of asthmatic children will also score more highly than the mothers of controls on the pathogenic scales of the P.A.R.I., an instrument to measure psychologically damaging attitudes to child rearing and family life.

Clinically, mothers of asthmatics are thought to have conflicts centring on their own unresolved dependency needs, and Hypothesis 3 predicts that these needs will show up more frequently in the thematic stories produced by asthmatic mothers and controls. They will be more concerned with assertive and affection seeking behaviours, as evinced by their phantasy productions. The fulfilment of their needs will be more often threatened by domination and rejection from those around them and from their own perceived inadequacy. Their stories will most often end unsatisfactorily and the behaviour used to overcome threats will most often be evasive or negative.

Hypothesis 4. This predicts that, apart from maternal rejection, asthmatic children will have experienced significantly more unsettling environmental experiences than will control children. The experiences considered to be most unsettling in that they might threaten permanent separation from the mother are:

(1) Actual separation of mother-child, due to illness and removal to hospital, or to hardship, domestic crisis or holidays. Of greatest significance will be experiences in which the child is removed from its home to a strange environment—either hospital or nursery.

(2) Moves from one house to another.

(3) Deaths in the family of loved relations which remind the child of the impermanence of its parents.

Hypothesis 5. This relates to the relationship to be found in the asthmatic group between scores of maternal rejection, unsettling environmental experiences and perceived child problem behaviour.

It is predicted that child problem behaviour—as perceived by the mother—will increase as a function of the mother's own rejection and the number of unsettling environmental experiences the child has had to sustain.

CHAPTER XIX

Previous Investigations of the
Child and his Mother

The first empirical study of personality characteristics of child asthmatics was contained in a more general study of hostility in allergic children. It was published by Miller and Baruch in 1950, and the conclusions were based on interviews with parents, and play and interview sessions with children. A control group was used but no matching for personal characteristics such as age, sex or intelligence quotient was made. Conclusions based on this study must therefore be regarded as extremely tentative.

Ninety allergic children, fifty-five of whom had asthma, formed the subject group. Fifty-three children referred 'from various sources for diverse problems' formed the control group. Six different methods of expressing hostility in behaviour were described, and the children were rated on the extent to which they showed any or all of the different types.

Allergic children showed significantly less outward going hostility than control children, even in indirect and displaced forms. Instead they displayed significantly more hostility against themselves, and exhibited a greater amount of blocking, that is, bringing out hostility only with hesitance, or withholding it. The authors concluded that the asthmatic child is guilty and anxious about his hostile feelings and is frequently in conflict about expressing them. He seeks to punish himself for them and to quote the authors: 'Here is probably where his allergic constitution comes in. It becomes useful to him, he can muster it to his aid.'

The authors do not attempt to explain this supposed relationship between allergic manifestations and guilty hostile feelings. Nor do they try to relate either of these to the rejection which they deem to be present in eighty-nine of the ninety mothers of allergic children they studied. In this respect the study, whilst interesting, is thought to be inadequate.

In the same year, 1950, Cohen and Little published the results of an experiment into differences in the level of aspiration behaviour of asthmatic and non-asthmatic children, and of their mothers' aspirations for them. Using a simple dart-shooting task, a group of thirty asthmatic children was compared with a control group of thirty children carefully matched for age, intelligence, school placement and socio-economic status. The mothers of each were asked to predict, without their child's knowledge, the score they expected their child to earn on each of a series of twenty trials. Each child was also asked to estimate his score on these trials.

The results suggested that both asthmatic children and their mothers set significantly higher goals than control children and mothers. There was little difference between the levels of aspiration of asthmatic children and their mothers, but the mothers of control children set goals reliably lower for them than the children set for themselves.

To explain these differences in the behaviour of asthmatic and non-asthmatic children, Cohen and Little refer to Holt's (1946) work on level of aspiration which suggests that defence is the determinant in goal-setting behaviour. Noting that Sears (1940) found consistent low positive goals in her secure children, they suggest that this control group feels more secure than their asthmatic group and therefore has less occasion to over-defend itself in its goal-setting.

Cohen and Little note that the asthmatic child's mother not only set a goal higher than his achievement level, but failed to modify it in the second half of the test, as compared with the control mother whose bids were nearer to the level of the child's actual performance, and who lowered the bids in the second half. Cohen and Little draw from this the conclusion that: 'The mother, rejecting her child either because he is ill or for some other reasons, deals with her guilt about such feelings by over-protecting her child.'

In the circumstances, this conclusion would appear un-warranted. No evidence is produced to substantiate the idea that over-protection produces high goal-setting behaviour, indeed, logically over-protection might be expected to produce the reverse, that is, low goal-setting behaviour. Similarly, no proof as to the existence of over-protection or rejection in these mothers is put forward.

A further possible explanation for the observed differences in goal-setting behaviour of the asthmatic and non-asthmatic children—and one not mentioned by Cohen and Little—is that asthmatic children are frequently first children. No attempt was made by Cohen and Little to control this possibly selective positioning within the family, yet it has been suggested (Schacter 1963) that the level of aspiration of first children, and their mothers' expectations for them differ from those of second and other children.

Harris, Rapoport, Rynerson and Samter published in 1950 the findings of an observational study on asthmatic children. They compared twenty-two asthmatic children, with seventeen children suffering from allergic rhinitis and fifty-six children who had been referred because of acting-out problems. There was no attempt made to match groups on characteristics and consequently, as in the work of Miller and Baruch already described, the results of this study must be regarded as extremely tentative.

Certain variables of child behaviour were rated by the children's teachers and the mothers were interviewed, but no details are given of rating schedules. The results suggested that asthmatic children were somewhat fearful in their attitude towards female authority, and never displayed aggression towards their teachers. Two thirds of them had difficulty in crying and these children were also thought to have some further difficulty in confiding in the mother. The authors attributed the difficulty in crying and in confiding to the mother's personality; children who were inhibited were thought to have mothers who were intolerant of unusual behaviour and reacted angrily upon provocation. Non-inhibited children had mothers who were more tolerant of behavioural deviations, and suppressed their own infrequently felt anger.

The authors thought that the mothers of asthmatic children were somewhat more over-protective than the other mothers, though they felt this attitude might be more a characteristic of mothers who faithfully bring their children to medical clinics (from which they drew their subjects) rather than simply a characteristic of mothers of asthmatic children.

The authors suggested that mothers of asthmatic children identify with their children less than mothers of rhinitic children and suggested that this might be due to rejection on their part. They did not investigate the relationship between rejection and lack of identification, however. Their observations further suggested that mothers of asthmatic children handled sexual information and education rather unsatisfactorily, and that their husbands tended to be more passive and easygoing than those of the children referred for acting-out problems.

Whilst the authors are clearly in no position to make definite conclusions as to personality differences between asthmatic and non-asthmatic children, dependent upon differences in maternal personality, their observations are certainly suggestive of possible areas of conflict.

Bostock (1956) in an equally uncontrolled observational study added further information on the incidence of rejection in the maternal group. Of the thirty-eight mothers of asthmatic children interviewed, twenty-two admitted an unwelcome baby. Eight further cases were thought to involve 'probable rejection' of the child. Only eight mothers of asthmatic children were 'accepting', and of these, seven regarded children as more than usually precious. No definition of acceptance or rejection is given, but Bostock appears to equate lack of adequate breast-feeding with rejection, a concept which is undoubtedly questionable. (For a more complete exposé of the problem see Appendix 1.)

Half of the mothers showed evidence of marital conflict, a majority were dominant partners in their marriage, and over half of the mothers said that they had experienced an unsatisfactory relationship with their own mothers. Bostock did not relate the 'undue tension' in the maternal group to the emergence of the child's illness however. Instead he explained this in terms of heredity, and shock following hospitalisation for the first time (frequently after a tonsillectomy), or the mother's return from hospital with a new baby, or long periods of crying alone.

Bostock showed the T.A.T. pictures to the thirty-eight asthmatic children he studied and noted phantasy hostility directed towards the mother, and also some evidence of rebellion against parental planning. No details are given of the frequency of these themes in the T.A.T. protocols.

Two allergists, Harris and Shure, set out in 1956 to refute the notion that distinct personality types are specifically predisposed to certain diseases. From a normal school population of 1,263 children aged six to twelve years, they selected twenty-five with asthma and twenty-five control children of the same age, class (at school) and socio-economic status. They asked each child's teacher to report on his emotional growth, social adjustment, work habits and special abilities and interests.

On the basis of the teacher's reports, they noted as much deviation in the emotional and behavioural patterns of the asthmatic children as of the controls. In only one instance did there appear a difference between groups, asthmatic children appeared less in need of praise and affection than control group children. No details are given of the method used by teachers to assess the children, and it is therefore impossible to judge whether the apparent absence of personality differences between groups might be due in part to lack of specific rating categories.

In 1956, 203 child asthmatics under sixteen years of age, were studied by Rees, as part of a larger study of the incidence and relative importance of various possible factors in the aetiology of asthma. The group was unselected and controlled by a group of children admitted to hospital because of accidental injury.

Rees noted that before the age of sixteen, there were twice as many boy asthmatics as girls. A history of allergy was noted frequently in the girl asthmatics, but not in the boy asthmatics. Girl asthmatics were also thought to be very unstable and ill-adjusted as compared with the control girls.

Rees rated a number of personality traits on a three-point scale and compared the asthmatic and control groups. He found a higher incidence of very anxious personalities in the asthmatic group, and a higher number of individuals rated as being very timid, obsessional and sensitive. There was also a higher incidence of neurotic symptoms in the asthmatic children, particularly the boys.

Rees suggested that more than one aetiological factor is present in a large proportion of childhood asthma. Psychological factors played an aetiological role in between 61 to 76 per cent of cases. He further suggested that parental influences were important in determining emotional reactions, which precipitated attacks of asthma in children. Overprotection was the most common faulty attitude. Parental overprotection was found significantly more often in the asthmatic than in the control group. Other faulty attitudes of the parents, such as rejection and perfectionism, also occurred but less frequently than over-protection. Rees noted that these parental attitudes antedated the onset of the asthma, and he found that guidance for the parents was the most effective therapeutic method of treating asthmatic children.

Long and colleagues (1957) produced a fascinating experimental study to explain why children with intractable asthma are often symptomatically relieved by admission to a hospital, even though they have the same medication in the hospital as they received at home. Because of the frequent claim by allergists that removal from house dust whilst in hospital is sufficient to explain remission of symptoms, the authors devised a test to discover whether sensitivity to house dust is the only factor necessary for the production of asthma.

Using eighteen subjects, asthmatic children aged between six and twelve years, they circulated dust collected from the child's home in its hospital room at night. This house dust normally produced a skin sensitivity reaction in fourteen of the children. At the time of the testing, no evidence of respiratory change was perceived in the children although the rooms were heavily sprayed. Indeed one child who lived above a bakery and was markedly sensitive to wheat, had flour sprayed heavily into her room, without any respiratory changes.

The authors concluded that allergic sensitivity was not sufficient to precipitate asthmatic attacks in their sample. They tested an alternative hypothesis, that children with asthma as compared with control children would display 'a stronger wish to return to the state of closeness to the mother that existed before birth'. To test this suggestion, the authors compared the number of claustral phantasies produced in response to T.A.T. pictures by subject and control children. They found that the asthmatic group produced three times as many claustral symbols and claustral themes as the controls.

They also noted that asthmatic children told more stories centring on dependency needs than controls, who by comparison produced more stories relating to needs for achievement. In addition, they suggested that the asthmatic children perceived this dependency wish as dangerous. More of the asthmatic subjects as compared with controls described the hero in the projective stories as ill when at home, or as improving when away from home.

Believing that the psychoneurotic symptoms, as often stressed as being peculiar to the asthmatic personality, might relate more to the fact of being chronically ill than to the specific illness, Neuhaus (1958) decided to compare an asthmatic group with a cardiac group.

Thirty-four asthmatic children were compared with the same number of cardiac children and with groups of healthy matched controls. Both groups were also compared with groups of their brothers and sisters and all children were given three separate personality tests. On the basis of the scores obtained the authors concluded that asthmatic children were more maladjusted than control children and exhibited marked traits of anxiety, insecurity and dependency. No difference was found between the sick children and their brothers and sisters, suggesting either similarities in personality due to constitutional or family factors, or some generalisation of the sick child's personality characteristics, because of his presence in the family.

Similarly no significant difference in personality patterns was found between the asthmatic and the cardiac children, suggesting to the author 'the existence of personality traits common to both illnesses and conceivably common to protracted illness in general'.

Fitzelle (1959) focused his attention on the personality characteristics of the parents of asthmatic children, but could detect no differences between them and a group of control parents. In attitude to marriage and incidence of divorce or marital unhappiness, there was also no apparent difference, although the age of the asthmatic mother was considerably higher than that of the controls. Mothers and fathers of asthmatics were also more inclined to feel mild dislike, or only mild attachment to their own parents. Significantly more of the asthmatic parents had suffered from some allergic condition as compared with control parents.

When the two groups of parents were asked about their children, Fitzelle noted that asthmatic parents ascribed to them nearly twice as many nervous symptoms. Fifty-five per cent of the mothers reported that asthmatic attacks sometimes or frequently followed a nervous upset. Fitzelle did not specify the manner in which his control group was selected and the significant difference in ages between asthmatic and control group mothers might possibly indicate a real difference in personal characteristics of the two groups, which would render conclusions based on these results extremely tentative.

One of the most carefully controlled studies in this field was completed by Alcock in 1960. She compared twenty-five asthmatic children with twenty-five emotionally disturbed, twenty-five 'normal', and twenty-five chronically ill children, all matched in terms of age, sex, intelligence, and socio-cultural environment. Unfortunately one crucial variable—ordinal position within the family—was not controlled. Alcock gave the Rorschach to each child, and the results were independently assessed.

On the basis of the Rorschach responses, Alcock concluded that the general personality characteristics of the asthmatic children are marked sensitivity in human relationships, lowered reactivity and tension without appropriate release. She noted considerable shading shock, a characteristic commonly found in adult cases of severe depression. She noted a further characteristic of depression—lowered reactivity—both in the Rorschach responses and also in their apparent inhibition of intellectual performance. Alcock concluded: 'Repressed anger and consequent depression are major features in the psychogenesis of the asthmatic personality which may thus be regarded as a predisposition to the disorder.'

Owen (1961) designed a fascinating experiment to discover whether or not the sound of the mother's voice would evoke significant respiratory change in a group of asthmatic children. This experiment clearly does not attempt to shed light on the personality structure of the asthmatic child, but it affords considerable evidence of the crucial nature of the mother-child relationship for the child's bodily functioning.

Twenty asthmatic children were matched for age and sex with twenty children suffering from other organic illnesses, and pneumographic tracings of each child's respiratory patterns were made during two ten-minute experimental sessions. In each session the child listened to the tape recordings of two voices, that of his own mother and that of the mother of his matched control. In one session each of the voices was heard reading a story which was non-threatening in content. In the other a story possibly threatening in terms of the theme of mother-child separation was read. The children were compared as to the amount of change in respiratory pattern which occurred when the unknown voice was replaced by the mother's voice. The asthmatic children showed much greater change, and also showed more abnormal patterns of respiration as a result of hearing their mother's voice on tape. These changes occurred irrespective of story content, thus Owen attributed all significant differences between groups, to the greater significance of the mother's voice for the asthmatic children.

A final study of the mother-child relationship in bronchial asthma was made by Margolis in 1961. Twenty-five mothers of asthmatic children were compared with twenty-five mothers of rheumatic children and twenty-five mothers of relatively healthy children seen in surgery outpatients. No criteria for matching were given, and testing was done in small groups in the hospital.

Margolis found that asthmatic mothers exhibited more evidence of psycho-sexual conflict when tested with the Blacky pictures, than did the controls. He thought that they had sustained disturbances in their oedipal relationships and were more orally erotic than the controls. Asthmatic mothers were thought to be more closely identified with their own mothers as the disciplinary figure in the household, and they were thought to show greater evidence of rivalry with brothers and sisters, particularly rivalry because of fear of loss of parental affection.

Margolis tested his groups with the Parent Attitude Research Instrument, but found only one significant difference between groups. Asthmatic mothers scored more highly on the dependency-on-the-mother scale. Margolis concluded that whilst mothers of asthmatic children appeared to be more emotionally disturbed than mothers of non-asthmatic children, the differences were slight and a replication of the study was essential·

From an analysis of previous empirical work, it must be apparent that the results so far obtained appear highly conflictful. Some studies appear to substantiate the clinical insights discussed previously, some negate them. Frequently the haphazard method of selecting control samples, and the subjective method of scoring data suggest serious sources of error in the results obtained. Whilst fascinating fragments of information have been gathered relating to the personality needs of the asthmatic child and his mother, it is suggested that there exists as yet no conclusive or complete view of the relationship, and its place in the aetiology of childhood asthma. It is to overcome this lack that the present empirical study was undertaken.

CHAPTER XX

The Personality Needs of
Asthmatic Children

The first hypothesis suggests that asthmatic children are more unsettled than control children. Testing of this hypothesis proceeded in three stages:

(1) An estimate of the degree of unsettledness shown at school was made by means of the Bristol Social Adjustment Guides, filled in by class teachers.

(2) A comparison was made of the number of behaviours indicative of anxiety (for example, night fears, jealousy of siblings, excessive temper tantrums) shown at home and reported by mothers in answer to questions concealed in a questionnaire relating to the child's development.

(3) A comparison of the conflicts and fears underlying this behaviour was made by means of an analysis of themes produced by the children in response to twelve T.A.T. pictures. An overall analysis and comparison of needs, emotions, threats, actions and outcomes was made and also a specific analysis of themes relating to parent-child relationships.

Subjects

Twenty-five children who were referred consecutively to the de-sensitising clinic, and to the in-patient wards of the Ava Wing, Belfast City Hospital were seen by the author, and form the asthmatic group. No attempt was made to select cases whose aetiology was presumed to be essentially psychological, nor to obtain only those cases whose disease history was of long duration, and a serious nature. The Asthma Group represents —in so far as any *small* group is able—a cross section of the school-age child asthmatic population of Northern Ireland, as seen by a paediatrician working in a hospital setting. (For personal details of asthmatic subjects, see Table II.)

The control group represents a group of twenty-five non-asthmatic children matched individually to the asthmatic

TABLE II

PERSONAL DETAILS OF SUBJECTS IN THE ASTHMATIC GROUP

Subject	Sex	Age	I.Q.	Ord. P.	No. Sib.	Father's Occupation	Length of Illness in Years
1	M	8·11	95	2nd	2	Civil servant	4
2	M	13·6	98	1st	2	Sales rep.	7
3	M	12·11	98	1st	3	Labourer	0·5
4	M	10·2	115	1st	1	Teacher	6
5	M	9·5	94	1st	–	Bus conductor	6
6	M	9·4	102	1st	2	Mate—Merchant Navy	7
7	F	12·2	84	1st	6	Labourer	7
8	F	9·9	110	3rd	2	Civil Servant	6·5
9	M	13·0	105	1st	6	Barman	10
10	M	6·10	90	1st	2	Bricklayer	4
11	M	9·11	—	1st	3	Lorry driver	7
12	M	8·1	105	5th	6	Registrar	4
13	M	13·2	96	1st	1	Air controller	11
14	M	11·10	104	1st	1	Bus driver	7
15	M	11·6	88	1st	5	Unemployed	11
16	M	6·4	—	3rd	4	Excavator driver	3·6
17	M	9·4	90	2nd	3	Donkeyman M.N.	7
18	M	14·9	72	6th	7	Unemployed	4
19	M	7·6	—	1st	2	Aircraft inspector	5
20	F	11·6	94	1st	2	Sailor M.N.	2·5
21	M	10·2	99	4th	3	Cargo super.	9
22	M	12·4	109	2nd	9	Docker	6·6
23	F	5·3	—	1st	1	Engineer M.N.	2
24	M	6·3	—	5th	8	Labourer	3
25	M	12·9	98	2nd	6	Labourer	8

Total number of males = 21*
Total number of females = 4*
Mean age = 10·1
Mean I.Q. = 97·3

Ordinal Position:
1st = 15†
2nd = 4
3rd = 2
4th = 1
5th = 2
6th = 1

* Difference significant at the ·001 level Sign Test.
† Difference significant at the ·01 level using the Kolmogorov Smirnov one sample test (2-tailed).

children. The variables considered to be important in selecting a control child were:

(1) age (within six calendar months of the asthmatic child);

(2) sex;

(3) intelligence quotient (as measured by the progressive matrices) and school achievement (as rated by the teacher);

(4) socio-economic status and religion;

(5) ordinal position and number in the family (approximate);

(6) extent of illness.

Where the subject child was seriously incapacitated by his illness, another chronically ill child was selected with whom to compare him. Where the asthma represented a minor disturbance in the child's life, a child with a normal illness pattern was selected with whom to compare him.*

The selection of control children was made through the school which the asthmatic child attended. The Head Teacher was approached, and the nature of the study explained to him and his co-operation obtained in selecting a control child matched in terms of the specified variables.

Unsettledness and maladjustment displayed in school

The class teacher of each pair of asthmatic and control children was asked to fill in a Bristol Social Adjustment Guide for each child. In selecting the control sample, care was taken not to choose children in school classes other than those in which the asthmatic child worked, thereby avoiding a possible source of error in rating Bristol Social Adjustment Guides.

Twenty-four pairs of Adjustment Guides were returned to the author and the results obtained were subjected to statistical analysis, using a one-tailed Wilcoxon Matched-Pairs Signed Ranks Test.

Two syndromes were found to yield statistically significant differences between the groups. They were the syndromes of

* A comparison was also made of the previous school attendance records, because it was felt that children who were frequently absent from school might display a greater degree of unsettledness upon their return to school due to the difficulty of reintegrating into the school community. A statistical comparison of the actual number of school attendances was made using a two-tailed Wilcoxon Matched Signed Ranks Test. No significant difference was found between the attendance figures for the two groups.

unforthcomingness (differences significant at the .05 level) and the nervous symptoms score (difference significant at the .05 level). Two other syndromes, the depression, and the unconcern for adult approval syndromes, also yielded substantial differences between groups. From these results therefore it would appear that in school asthmatic children appear to be inhibited, lethargic and lacking in interest. There appears to be an inhibition in their 'normal striving for personal effectiveness' (Stott 1964). They appear to defend themselves against any new experiences, and generally to lack confidence in all challenging situations. As a group, they appear to have lost interest in wresting approval from the adults around them, possibly suggestive of some kind of early deprivation of affection.

These conclusions are further substantiated by an analysis of the individual B.S.A.G. items. The total number of respondents in both groups presenting each behavioural item was noted, and the results were analysed statistically using a Sign Test.

Asthmatic children were more often described as 'being outsiders' (difference significant at the ·016 level). They were thought to be frequently 'on the fringe' of classroom cliques. In addition, they were frequently described as apathetic, and they tended to lack interest in school work and class activities. Many of them were thought to work only when they were being watched or compelled to do so. Some of them showed a tendency to copy their classmates' work.

Several short descriptions of asthmatic children are now included. These show the depressive and unforthcoming aspects of the children's behaviour in school.

John was a slight, pale, wiry-headed eleven-year-old who attended a special open air school because of his delicate physical condition. Dirty, and inadequately clothed, he was the first of a family of six children, and was, at the time of testing, living with his own and six other families in a temporary hostel for the homeless. He was diagnosed as asthmatic at three to four months. Before this he had already been hospitalised for suspected gastroenteritis and had abscesses around his eyes, which his mother attributed to lack of sleep due to frequent moves.

In school, John showed considerable evidence of depression and unforthcomingness, and in addition slight unconcern for adult approval. He was submissive, and somewhat distant, tending both to shun others, and also to give in to them too easily. He never made the first approach in greeting or during lessons, instead he waited to be noticed or asked. When forced to speak, he would mumble shyly and awkwardly. His mood was variable, sometimes he would seem eager, and at other times he couldn't be bothered to join in class activities. He lacked physical energy and frequently appeared apathetic, or when at games, too sluggish or lethargic to participate. Possibly because of this lack of involvement he was constantly on the fringe, an 'outsider' in his own class. He tended to play childish games, frequently with younger children. His teacher formed the impression that he deliberately minimised his contacts with her, and she felt that he was frequently watching and assessing her. She remarked that she had never seen him smile.

William N. attended the same open air school as John, but was in other respects very different. A well built thirteen-year-old, he had developed his asthma at the age of two-and-a-half. He was the first boy in a family of two, his mother having lost a boy baby at birth, two years before William's conception. His father was a technician employed in aircraft manufacture, and the family enjoyed a slight degree of physical comfort. William's mother expressed sorrow at his illness and said that she personally believed that he would never work. This gloomy prediction was totally at variance with the prognosis made by the consultant paediatrician. Mrs N. encouraged William to 'rest up' on a sofa in the family living room, and she brought all his meals to him there. In school his Head Teacher thought him lazy, for despite his own quite considerable physical strength, and above average intelligence, he could never be compelled to work or attend for very long.

He showed considerable unsettledness in school, his behaviour reflecting both depression, hostility towards adults, unconcern for their approval, and in addition, a real need for acceptance and approval both from adults and other children.

He was described as lacking in interest, apathetic, and

tending to slump and loll about. At games he was always sluggish and lethargic and tended to shrink from any active play. In class, he would only work when watched or compelled. She noticed that he always bore a grudge against anyone who punished or chastised him. In his relationships with other children he tended to tell tales and to be a spoilsport, and he was consequently an 'outsider', unwelcome in any group, and mostly on bad terms with everyone else.

Despite this obvious hostility, William was concerned with gaining affection. He was over-eager to greet his teacher, and over-friendly towards her. He tended to talk excessively to her, and was always finding excuses for engaging her attention, and for hanging around her. He frequently craved her sympathy. Similarly, he bragged to the other children, tending to play the hero, and liking to be the centre of attention. This ambivalence of affection obviously increased his nervousness, and he tended to stutter.

Brian C., the last of these brief portraits based on teachers' observations, was the fifth child in his family and had a younger brother and sister. He had been born with eczema and had to have his hands in splints from birth. He was also described as 'chesty' from birth and developed his asthma at four-and-a-half years of age, just when his eldest brother's asthma was remitting. At this time he also became enuretic. At the time of testing, Brian was eight and was about to be given a place in a residential school for asthmatic children. His mother noted that his younger brother was showing signs of developing asthma also.

In school Brian was unforthcoming to the point of withdrawal and depressed and nervous. His teacher described him as too timid to be naughty and remarked that he could never get a word out of him. Brian tended to mumble shyly, and associated only with one other child. He never appeared friendly or eager, and had never greeted his teacher spontaneously. He was apathetic and lacked interest and would only work when compelled to do so. He was thought to be babyish, mispronouncing many simple words, and he was described as an 'outsider' in his group. To his teacher, and to me, he appeared 'lost', and decidedly sad.

Unsettledness of asthmatic children when compared only with controls who are healthy

A relationship appears to exist between the experience of chronic illness and the appearance of behavioural unsettledness. Neuhaus (1958) suggested that it was this relationship, rather than some underlying emotional conflict, which accounted for the apparent anxiety reflecting personality variables of the asthmatic child, and his work suggested that studies using only quite healthy controls would yield greater differences between asthmatic and control groups, than studies using chronically ill controls.

Because of this suggestion care was taken in the present study to select a child with a comparable length of illness to control each chronically ill asthmatic child. Despite this, statistically significant differences were found between groups —the asthmatic children appearing more nervous and unforthcoming than the controls. But the question remains as to whether the subject children would have appeared more unsettled if they had been compared with only healthy controls, as Neuhaus' work suggested.

In an attempt therefore to further investigate the relationship of chronic illness to observed behavioural unsettledness the scores of the asthmatic and control children were again compared statistically, but this time the scores for the five chronically ill control children were excluded from the group. The Mann Whitney test was used and a Z value was computed for each comparison (n.S = 24, n.C = 19).

On this testing five syndromes yielded significant differences between groups. Unforthcomingness became more apparent (P = ·008), so also did the nervous symptoms displayed by the asthmatic children (P = ·036). In addition, asthmatic children appeared withdrawn (P = ·023), affection seeking (P = ·05) and unconcerned with adult approval (P = ·045).

This apparent inconsistency in results may serve to explain the conflicting findings of previous studies. Studies using chronically ill control children produced fewer differences in personality variables than investigations which compared asthmatic children with healthy controls only.

This conclusion would suggest that the experience of chronic illness tends to unsettle a child. Possibly frequent absences from school, and an inability to withstand physically the rough and tumble of the classroom may account for the symptoms noted by teachers in all chronically ill children, whether asthmatic or otherwise.

The discrepancy in results on the two testings highlights the need to match subject and control children on all possible personal variables before any reliance can be placed on the findings obtained from investigations of their personality needs.

Unsettled behaviour observed in the home

Material on the reported unsettled behaviour displayed by each child at home was abstracted from the interview questionnaire which I used when talking to the child's mother. The number of affirmative answers made by mothers to questions relating to problem behaviour was compared statistically for the two groups, using the Sign Test.

Mothers of asthmatic children consistently described their children as problematic. They were thought to have been problems as infants (significant at the ·046 level), as toddlers (·02 level), and at the time of the present study (·046 level). When an overall analysis was made of the responses for each child on all the eleven questions indicative of problem behaviour (for example night terrors, sibling rivalry, obsessive daytime fears) and a statistical comparison between groups was made, using a one-tailed Wilcoxon Matched-Pairs Signed Ranks Test, a high level of significance was obtained (·005 level). The results suggested that asthmatic children, as seen by their mothers, were more disturbed in their home setting than the control children.

From an analysis of the supplementary information given by mothers and compared with the aid of the Sign Test, it was obvious that as infants asthmatic children tended to be poor feeders (significant at the ·031 level), and excessive criers; as two to three-year-olds, more inclined to temper tantrums, crying and unsettled behaviour. They were more inclined to show jealousy when the next child in the family was born, and this jealousy tended to persist, and in some cases became a generalised dislike of brothers and sisters. At the time of the study the subject children showed themselves as more moody, depressed, stubborn and inclined to tempers than controls. They also showed more evidence of night fears and restless sleep than the controls. In the play situation significantly more asthmatic children showed a preference for play outside the home (difference between groups significant at the ·046 level using the Sign Test). This preference for play away from home had also been apparent when the asthmatic child was quite small (difference significant at the ·029 level, using the Sign Test).

Case histories of typical asthmatic children are given in Chapter XXII (p. 224) where it is possible to relate this supposed deviancy on the child's part to his mother's initial emotional and behavioural responses to him. Child problem behaviour is then viewed as an extension of disturbed maternal behaviour.

Underlying needs, threats and emotions

A comparison of the child's needs, and the threats underlying his behaviour was made by means of an analysis of the themes produced in response to twelve T.A.T. pictures from Murray's standard set.

The pictures were administered by the author individually, usually in the child's school, although a few of the asthmatic children were seen as in-patients in the Belfast City Hospital. The test was prefaced by the 'warm up' procedure described in the first section of this book (p. 41), and the instructions given to each child were similar to those already described earlier. No refusals were encountered by the author, whether the subject was seen in hospital or in school.

Scoring of the T.A.T. protocols used the method outlined by Cox and Sargent (1950) in a slightly modified form. Rating of protocols was done by the author, and by two independent post-graduate clinical psychologists. Differences between items scored by the two groups were analysed by means of a one-tailed Wilcoxon Matched Pairs Signed Ranks Test.

The results obtained suggested that the emotional tone of the stories told by asthmatic children was significantly more sad (·001 level), and more anxious (·03 level) and full of conflict. By contrast the control children told stories of a happier (·025 level) and more positive nature (·001 level).

In accordance with clinical observations, the asthmatic children in this group showed a significantly greater need for assertion than did the controls (·001 level).

Asthmatic children, as evinced by their T.A.T. themes, see the environment as more threatening than do the controls. They showed significantly more fear of their own guilt (·005 level), their own mental inadequacy (·04 level) and their own motivational inadequacy (·025 level) all of which prevented satisfaction of their needs. They were significantly more aware of their own inadequacy than were the controls (·001 level). In addition they felt more threatened by the external environment (·005 level) and particularly by the domination of others (·036 level).

By comparison with the controls they were less prepared to take positive action to secure their needs, and were more inclined to see their efforts to secure personal satisfaction as meeting with only modified success (·04 level). Controls gave significantly more successful outcomes to their stories (·01 level).

The following illustrate the assertive stories recounted by the subject children. The first seven were told by a ten-year-old boy, whose asthma began when he was nine months of age. Previously, at six months, he had been in hospital for pneumonia. Both stories relating to parents deal with parental opposition to the child's career decision. In both cases the child succeeds, but success becomes a mixed blessing.

(2) 'Once upon a time there was this girl who wanted to be a school teacher but her mother wanted her to be a nurse—so she ran away and went to California, where they were looking for school teachers. She applied for the job and got it, and all the children at the school liked her, and she taught them a lot of subjects they had never been taught before. The class she taught was a low class but soon she was up with the high ones. She had to leave the school to go to New York and teach science to soldiers, for the war was almost coming and they had to learn a lot of things. She was very poor at the start but she soon had a lovely car and home. She married a Russian soldier and was to go to Berlin with him. Then she fell ill and was taken to hospital, and after two days she died and was buried in California where she made her first start.'

(3) 'One day there was these two boys, aged fifteen years old, were

in a home because they cut a man open with a razor blade. The man was called Mr Jones, who lived in an army hospital. He was a plastic surgeon who made other people's faces better and one day he went to visit the two boys who had tried to cut him up—they threatened to shoot him, and he sent for the police. They found they were insane and they were checked and put in a mental home, and one day they got out of control and had to be put in chains. They shouted and screamed and did everything for attention but it did not do any good and they soon gave it up and were soon better again.'

(4) 'One day there were these two lovers in a surgery waiting to be seen—for they were married of course and she was going to have a baby. They found the doctor would pay no attention to them at all—and he sent them out and the man wanted to kill him. He went one night and killed him but when he went home he found his wife strangled. The doctor did it. When the police came it was found the doctor was mad and they dropped the case.'

(6) 'This young child who attempted to commit suicide by jumping off a roof. She wanted to kill herself for her baby had died two weeks ago. It died of smothering—though the doctor said it would be alright. And she wanted to commit suicide. But her husband went up onto the roof and brought her down to the doctor who soon fixed her up.'

(14) 'In New York there was this tragedy of two young boys who were breaking into shops and houses and hotels. They were stealing money and other things—and the police were out looking for pictures of the boys who didn't care what happened to them, and had stolen £26,000 and property. One night they tried to break into this house. They made a noise and the man phoned the police, who arrested them, and they served six years in jail.'

(16) 'Once upon a time there was this man and his son who lived in a cottage. The boy's father was a solicitor and he wanted his son to follow in his footsteps, but his son wanted to study the stars. But he wouldn't let him, so he ran away to New York, and was soon very good. One day he came to his father and told him what had happened. His father wouldn't speak to him, and threw him out of the house, and felt very sad. Then he told his father he would follow in his footsteps and his father taught him the soliciting, and he won many cases, and one day his father took a heart attack and was taken to hospital and was given blood transfusions, but it didn't help. His father left his son plenty of

money and books, but it didn't help. He wanted his father—but his father was very ill and soon died, and his son buried him in his own garden.'

(18) 'One day there was this man who threatened to blow his brains out with a revolver but he was too nervous to do it. They sent for doctors who found he was suffering from a head injury which he got from a car. He was still ill, and he didn't know what he was doing, and in a few days he blew out his brains with a revolver his father had given him as a child.'

The following stories are taken from the protocol of an eleven-and-a-half-year-old girl, who had developed her asthma two years before the testing. At this time she heard that her mother was expecting another baby, and also she was taken to live with an uncle whose wife had just deserted him, leaving him with three small children.

(2gf) 'A long time ago in a village called Rocky Green, there was a young girl whose father owned it, and there was this young man called Jason, who lived in a very poor farm at the end of the village. Jane loved Jason but her father would not allow her to marry him as he said he was not good enough for her. But they met secretly and Jason said he would go and ask her father could he marry her, but she said it would be no good. They were watched by Jane's father's servant who went and told his master, who was in a rage. He told Jane if she saw Jason again he would have him thrown out of the village. So the next time they had to be even more careful. Jason said he would go and ask her father again—but she said no it would do no good. So next day she went into Jason's house but he was not there, and it was very dusty and there was a note saying: "I'm not coming back for your father would never let me marry you. Good-bye for ever, Jason." She ran back home and said she hated everyone—her father and everybody. Her father heard her crying and heard what was wrong, and said she was better off without him, and she said she would run off and marry him, and he said he would lock her up till she saw sense and he tried to comfort her, but she would not have his arm around her and went out, locking the door. She saw Jason going by on a cart, but he could not hear her and so she tried to get out, and she crept out after dark, and ran off on a bus, leaving a letter for her father saying she had gone out to marry Jason, and seeing he hadn't let her marry him there, she had gone away. The father wept when he read it and threatened to sack his servant if he said they were better off without her. The father followed them and found Jane and Jason together, and Jane was trying to persuade Jason to marry her and the father said they could come home and be married in the little town.'

(5) 'Once upon a time there was a man and his wife and a little girl and they lived in a nice house at the end of the lane in Millingtown Lane and it was always bright and one day the mother took sick and they called the doctor who said she had a fever and it was very bad and it got worse and they heard the mother moaning, and called for the doctor, and Jane didn't know what was wrong. She was only five. The doctor stayed with her for two hours, and then he came downstairs very sad and said her mother was dead, and he would arrange for the funeral. At the end of the week it was all over, and the little girl went to school again. For a year the father and the little girl went each week to tend to the grave and lived happily together, and then the father married again—a wife who was very cruel and just wanted the father's money. She hoped the little girl would die and then she could get all the money, and she kept Mary without food and locked in her room. But she never told her father who was ill in bed. She told him she was keeping her well. Then one day her stepmother brought a beautiful vase which had cost a lot of money and then Mary knocked it over and broke it. She didn't know what to do. She was so scared. She sat down and tried to put all the pieces together. And then her mother arrived, and it was her mother looking so angry—and her mother said "I've never been so insulted as I have today" and she stamped upstairs, and Mary said she wanted to speak to her, and Mary told her of the vase, and she hit Mary in the face. The father heard all this and came downstairs, and the stepmother tried to say "Mary had done it on purpose" and then the father took Mary in his arms and asked what was the matter, and Mary told him of the bread and water and things, and Mary's father said "I don't like you any more" and he told Mary to go to some friends in the next village for a fortnight and meanwhile her father got rid of her stepmother and got a housekeeper who was plump and jolly and Mary liked her, and her father did too, and Mary's father married her and they lived happily ever after.'

(9gf) 'A short while ago there was this mother with a little girl who went to a school called St Clare's, and it was a good school, and she loved it. But her mother and father decided they would take her away from the school for it was wearing her down, and making her tired, and her father who was going on a boat to Africa said he would take her with him. But the mother said no, it would be no rest for her. But the girl went, and on the ship it was very rocky, and she felt sick, and when she went to find her father he was gone, and she fell and hit her head, and the boat sank and her father took her in a boat and they got inland and they wandered around and found a white lady who couldn't get off the island. But next day a boat came and they were safe, and the girl went back to St Clare's and told them about the boat and she was never sick again.'

(Several months before this story was told the subject had been moved from a normal intermediate school—a very new and well equipped one—to a much smaller open air school. It is possible that this move formed the basis for the story.)

(14) 'Once upon a time there was a little boy called Jimmy and he had a new little fellow come into his street, called Bobby, and he was blind and couldn't go to school. His mother took him everywhere, and one day Jimmy said: "I wish I was blind. I don't like school and I wouldn't be smacked, and you'd be nice to me and do everything," and so Jimmy prayed hard he'd be blind, and the next day he went to school in the bus but it crashed and all the glass broke, and everything was alright except for one thing. Jimmy was blind and he was really very pleased, except that he began to miss playing with his friends and seeing things and he wished he hadn't been blind and it wasn't nice at all, and he started to cry. But his mother came up and said God was fair and he would soon get used to it; so he kissed his mother and went to sleep.'

(16) 'Some time ago there was a little black boy called Bobo and Bobo's father had come into some money and he sent Bobo to a white school, and everyone jeered and laughed, and one boy was very nasty and pretended to be his friend, and when they were down on the beach, he told Bobo that he was black—really a savage—and all the others would throw things at him if he came back to school. But Bobo had a boat and had taken his friend to an island, and Bobo said if he didn't take what he had said back, he'd leave him alone and take his boat away. But the boy jeered the more and said he was dirty and nasty and black and really a savage. So Bobo went and took the boat and left the white boy alone and the waves came up and the wind blew and the police began to look for him. But Bobo said he'd taken the boy home

and didn't know where he was. But then Bobo heard the beach was flooding so he went to the boy's mother and told her, and they went and rescued the boy and put him in the boat—and the men scolded Bobo, and said they'd drown him if he did it again. The doctors were scared he might die—and Bobo was scared for if he died he might be sent back to Africa, and Bobo's parents scolded him very much and the white boys jeered at him no more, for they were scared what he might do to them, so they never spoke, and he became friends with the white boy and they lived happily ever after.'

(18) 'Once upon a time there was this old lady and she lived in a very big house with her daughter and her daughter was wicked, but the old lady was slowly dying and the doctor came to see her every month. But the daughter thought if she had the house soon she could have a good time, and she told her mother that she was dying and worried her, and then she said to go and have a bath, and the daughter opened all the windows and gave the mother a cold, and then she gave her asprins, and doctor had said she was to have no tablets. Then the mother decided she was hungry and tried to go downstairs, but she tripped and fell downstairs—and she was dead, and the daughter felt ashamed for what she'd done. The doctor came and he knew what the daughter had done, but he told nobody, for he knew the daughter would punish herself in her own way by living a life of misery.'

A final story is added, because it very clearly illustrates the real fear of parental punishment and discovery of supposed misdemeanours. This kind of theme was found frequently in the children's stories. This is the story of a twelve-year-old boy, Michael, who was diagnosed as asthmatic between three and four years of age, and who had previously been bronchitic.

(14) 'It was bright on the first morning of May and Frank stepped outside the door of his house. His mother told him to behave and not get up to the general tricks. His mother was used to hearing complaints about him. Frank did not like this much, and went off in the direction of the town shops. On his way he passed the greengrocer's and sitting outside the shop window was the barrel of apples. Frank was very much tempted by the apples and took one. He knew his mother had told him often not to do this, but Frank could not resist temptation. Luckily for him he was not seen by the greengrocer, Mr Thompson. Frank had

different ideas and ran away into a bomb site and contentedly ate the apple. On the way home again he saw Mr Thompson leave the shop with a box and heading towards Frank's house. Frank was terrified at the thought that Mr Thompson knew about his stealing the apples. Frank raced to his house and slipped in the back door and ran all the way up to his bedroom. He slammed the door behind him and stopped against it breathlessly. A knock was heard at the door. Frank assumed it would be Mr Thompson. He was right. But Mr Thompson had only come to deliver a box of apples. Frank's heart beat loud because he became very frightened. The door shut again. Frank thought this was Mr Thompson talking to Frank's Mummy about him stealing an apple from his shop. But really it was just the greengrocer leaving the house. Frank's room started to get dark for no apparent reason. He groped to find his way around the room but he could not make anything out. Frank had forgotten about the greengrocer and was now even more frightened of the sudden darkness. Suddenly he fell over his bed. At least he knew of his whereabouts in the room. He started off again to look for the window. He groped round the walls punching everything in front of him. All of a sudden his head hit something but this was only another corner of his room. At least now he was near to the window. Smash! went the window as he put his hand through a pane of glass in the window. The window opened immediately and the room was once more filled with light. But Frank now had another problem. It was worse to pay for a broken window than an apple.'

Themes relating to parent figures

From the themes related in response to the T.A.T. pictures, stories relating to parent-child relationships were abstracted and subjected to further analysis. Nine scoring categories were devised, and have already been described in the first section (p. 49). A statistical analysis was made of the scores yielded by the two groups using the Wilcoxon Matched Pairs Signed Ranks Test.

From the analysis it was possible to conclude that asthmatic children tended to view parents as more punitive than did control children and showed a significantly greater need to get away from them, coupled with a fear of their own assertiveness (·03 level). By contrast, control children saw their parents as significantly more helpful (·025 level).

Several stories illustrative of the asthmatic child's perception of parent figures as punitive have already been given, but because of the enormous importance of these negative perceptions, further examples are added here. Almost invariably in these stories the child sees himself as guilty, and this justifies the parental hostility.

(3) 'This young boy has been sent to bed because of something he's done wrong, and his mother has sent him to bed but the young boy is not tired as he lies beside the bed and feels sorry for himself, and tries to find the error of his ways.'

(6) 'This man is a detective. He has come to tell the lady something which is very hard to do. The lady is insane and unknowingly she killed her own son for his money. No one can blame her for she is insane, and the detective has been left the job of arresting her and bringing her to an asylum.'

(3) 'Once upon a time there was this young boy. He went out every night and played with his rough mates. His mother did not like this and thought he might get into trouble, and when the boy came in his father told him not to go out with them no more. He said "O.K." but still went about with them, until one day his father found out that he broke windows, and broke into shops and got caught by the police. The boy was lucky getting off when he got to Court, and his father kept him in his room. He was not allowed out for weeks.'

(6bm) 'One day in the year 1948 during the war, there was a woman who had three sons. She wanted another son and she adopted one. The one that she adopted wanted to go to war when he grew up, but she did not like it. She said "You cannot go to war because you might be killed", and then one day he sneaked out of the house with two of his brothers. He went and joined the army. Then one day they were walking through a town, and three of them got captured by surprise. The adopted son escaped from the soldiers and told his mother what had happened. Next morning in the papers it said two boys, young men, would be court martialled for deserting camp during the war. Their mother wanted to go to see them but no women were allowed—just men. She said to her adopted son and her other son to go and find out what happened. They were going to be whipped, and one of them got his punishment, and the other one tried to escape and got shot. When she heard of this she threw her adopted son out and he had to go somewhere else.'

(3bm) 'In the picture is a girl called Mary. She is leaning against a sofa and looking as though she was crying—perhaps because her father has hit her or just because she is sad. She has black hair and is wearing a jersey or pullover. There is a belt round her waist which holds up her dress and she's wearing a pair of light shoes. If she's sad she thinks she wants to get away from her mother and father for they always hit her. She also thinks that if she had a different mother and father life would be better.'

(3bm) 'After asking his father could he go to the circus, Jim's father said "No, you cannot go to the circus, because you did not do as I told you," so Jim went up to his room and sat down on the floor to think. Later when his mother and father and brother were going to the circus he climbed through his window. He followed them on his bike and they turned the corner which led to the bus stop. They got on the bus. He pedalled as fast as he could after the bus. When it reached the circus he was relieved because he was quite tired. They got off the bus and went to the circus. Jim creeped in behind a man so he would not be seen by the ticket collector. After the circus was over he rushed out, jumped on his bike and made for home. The bus was not far behind him. If it caught up with him, he would be found out. He took a short cut through a rocky lane. When he got back he put his bike in the shed and climbed through the bedroom window. But he was too late, for there, waiting for him was his father, who said he was to go straight to bed and get no supper.'

(3gf) 'Her mother might have hit her and she's run off crying. She might be going away. Her mother's hit her because she done something wrong. She might have broke the cup or something of her mother's. Or she's run out of the room crying.'

(6bm) 'A woman is looking out of a window and she sees someone get knocked down and the man—he's a doctor—and he wants to go out and save it. It's a wee baby, and the mother says "No". She won't let him out, because he's left his stuff in the surgery. And he wants to go out and begs his mother and she won't let him go out, and he looks worried. And another doctor passing in his car goes out to it, and he lifts up the wee baby, and the man slips out while his mother is still at the window, and runs down the stairs and out into the road, and does everything he should to help the wee baby, and they get into the doctor's car and go to hospital with it. And they stay to hear what happened to it and the wee baby doesn't survive, and the doctors are all worried—puzzled—

especially the one whose mother wouldn't let him go in the first place.'

(13b) 'This wee boy and he's wondering where his mother is and he was put up to bed for being bad, and he didn't know that his mother was out, and he sneaked down to the kitchen and he found the door open and he sat there wondering where his mother was—and there was no friends for miles and miles away. Just a wee wooden shack where he lived, and he wondered and wondered where his mother could be, and about two o'clock his mother returned. The wee boy ran out to meet her, but the mother didn't talk to him. She just went into the wooden hut and then she gave him his tea, and then he went up to bed and the mother called him down and asked why he was going up, and he said "Because I crept out in the afternoon." And she said "That's alright, you can stay up if you want." But the next day it was his birthday and his mother had baked him a huge big cake and brought lots of presents, and that there was the first happy day the boy had had in his life.'

(18) 'This man here he doesn't want to see nobody and somebody is bringing him back. But he doesn't want to see somebody, and he turns his head. And the person he doesn't want to see is his mother because she threw him out of the house when he was a baby, and he was brought up in a hospital. And these people who brought him up in the hospital want him to see his mother for she wants to repay what she's done. But he says "No! not after what she's done." But these men say: "You must," and they try and scare him, and he says "O.K.—if it's all that important." And he goes to see his mother, and she's pleased—and the both of them. The man said to his mother, "Do you know I haven't very long?" and his mother said "What are you talking about?" and the men shake their heads, and the man said "Could I go home?", and the mother said "Certainly, if you want to" for the man said "I haven't very long to live." And so the mother took him home. It wasn't true—and the men had only said that there to scare him, so that he would go home with his mother, and he believed them.'

The picture that emerges from this three-fold study of the personality variables of asthmatic children is clearly in accordance with that formulated in the clinical literature, and summarised by the first Hypothesis.

Asthmatic children display more unforthcomingness, more backwardness and more nervous symptoms in school than controls. At home they are moody and depressed, more jealous of their brothers and sisters, have more night fears and temper tantrums than controls.

Beneath this unsettled behaviour lies a need for self-assertion, which they perceive as being thwarted both by their own inadequacy, and by the threatening—particularly dominant— nature of their environment. The unsuccessful struggle for independence produces more conflict and depression in their stories and a tendency to avoid positive action and to expect only modified success in their ventures.

By comparison with their control group, asthmatic children are significantly less affection seeking. Control children see their parents as helpful, whilst asthmatic children are more inclined to expect punishment from their parents and express a greater (though fear provoking) need to escape from them.

A possible explanation for the discrepancies obtained by previous studies was suggested by the statistical comparison of the social adjustment scores of asthmatic children and perfectly healthy controls only. Though greater unsettledness was found in the asthmatic group when compared with the group of children matched for degree of incapacitation due to illness, when the comparison was made with healthy controls only, the difference in degree of unsettledness became more apparent. Some intensification of unsettledness seems to result from illness.

CHAPTER XXI

The Relationship between Length of
Illness and Degree of Unsettledness

The second hypothesis explored the possibility that although some degree of emotional conflict and consequent unsettledness of behaviour might exist, before the illness, and be a factor in its aetiology, the illness itself might modify the initial conflict.

Three possible results might be anticipated at the outset:

(1) Unsettledness might increase along with the length of the illness. This might occur because of the frustration inherent in illness.

(2) Unsettledness might decrease with the length of the illness. The possibility for dramatic acting-out permitting expression of, and therefore lowering, the subject's anxiety level.

(3) The degree of unsettledness might not depend on the length of illness.

To test these relationships the asthmatic group was divided into two halves according to the length of their illness. Group One had a mean illness length of 3·7 years. Group Two had a mean illness length of 7·7 years.

A comparison was made of the unsettledness scores of the two groups derived from the Bristol Social Adjustment Guides. Several traits—noticeably the affection seeking, the hostility, and the unconcern for adult-approval syndromes—seemed to be more prevalent in the children with the longer illness length, but when the two groups were compared using the Mann Whitney Test, these differences were not statistically significant.

Only one criterion of unsettledness—the score for the nervous symptoms syndrome—appeared to approximate significance between the groups—this reached the ·06 level. Before it was assumed that nervous symptoms increased with the length of asthmatic illness, two further checks were made. The subject and control groups were divided into two by age, and a comparison made of the adjustment guide scores of the younger and older subject children, and of the younger and older control children. In both groups there was a slight suggestion that unsettledness tended to increase with age, and the older control children displayed more nervous symptoms than the younger controls (difference significant at the ·06 level).

On the basis of this further testing, it was impossible to conclude that the length of illness alone produced an increase in nervous symptoms. The suggestion is therefore made that nervousness found in children suffering from asthma may increase as a result of the stress of growing older rather than as a result of the length of the illness.

As a further check some of the scores obtained for the asthmatic children on the T.A.T. were compared with the length of the child's illness, and with its age (a Mann Whitney Test was used). The only significant difference between children with shorter and children with longer illnesses was in their fear of the external environment. Asthmatic children with a longer history of illness appeared to perceive the world as significantly more threatening than the children with a shorter illness (·051 level).

This finding was checked by comparing the same T.A.T. category score for the asthmatic subjects divided by age, and for the control subjects divided by age.

The results obtained suggested that the older asthmatic subjects tended to view their environment as threatening to their needs (significant at the ·03 level), and so also did the older control subjects (significant at the ·01 level).

From these statistical analyses one must conclude that no definite relationship exists between length of illness and degree of unsettledness.

Nervous symptoms and seeing the environment as threatening do increase with the length of the illness. But both increase in control subjects as they grow older. Whilst the frustrations of the illness may be a contributory factor, the results suggest that the frustrations inherent in growing up in our culture seem to play an equally significant part in the moulding of these personality needs and fears.

CHAPTER XXII

The Asthmatic Child's Mother
and her Attitude towards him

The clinical literature suggested that mothers of asthmatic children would be more rejecting towards their asthmatic children than mothers of control children. Several indices of primal rejection were therefore devised and questions relating to their incidence were integrated into the questionnaire given to all mothers, the assumption, formulated in Hypothesis 3, being that mothers of asthmatic children would display more rejection than control mothers. It was also assumed at the outset that mothers of asthmatic children would display more psychologically damaging attitudes to child upbringing when presented with the Parent Attitude Research Instrument.

Equally it was thought, on the basis of previous clinical studies, that mothers of asthmatic children would show evidence of unresolved dependency needs which would make it difficult for them to handle their children adequately. These needs would probably stem from an unsatisfactory relationship with their own mothers, and would show up in preoccupation with assertive and affection-seeking needs, and fear of domination and rejection in their Thematic Apperception Test protocols.

To test these assumptions the mothers of the twenty-five asthmatic and the twenty-five control children were approached and asked to assist in the investigation. None of the mothers refused.

As described in the first section of this book, the materials used for testing were the questionnaire, consisting of fifty-seven questions devised by the author relating to the child's early development, and the 115 statements contained in Bell and Schaefer's Parent Attitude Research Instrument, to which the mothers responded orally. Twelve pictures taken from Murray's

Thematic Apperception Test were also given and the mothers' oral responses were noted.

Testing

All testing was done individually and in the privacy of the mother's own home. As also explained in the first section of this book, the test materials were presented in a manner likely to focus the mother's attention initially on the individual child, and only later on the wider issues covered by the study.

I told asthmatic mothers that the investigation was part of a general hospital study into sick children, and that I was collecting general information about asthmatic children and how they behaved at home. I also said that I would be interested to know about the mother's views on child upbringing.

I approached the control mothers by saying:

'I am doing a study of children suffering from asthma, and I have been visiting their mothers and asking them to tell me a little about their children's behaviour at home. I want to be sure that the conclusions I come to apply only to children with asthma and not to all children, and therefore I have compared each asthmatic child with another child of the same age and sex, taken from the same school. Your child was chosen by the Head Teacher, as being the child most like the sick child I am interested in, and therefore, I wonder if you would mind if I talked to you for a little while about (name) and asked you the same questions I have been asking the sick child's mother.'

Questionnaire material

Because of the controversy that exists in the clinical literature as to the primary or secondary nature of maternal rejection in the aetiology of asthma, an attempt was made to evaluate deviant maternal attitudes and behaviour during pregnancy and in the early months of the infant's life before the onset of the illness.

Nine questions were taken as indices of rejecting behaviour on the mother's part. Responses to them were elicited from the mothers during the completion of the Questionnaire, and group responses were compared statistically using the Sign Test.

The results obtained suggested that significantly more asthmatic mothers thought of their pregnancy as difficult (·006 level), the major reason for their discomfort being excessive sickness 'all the time' (·004 level). More asthmatic mothers described their pregnancy as 'unplanned' (·011 level) and were emotionally upset during it. This upset was sometimes caused by their own 'nervousness', but more generally it was ascribed to adverse environmental factors such as bad housing, and death in the family.

After the baby's birth more of the asthmatic mothers stuck to rigid feeding schedules (·011 level) and experienced problems in feeding the baby (·035 level). A third of the mothers reported that their infants had been slow, poor feeders, or had refused milk or other foods. Other infant problems were also noted (the difference in the total amount of problem behaviour between groups being significant at the ·046 level) especially poor sleep, and considerable crying.

A statistical comparison of the total rejection scores obtained was made for the two groups using the Wilcoxon Matched Pairs Signed Ranks Test. The results obtained suggested that the asthmatic mothers were more rejecting than the control mothers (significant at the ·001 level, using a one-tailed test).

This result seems to bear out the assumption made at the outset of the investigation that asthmatic mothers tend to reject their infants before the onset of the illness. Only two mothers out of the twenty-five studied had children who had developed asthma before the end of the first year. In one case the baby developed it at three to four months, in the other the baby produced asthmatic symptoms at nine months. Both these mothers had already shown signs of rejecting their pregnancy, and the rejection existed before the illness, and was certainly not a reaction to it.

The following are case histories which show this early maternal rejection and subsequent difficulty with the infant.

The first case history is that of Mrs R. and eleven-year-old John, whose behaviour in school has already been described in the previous chapter. John was the first child in a family of six. During pregnancy it was found that Mrs R. was acutely anaemic and she was given treatment to relieve this condition.

John was not a planned conception, but Mrs R. said that she 'didn't mind too much' when she realised that she had conceived. Labour was normal and full term, lasting only ten hours. John weighed four pounds four ounces at birth, and remained in the premature nursery for three weeks of life. Within a month of returning home he returned to an isolation hospital with gastroenteritis. Asthma was suspected at three to four months of age, by which time John was reported as having 'abscesses' around his eyes from lack of sleep. Mrs R. said that, because of John's crying, people kept evicting them. They moved from one room to another. Mr R. had a labouring job at the time, there was little money on which to live, and with the persistent removals, John's early life was 'nerve-wracking'.

By nine months John still weighed only four pounds, and had been taken into hospital on several occasions. He was bottle fed on demand, and weaning was not attempted until he was eighteen months. He was a 'bad sleeper—always waking up. He cried and cried all the time' and Mrs R. found him very difficult to manage. Motor milestones were normal, except for walking which was slightly delayed. John did not respond to pot training until he was three years old, but Mrs R. said that she did not commence training until he was two-and-a-half years old, realising that he was 'slow of himself'.

The next child was born when John was two years and three months, and Mrs R. went to hospital for the confinement, finding John a 'wee bit upset' when she returned home. He wouldn't 'take' to her after this and it took several months for his dislike to wear off. Subsequently he was thought to be a bit uncertain in his relationships with his brothers and sisters even at the time of testing. He was not overtly jealous of them, however, possibly because his mother treated him as 'very much his mother's pet'.

John had been subject to nightmares throughout childhood, and as a small child he would jump up screaming and shouting in his sleep. On the two nights before my enquiry he had jumped out of bed, shrieking that 'he was choking and smothering'. Nightmares were thought to be worst, and so also were daytime fears, whenever there was fighting in the family, and whenever John returned from a hospital visit, which was quite

225

frequently as Mrs R. had no means of nursing him in her one overcrowded room.

At the time of testing Mrs R. described John as 'very, very moody—a funny sort of-type of child.' She was flattered by his very real need for her, and said that she was 'very, very sorry for him at times'. She always tried to give him anything he wanted, he was 'not a greedy child. He just wants wee odd things'.

Mrs R. never beat him when he was naughty, but talked to him. Despite this, any type of checking brought on crying and asthma. He always 'worked' himself up when chastised.

At the time of testing, John's asthma appeared to be precipitated by any form of family quarrel or argument, particularly arguments in which he was involved, or fights between his mother and father during which he always took his mother's part.

Paul C. was nine at the time of the testing and was the first in a family of four. His father was a lorry driver and the family lived in a small neat terrace house on a new housing estate. Paul had eczema from four months of age, and was in hospital for this condition twelve times before the age of five. On one occasion at two years of age he spent nine months in hospital, only to return home for two days and was then rushed back into hospital, developing asthma there. There was no family history of allergy or asthma.

Mrs C. became pregnant within the first month of her married life. 'I was caught right away'—but said she was delighted. Throughout the pregnancy she was very badly sick, and suffered from high blood pressure towards the end. During this time she was very unsettled. She and her husband moved seven times while she was pregnant. 'We knocked about in rooms. Some had rats and we had to move.' The labour took twenty-seven hours and Paul was forceps delivered. He weighed ten pounds and Mrs C. breast-fed him for three to four months. He was then weaned on to a bottle, feeding times being regular. Motor milestones were normal and he walked alone at eleven months. From earliest days his sleep was poor, and after four months when he developed eczema, he would lie in his cot scratching and crying. His toilet training began at nine months and was completed before two years of age by the nursing staff at the hospital.

When Paul was almost two years of age and away in hospital for eczema, a younger brother was born. Mrs C. told him about the expected arrival beforehand and when Paul returned home she said 'He was delighted. He would let no one near him. He stood in front of him with his two arms out'. Perhaps she misconstrued his emotions somewhat, because subsequently he frequently complained 'You love him too much'. It was at this juncture that Paul developed his asthma.

At the time of the study Paul was described as 'cranky sometimes. He cries for nothing'. When in a bad mood, or when punished, he would start to scratch himself or cough. He never had nightmares, but was afraid of rain or grubby children. He said they were 'full of germs'. His mother worried a lot about his illness and hoped he would outgrow it.

Finally, the case history of five-year-old Julie S. the first of two girls, who developed asthma at the age of three. There was a family history of asthma and bronchitis, and Mr S. had contracted T.B. during the war. Before the asthma developed Julie 'was not even subject to colds', and Mr and Mrs S. had left her quite happily in the care of her grandmother for three days, whilst they went off for a short holiday. When they returned Mrs S. noted her harsh breathing and gave her an antibiotic which she vomited. She then had a bad asthmatic attack.

Julie was conceived before her parents were married. Mr S., then a Merchant Navy engineer, had returned for a four-month trip when Julie's mother discovered that she was pregnant. She was desperate, but there was nothing she could do except wait for his return. At that time she was in her early thirties, and living at home. Her parents were appalled, and also her grandmother who had brought her up. A nervous woman anyway (she had had chorea for eight years as a girl), Mrs S. was distraught. She was sick throughout the nine months and had severe heartburn. Julie weighed six pounds six ounces when she was born, but the labour was long—forty hours, and she was forceps delivered. Mrs S. was very nervous at the thought of caring for Julie herself as she had had no experience with young babies. She breast fed by demand for a month, and then transferred to a bottle because in this way she was 'better able to gauge' how much milk Julie was getting. Weaning began at four-and-a-half months, but Julie was allowed a bedtime bottle until she was two-and-a-half years old. There were no feeding problems during infancy, but at the time of the study her appetite was so poor that her mother said 'I must get food into her. Even if I sit for an hour with her on my knee. I must keep her strength up or she is going to be ill'. Motor milestones were normal and Julie walked by ten to eleven months. Toilet training began at birth and was said to be complete at eighteen months. No punishment was given. Mrs S. never let Julie cry, and always picked her up whenever she was restless. She thinks she may have done too much for her.

From earliest days Julie was 'temperamental' and Mrs S. said she always gave in to her. She was a 'nervous, highly strung child' who was never very affectionate towards her parents. At the time of the study her mother remarked 'Sometimes she does seem hostile'. But Mrs S. was not able to associate this hostility with anything specific.

Julie was twenty months when her sister was born in hospital. When Mrs S. returned home she thought 'Julie would run to me and cuddle me. I wanted her to do that. But she drew back and wouldn't. Gradually she came round and took more interest in us'. At the time of testing Julie was said to be the best of friends with her sister and to be very fond of her father. Mr S. had in fact abandoned his seagoing career because Julie, then aged three, had suffered a couple of asthmatic attacks whilst he was away. Both he and Mrs S. said they were 'crazy' about Julie, and would do anything to help her. Despite this, Mr S. had a drinking problem which increased in severity after he came ashore. Frequently he would promise Julie not to drink or not to stay out late—'with disastrous results!' The promise would be broken, and 'Julie thought he was lost and cried and cried'.

At the time of testing, Julie was subject to frequent nightmares and needed the light on in her room all night. She frequently dreamt that an old woman would come to take her away, and became so frightened that nothing would console her.

Mrs S. said that she no longer smacked Julie, although she used to before the development of her asthma. She noticed that before and during an attack Julie 'became more demanding about everything—even the silliest, tiniest things'. To comfort her, Mrs S. would stay with her all the time, even to the extent of sleeping with her. She blamed herself for the development of the asthma, because it began so dramatically on her return from her three-day holiday away from Julie. Consequently since then she and Mr S. had never left Julie.

Attitudes to child rearing, as tested by the Parent Attitude Research Instrument

The prediction was made at the outset that mothers of asthmatic children would score more highly than the mothers of controls. on the pathogenic scales of the Parent Attitude Research Instrument, a questionnaire designed to measure psychologically damaging attitudes to child rearing and family life.

This test contains 115 items which yield scores on twenty-three sub-scales, three of which may be considered satisfactory child rearing attitudes and twenty of which are thought by the authors to be damaging to the healthy development of the child. All mothers were asked by the author to select the most suitable response for each item from four categories: 'definitely agree', 'mildly agree', 'mildly disagree' or 'definitely disagree'.

Scoring was made in accordance with the centroid values produced by Schaefer and Bell, and the differences between groups for each scale were analysed statistically using the Wilcoxon Matched Pairs Signed Ranks Test.

The results were in accordance with the initial assumption. Mothers of asthmatic children scored significantly more highly on fourteen of the twenty pathogenic scales in the P.A.R.I.

Eight scales yielded extremely significant differences between groups. They were:

Fostering Dependency	(·001 level)
Ascendancy of Mother	(·001 ,,)
Acceleration of Development	(·001 ,,)
Avoidance of Communication	(·001 ,,)
Seclusion of Mother	(·005 ,,)
Martyrdom of Mother	(·005 ,,)
Suppression of Sex	(·005 ,,)
Breaking the Will	(·01 ,,)

Also significant were the differences between groups for the scales relating to fear of harming the baby (·025 level), marital conflict (·025 level), strictness (·05 level), deification (·05 level), suppression of aggression (·05 level), and dependency of mother (·05 level).

As a group therefore asthmatic mothers saw their parental role as a dominant one. They did not feel it necessary to explain their decisions to their children, they believed themselves entitled to complete obedience, and they felt it was their duty to suppress all instinctive actions in their children, in particular their sexual and aggressive tendencies. They wished to maintain their children in a state of complete dependency upon themselves and yet at the same time they wished them to develop as quickly as possible. They were fearful in their role as mothers, still dependent on their own mothers for guidance, and they expressed some dissatisfaction with their marital state.

These conclusions, based on the P.A.R.I. results, were borne out by much of the anecdotal material produced by asthmatic mothers in response to the questionnaire. For example:

Ascendancy of mother. Question 48 of the questionnaire related to punishment of the child when he was naughty. The mothers were asked who normally punished the child. Mothers of asthmatic children more often said that they normally punished the child (·001 level, using the Sign Test). Control children, by contrast, were punished by 'either parent' significantly more often (·006 level, using the Sign Test).

Similarly, asthmatic mothers as compared with control mothers, when questioned as to which parent had the 'greatest say' in their child's life, more often said themselves (difference significant at the ·059 level, using the Sign Test).

Martyrdom of mother. Responses to Question 53 of the questionnaire bore out the contention that frequently the mother regarded herself as a martyr to the child's illness, and in some cases openly resented the illness.

The remark passed by one mother was particularly indicative of this: 'I feel rotten about it really, if only there was something I could do, that is the only thing that comforts me, that

I have done everything for him possible'. Later she added: 'I sometimes feel I do too much for him; he would just stand there and let you do anything for him'.

Another mother commented: 'You just keep on doing things for him, and he won't do anything for himself.'

Another mother commented on her child's early days: 'Sometimes I think I did too much; I picked her up whenever she cried.'

One mother commented: 'To tell you the truth, the doctors said I'm at breaking point—it's got me down terrible—I'm cross and I'm worried. I can't get it out of my head. There is a dread on me about her.'

Suppression of sex. Whilst no questions relating to this topic were contained in the questionnaire, mothers frequently confided their distaste concerning sexual information. One mother said that her greatest fear was to teach her child the 'dirt' of sex. There seemed to be some agreement that facts relating to the infant's days in the womb could be related, but no information could be given regarding conception. Many mothers agreed with the P.A.R.I. statement that 'sex is the greatest problem to be dealt with in children'.

Breaking the will. Frequent criticisms of self-willedness were levelled at asthmatic children. One mother said: 'He's very wilful. He likes his own way and he won't love me if he doesn't get it—he's just awkward.'

Another mother added: 'She's beginning to have a mind of her own. She knows what she wants and is determined to get it.'

The illness seemed to give some children a substantial weapon for getting their own way. For example one mother confided: 'He's very stubborn. He likes to have his own way. If you chastise him he starts coughing.'

Another mother whose child had eczema in addition to asthma said: 'If you don't do what he wants, he starts to scratch.'

During illness one mother noted: 'She becomes more demanding in everything—even the silliest thing.'

When this child's temperature was up one point this mother

decided to keep the child at home (the child is enrolled in a special open air school for sick children) but the girl had hysterics and the mother had to allow her to go. This mother also commented: 'I must get food into her—even if I have to sit for an hour with her on my knee—I must keep her strength up or she is going to be ill.'

Perhaps the best summary of the situation is a comment made by one mother about the speed with which her child could recover from an attack. She found that: 'A new toy brings him round rightly. He likes you to bring in things and tell him you'll buy him something.'

Seclusion of mother. A number of mothers reported proudly that they had no life outside their own homes. One mother said that twice she had gone out at night only to return to find the child in a state of collapse. She vowed that she would never leave him again.

Another mother reported: 'I think if I leave her something seems to happen.'

Fostering dependency. Sometimes the mothers explained this tendency in terms of illness: 'I cling to him more than the rest of them—more for the pity of him.' Later she added: 'He has to have me at home whenever he's been out at school—if he comes home to closed doors, he would die.'

At other times the need to keep their children infantile was explained simply in terms of the pleasure it afforded the mother: 'He's still very much mother's pet.'

Another mother of a teenage boy who had just left her husband added, with quite obvious satisfaction: 'He's more like a wee baby now. He wants to stay with me all the time—even in bed, says his stomach is sore, and gets in beside me and goes to sleep.'

One mother attributed her child's subsequent illness to 'pampering'; 'I imagined I pampered her too much as a small child, and now I add two and two together and realise that is why she has asthma.'

The illness may well afford the asthmatic mother further opportunities for maintaining dependency in her children. At least half the mothers said that they alone could assist the

child when he was suffering an attack. One mother commented:
'*We* get over it by sitting down—making him sit very quietly
with no one in the house—and then *he* and *I* can get over it
in half a day now.'

Acceleration of development. Several parents complained that the
illness might prevent the child from adequately realising his
intellectual potential. One mother said that her husband forced
the child in the hope that he would pass his eleven-plus. The
child worried a lot about his school work, and tried to do more
than he was able, but still the father urged him further. 'But
Dad would never make a school teacher, he loses his temper
too easily.'

Clearly, both from the results of P.A.R.I. testing, and from
the spontaneously produced remarks of mothers during the
interview, it must be apparent that asthmatic mothers were
often far from accepting in their attitude towards the upbringing of their children.

Underlying needs and conflicts of asthmatic and control mothers

The clinical literature stressed the unresolved dependency
needs of asthmatic mothers. The assumption was made therefore that these mothers would display significantly more
assertiveness and affection seeking than controls in their T.A.T.
protocols. It was also assumed that they would view the world
as more threatening than the controls, and would be particularly fearful of the domination and rejection of others.

Accordingly all the asthmatic and control mothers were
given twelve pictures taken from Murray's standard T.A.T.
set. I recorded all responses in the usual way and analysed
them by a slightly modified version of Cox and Sargent's
scoring methods. Between group differences for each scoring
category were analysed statistically using the Wilcoxon
Matched Pairs Signed Ranks Test.

The results suggested that asthmatic mothers showed a
significantly greater need for assertion than the mothers of the
controls (·001 level), who by comparison, show a greater need
for success and achievement (·001 level).

In contrast to the original assumption, the mother of the

asthmatic children did not appear to differ from the mothers of the control children on the need for affiliation.

As predicted, however, they viewed the external environment as particularly threatening (·01 level), and were especially fearful of hardship (·05 level), domination by others (·025 level), and rejection (·05 level). In overcoming these threats to their need for assertion they took significantly more evasive action than the controls (·025 level), who by contrast took more positive action (·05 level). Mothers of asthmatic children expected to meet with failure (·025 level) or only modified success (·05 level) more often than the mothers of control children.

The anxiety engendered by this strong need for self-assertion, and the real fear of rejection or domination are apparent in the following T.A.T. stories related by the mothers of asthmatic children.

The first nine stories come from the protocol of Mrs R.—the mother of eleven-year-old John whose behaviour, both at home and in school, has already been described. Mrs R. lived in one large barracks-like room with her husband and six children. Mr R. was unemployed and the family had sustained so many house removals that Mrs R. had lost count. At the time of testing she was living in a temporary hostel for the homeless.

(2gf) 'This girl here looks like as if this girl isn't wanted, and these two don't want her. But she may want to be on her own most of the times. She won't do much about it, just keep to herself. I would think maybe the girl thinks that the parents don't want her—according to her impression. The woman seems to want to be on her own all the time.'

(3gf) 'She seems to be scolded or pushed out—not wanted at all. I would find that if this girl was really more attended to, and taken by the parents, the child wouldn't feel so much unwanted. It all depends on really if the parents want the child. The child needs to understand it is wanted by the parents—just looks like our John at times.'

(4) 'A man. He looks as if he wants to be left alone on his own, but the girl wants to push him into doing something, but he doesn't want to be bothered. He wants to be left alone, and the girl is a bit selfish looking. She wants him to herself.'

234

(7gf) 'This one here. The child doesn't seem to be interested in the mother at all. The child just seems to be as if she did not know whether she was wanted or not, and I think the child's mind is just far gone. She's not interested in the mother.'

(8gf) 'This one here seems to be a very lonely person. It doesn't look like as if the person had anyone at all belonging to it. All alone all the time, just wants to be left alone mainly.'

(9gf) 'This one here, if this was a child, the child doesn't seem to like the mother too well, and she must think she's not wanted —otherwise if there wasn't anything wrong the child would not be running away from her.'

(14) 'This child here doesn't seem to want its mother or father, otherwise it would not be running away from them. Seems to be going outways. Mustn't really have much love for the child or it wouldn't have gone out of the window. Some quarrel between the child or the mother, or between the parents.'

(16) 'Well, if the child has had a lot of illness from the time he was a small baby, and if the mother was more lovable towards the child than the father, the child would come on better. If there was no quarrelling, and no selfishness between its mother and father during the illness, otherwise the child would ask more from the father during its sickness.'

(18) 'The mother of this child seems to be very pitiful and lovable by the child when it is crying, and the mother seems to be trying to help the child in the best way she possibly can. She looks to be very cross at what the child has done.'

The remaining five stories were recounted by different mothers, and give some indication of the many sources of marital tension which were mentioned in the themes.

(4) 'Puts me in mind of a man who doesn't want to do anything more with his wife. They've had a quarrel and she's trying to make it up—but he's not having anything. I think they might have quarrelled about that girl in the background. There may be nothing in it at all. The wife is making a mountain out of a mole-hill. There's nothing in it at all. I think eventually she'll see her mistake. I think it's her fault. She's jumped to the wrong con-clusion—but she may be the jealous type who could see no good in anyone where her husband was concerned.'

(2gf) 'The girl's worried looking anyhow—whatever she's up to. Does she seem to have quarrelled with her mother here, and be going off? I don't know what they could have quarrelled about. Perhaps she doesn't want to stay in the country. She wants to go off to the city to live and her mother wants her to stay and work on the farm. That could be her boyfriend there. No she probably wants to go to the city and have a career for herself.'

(2) 'That's a girl coming from school, and she's watching the man ploughing and the servant. It wouldn't be her mother standing there. It's in Africa, and she looks very thoughtful. She seems very angry or bitter. It doesn't seem to be about these people. It may be the mother has said something to her. She doesn't seem to be taking any interest or bother in her.'

(3) 'She seems to have been in trouble—she's going to have a wee cry just, soothing her nerves I would say. She might have had a row in their home over the children or with her husband. She just didn't get doing what she wanted to do. She seems to want to go outside and run away from it all.'

(4) 'He seems to be angry with her and she's trying to comfort him, and make him see her way. He seems to want it all his own way. They might have had a row over the children or other family problems. I think like that she talks to him the right way and he comes round to listening to her.'

CHAPTER XXIII

Unsettling Environmental Experiences
and the onset of Asthma

The fourth hypothesis assumed that asthmatic children would have sustained significantly more unsettling environmental experiences than the control children. Three experiences were thought to be most unsettling, in that they might threaten the child with permanent separation from the mother:

(1) Actual separation of mother and child, due to illness and removal to hospital, or to hardship, domestic crises, or holidays. Experiences in which the child was removed from its home to a strange environment—whether hospital or nursery—were thought to be of greatest significance.

(2) Moves from one house to another.

(3) Deaths in the family of loved relations, which might remind the child of the impermanence of his parents.

To test the significance of environmental experiences for the asthmatic children, three questions relating to each of the specific areas of separation were appended to the questionnaire and information relating to them was obtained from nineteen mothers in each group. Differences between groups were statistically analysed using both the Sign Test, and the Wilcoxon Matched Pairs Signed Ranks Test.

Early separation. The information relating to this topic was analysed in three ways: first, the number of mothers reporting separation at certain ages was compared using the Sign Test; secondly, the number of weeks of separation was compared for each age group using the Wilcoxon Matched Pairs Signed Ranks Test; finally, an analysis was made of the type of separation, that is, whether it was the mother, or the child, who was absent from the home. These results were compared statistically using the Sign Test.

On the basis of these comparisons it was obvious that significantly more asthmatic children were separated from their mothers during the three to five year stage ($\cdot$02 level). Asthmatic children were also apart from their mothers for a longer time both in the three to five year stage ($\cdot$005 level) and at the five to seven year stage ($\cdot$025 level). During these two periods it was the child who tended to be away from home, rather than the mother (difference for the three to five year stage being significant at the $\cdot$008 level, and the difference for the five to seven year stage being significant at the $\cdot$011 level).

Moves. Question 57 of the questionnaire sought information concerning the number and type of moves made by the family since the asthmatic and control child's conception.

The information given in answers to this question was analysed in two ways:

(1) The number of mothers reporting moves following the birth of the child was compared between these two groups, using the Sign Test.

(2) The difference in the total number of moves reported between the groups was analysed using the Wilcoxon Matched Pairs Signed Ranks Test.

The results obtained suggested that, compared with control mothers, more mothers of asthmatic children had moved house. The total number of these moves was three times as great as the number in the control groups. Whilst these differences between groups were not statistically significant they were in the predicted direction.

Emotionally disturbing deaths in the family. Question 55 of the questionnaire was: 'Have there been any deaths in your family or your husband's either in the nine months before (name) was born, or in the following years which might have affected you emotionally?' The information was analysed in two ways:

(1) The number of mothers in each group reporting emotionally disturbing deaths following the birth of the child, was compared using the sign Test.

(2) The difference in the total number of emotionally disturbing deaths reported per group was analysed using the Wilcoxon Matched Pairs Signed Ranks Test.

The results obtained confirmed that significantly more asthmatic children had sustained emotionally disturbing deaths in the family than control children (difference significant at the ·055 level).

On the basis of these enquiries it would seem that the fourth hypothesis is substantiated. Asthmatic children had more unsettling environmental experiences than control children, in particular they had been kept in hospital more often between the age of three and seven.

Obviously the measures used to assess unsettling environmental experiences were crude and probably extremely inadequate. Many less obvious incidents, which had passed without comment in the interviews, may have had an equal, if not greater, traumatic effect upon the child, for example, early and painful dental treatment possibly involving extractions, sudden accidental physical shocks, and either permanent or transitory separations from the father. A lengthier and more clinical interview might have revealed such incidents, but in a study of this kind such facts if present would have been hard to compare and measure statistically.

Perhaps the crucial issue raised by enquiries relating to unsettling environmental experiences, is the question of the part they play in precipitating or maintaining the illness. No questions directly concerning this topic were asked, but in the course of the interviews it became obvious that a large number of children had sustained one or more emotional shocks before the first asthmatic attack. Very frequently the mothers of these children were quite unaware of the possible relationship of these shocks to the onset of the illness.

Immediately before the onset of the first attack:

Ten children had been to hospital, the most frequently reported cause of such a visit being the removal of tonsils or adenoids.

Four children had been separated from their parents, either because of their own or the parents' holidays.

Four children had been faced with the arrival of a new baby in the family, whom they resented.

Three children had moved to a new house.

Four children had suffered a death in the family, either a grandparent living in the house or a brother or sister.

Three children had sustained a 'shock' which was recognised as such by the parent. In one case the child, who was unable to swim, was pushed into a pond by older children. In another case, the boy witnessed his alcoholic father beating up his mother, and in the final case the child's beloved sister was sent to a sanatorium.

In nine cases the mother described the onset of the asthma as 'sudden', with absolutely no previous symptoms.

By contrast, five other children had suffered from infantile eczema before the first attack, and eight other children had been suffering from a respiratory disease before the onset of the asthma. (In seven families there was a history of asthma, just as in seven of the control families.)

From this anecdotal material it would seem that in a substantial number of cases some sudden emotional shock appears to have preceded the first asthmatic attack. Whilst some children appear to have been physically vulnerable before the first attack, by no means all the children exhibited signs of a physiological predisposition to the disease. Considerable emotional upset, accompanied as it frequently was by somewhat harsh and unloving handling, appears to have acted as a catalyst unleashing the disorder.

It is interesting to note that subsequently the majority of asthmatic mothers reported emotional rather than purely physical stimuli to attacks. Six mothers thought that any general excitement could produce attacks, whilst twelve mothers cited specific situations of conflict, such as battles of will between mother and child, particularly those in which the child lost the tussle. Going to school, with an accompanying fear of lack of accomplishment, was also known to produce attacks.

CHAPTER XXIV

Child Problem Behaviour
as perceived by the Mother

The assumption was made in Hypothesis 5 that child problem behaviour as perceived by the mother, would tend to increase with the mother's own rejection and with the number of unsettling environmental experiences the child sustained.

This hypothesis therefore tests the suggestion that the more negative the mother's own attitude and the more frustrating the surrounding environment, the more unsettled the child will become, probably as a reaction to this unlovedness and upset.

In order to investigate this problem the existing data was analysed in two ways:

(1) The group of mothers was divided into two on the basis of the score they had obtained on eight of the questions relating to maternal rejection. Comparable child problem behaviour scores were compared using the Mann Whitney Test.

(2) A composite maternal rejection and unsettling environmental experience score was derived on the basis of the mother's rejection score, an above average separation from the mother.

The average for the asthmatic children was eleven weeks in the birth to seven year age range, an above average number of removals (on the basis of the total group score, two or more moves) and finally an above average number of family deaths (on the basis of the total group score two or more deaths).

Combinations of these scores were clearly very arbitrary, and could yield only a very crude measure of the total amount of emotional shock sustained.

(1) *Maternal rejection in relation to the child problem behaviour.* The

initial assumption was that mothers rating low on the rejection scale would be more likely to have children with low problem behaviour ratings. A comparison was therefore made of the problem behaviour scores of children whose mothers had lower ratings (N = 16), and children whose mothers had higher ratings (N = 9). A Mann Whitney One-Tailed Test was used, and a significant difference was found to exist between the two groups (·05 level). Children with most rejecting mothers were described by their mothers as showing most evidence of unsettledness at home.

(2) *Maternal rejection, unsettling environmental experiences and child problem behaviour.* The children were divided according to their composite rating for maternal rejection and unsettling environmental experiences. Two groups were formed, those with the least rejection and environmental stress (N = 7) and those with the most unsettling maternal and domestic experiences (N = 11). The child problem behaviour scores were compared for the two groups using a Mann Whitney One-Tailed Test.

As predicted, children with most rejection and most environmental stress were described by their mothers as exhibiting most problem behaviour when at home (difference between groups was significant at the ·005 level).

As a further check the unsettledness-maladjustment scores on the Bristol Social Adjustment Guide for the same groups of children were compared statistically, using a Mann Whitney One-Tailed Test. The assumption was made that the greater the score for maternal rejection and unsettling experience the greater was the child's unsettledness at school. This assumption was not borne out however by a statistical analysis of the results. As seen in school, there was little difference in problem behaviour between the two groups.

One possible explanation for these results is that the child's problem behaviour is a direct reaction against stress and rejection at home, and when this ceases, that is when the child is away from home as in school, he ceases to be a markedly problem child. It could also be that the mother's own negative attitude to the child influences her perception of him. She sees him as different because her own hostility has to be justified in some way. Whatever the reason, this lack of warmth on the mother's part and this tendency to see the child as difficult, cannot but make the relationship a strained one, and can do nothing to ameliorate any behavioural difficulties which the child may have.

CHAPTER XXV

Discussion of Present Findings

From our data we may conclude that asthmatic children are more unsettled than a carefully matched group of control children. This unsettledness is seen even in infancy by poor feeding, excessive crying and disturbed sleep. It persists throughout early childhood and is manifested in excessive temper tantrums, restlessness and crying. The asthmatic child as an infant is more inclined to be jealous of his brothers and sisters, and as an older child to actively dislike them. He is frequently described by his mother as a child who wants to be on his own, and as he grows older he becomes more moody, depressed, stubborn and insubordinate. At school he is seen to be more unforthcoming, and more nervous and backward than his class mates.

To some extent these signs of unsettledness may be common to all sick children, rather than to asthmatic children only. Chronically ill children in the control group exhibited similar characteristics to a lesser extent. No relationship existed, however, between the length of illness and the degree of unsettledness which the child exhibited. Asthmatic children are disturbed before the onset of their illness, and whilst the frustrations inherent in the experience of being ill undoubtedly accentuated the emotional conflict, they did not account for its causation.

As the clinicians predicted, the mothers of asthmatic children as compared with the mothers of control children are more rejecting in their approach to the child. Significantly more of them saw their pregnancies as unplanned, and were physically ill and emotionally upset during them. After the birth, they tended to be more rigid in the handling of the child than did the controls and to see their children as more of a problem particularly with regard to feeding.

Discussion of Present Findings

A relationship was seen to exist between a deviant maternal attitude, i.e. unwillingness to accept and love the baby, and the subsequent unsettledness of the child. Mothers who were most non-accepting had children who appeared to be most problematic.

It was found that this relationship did not extend to the child's observed unsettledness at school, a fact capable of interpretation in several different ways. Either the child is capable of expressing his unsettledness in different ways, i.e. having behaviour problems at home but not in school, or he is only seen as problematic by his mother, perhaps as a means of justifying her own rejection.

Clearly neither of these two explanations is sufficiently conclusive to explain the observed facts. As a group asthmatic children do tend to be more unsettled in school and particularly unforthcoming and backward, suggesting a defensiveness against anything or anybody strange, due to a lack of confidence. But the more apparent existence of emotional conflict at home—and as perceived by their mothers—suggests that for asthmatic children this is the real battleground. From the commencement of pregnancy these mothers viewed their babies as intruders, and in the course of the infants' ante-natal development they continued to cause their mothers sickness and inconvenience.

At this juncture, one might postulate some sort of chemical transmission to the foetus particularly during the later stages of pregnancy such that the mother's stress was transferred to the infant and its behavioural responses became more hyperactive and ill-controlled.

This postulated 'neural vulnerability'* might then account for the infant's gastro-intestinal difficulties, and for the excessive crying and restlessness reported by the mother. When faced with this type of infant the mother would find adequate justification for her initial rejection and, rather than modify her attitude to the child, she would treat it in the harsh and uncompromising fashion most likely to perpetuate rather than

* It is interesting in this context to note that as early as 1948 Dees and Lowenbach found that a quarter of the asthmatic children whose E.E.G.s they took showed a convulsive pattern for which no immediate cause could be demonstrated.

eradicate the infant problems. Alternatively, the previous maternal rejection and unyielding handling might in themselves be sufficient to produce the colic and restlessness reported in these infants.

From first days then the asthmatic child and his mother were at variance. The significantly high scores made by these mothers on the pathogenic scales of the P.A.R.I. (presumably a reflection of their unbending need to appear all important—either a reaction to the baby's supposed deviance or an extension of their own earlier rejection) could have done nothing to ease the tension. Mother and child were caught up in a spiral of maternal rejection—infant protest behaviour—further (supposedly justified) rejection and increased protest behaviour—which at the time of the study showed no indication of lessening.

This variance of mother and child would account for the child's problematic behaviour perceived at home, his own perception of his parents as punitive and threatening (as seen in his T.A.T. themes) and his desire to escape from his parents. The questions contained in the questionnaire relating to favoured play situations showed that asthmatic children, in contrast to controls, from early days displayed a significant preference for playing out of doors, away from their mothers. When away the child does not need to express his protest in any dramatic systematised way. The conflict with his mother may well underlie his reticence, backwardness, nervousness and slight depression observed at school, but away from her side it does not call for extravaganzas of unsettled acting-out. The frequently noted fact of 'no asthmatic attack in hospital' held true for all the children in this study who were seen in hospital, and was frequently commented upon by the mothers whose children went away to stay with grandparents or relations for their holidays. No asthma was found *away*, attacks commenced when the child returned. The attack seems to represent the behavioural protest employed by the child as a defence against, or as a means of modifying the mother's unswerving, dominant rejection.

It is this element of modifying the mother's behaviour that makes the child's use of asthma a meaningful form of protest. Without this element the employment of such an incapacitating

behaviour would be non-adaptive. As it is, the mother's dominance is immediately brought to a stop: all demands and criticisms of the child come to an end, the rival brothers and sisters
are at abeyance and the child and his illness become the pivot
of his mother's attention.

The questionnaire material abounds with ample evidence
for this contention. Most mothers either left the rest of the
household to its own devices whilst the child had asthma or
went out of their way to buy presents, for as one mother observed: 'a new toy brings him round rightly!'

Asthma modifies the mother's attitude to punishment and
the type of punishment, and the threat of an attack subsequently increases her tolerance of the child's misdemeanours.

The fact that the protest is a psychosomatic rather than an
anti-social one, suggests that the child may be too fearful in the
face of his mother's extreme dominance to invoke her wrath by
his own assertive behaviour, or he may feel too guilty to be
able to do so. Both these suggestions appear to be substantiated
by the significantly higher scores for 'threat of dominance' and
'threat of own guilt' found in the T.A.T. protocols of asthmatic
children.

A feeling of personal guilt may well arise in the child from
the conflict between his own need to protest against his non-
accepting mother, and his awareness of her unrelenting concern for his welfare. As a group asthmatic mothers take an
almost obsessional interest in the trivia of their child's existence.
This may be a reaction to the child's illness, or as the analysts
would suppose an unconscious compensation for the mother's
basic inability to love, or it may be a reflection of the mother's
inordinate need to assert herself. Compared with control
mothers, the mothers of asthmatic children show a significantly
greater need for assertion in their T.A.T. protocols and a corresponding fear of domination. The high 'fostering dependency'
and 'acceleration of development' scores shown in the P.A.R.I.,
reflect the mother's unremitting need to control her child's
existence, and not as has been supposed the mother's need to
satisfy a love-hunger of her own. Indeed, no significant difference exists between the asthmatic and the control mother's
need for affection as seen in the T.A.T.

Whatever the causation, the mothers of asthmatic children

hold greater sway over their child's existence than do the mothers of controls. Significantly more of them punish their children when naughty, decide what they are allowed to do, and see themselves as the preferred parent. The illness undoubtedly affords them a further opportunity to exert their influence, and the majority of mothers had a set plan for speeding recovery from attacks, in which they played a major part.

On the child's part, the illness represents the only permissible form of protest and control. Because the mother is so all-important in the asthmatic child's existence he could not protest effectively without excessive fear and guilt. This guilt is lessened by his illness ('for if you are ill, you cannot be naughty'), and the fear is allayed, for the protest will never be recognised as a protest ('for you cannot make yourself ill'). Any other form of anti-social acting-out would immediately be recognised for what it was and punished.

That asthma may represent a symbolic protest is substantiated by the fact that asthmatic children, as compared with control children, mirror their mother's needs for assertion. Unlike the controls who show a significantly higher need for affection, they display a significantly greater need for assertion, coupled with an increased awareness of their own guilt, physical, mental and motivational inadequacy. They see the environment as significantly more threatening, and are particularly frightened of environmental domination. In contrast to the asthmatic children described in the clinical literature, these children showed no significant fear of rejection.

It has been maintained (Stott 1958) that children faced with sustained rejection turn adaptively from affection seeking to assertive behaviour, and in this group of asthmatics it might be suggested that the child's rejection has been too long and continuous for him to be concerned any longer with fear of rejection and wresting affection from the environment. His primary concern is to escape to a situation where his basic needs can be met. His asthmatic symptoms may either mirror this need for assertion which he dare not express, or arise from the frustration of realising that he is physically and mentally inadequate to fulfil his needs for escape.

Frequently in the clinical literature mention is made of

breath-holding as a symptom of overwhelming emotion. As one of the basic physiological mechanisms underlying the asthmatic attack, it may well be a reflection of the child's emotional conflict. From the questionnaire material, it is apparent that the majority of children in this study sustained an overwhelmingly disturbing experience immediately before the first asthmatic attack. In a large majority of cases this was caused by the child's removal to hospital at an age before it could talk. Other causes were the arrival of a new baby, the family's removal to a new home, the death of a loved relation, or a physical trauma such as an unexpected dunking in a swimming pool.

Subsequent asthmatic attacks were attributed by the mothers to a variety of climatic conditions ranging from wet and cold, to dry and over-sunny. All manner of supposed allergies were mentioned, and half the mothers reported emotional causes, principal among which were attacks following conflicts with the mother.

In this context it is interesting to refer back to the evidence of significantly greater pregnancy stress among mothers of these children. If, as has been suggested lately, this produces neural abnormality (Sontag 1950)—for example, a dysfunction of the hypothalamus (Laufer 1957) such that large cortical areas are involved in responding to visceral stimulation otherwise served by relatively discreet areas—we have a readiness for subsequent neural abnormalities produced before birth. Dysfunction of the hypothalamus, particularly of the diencephalon producing as it does alteration in resistance at the synapses, results in the infants responding with greater than usual urgency to normal amounts of tension coming from the usual organic sources, such as hunger or a full bladder.

Many children would outgrow this deviant maturation (Caplan 1956, Laufer 1957) in the course of development but the asthmatic children in this study may well have been subjected to such an intensity of emotional shock, and subsequently to such sustained emotional tension, that the neural imbalance became accentuated and the asthmatic pattern became increasingly more difficult to control.

Had these children's mothers been more accepting at the outset and less rigid in their handling of their children, the initial neural impairment—seen in the colicky, restless infant behaviour—might have been outgrown.

The final and perhaps most fundamental of the questions for which an answer must be sought, is the question of why the asthmatic mother comes to treat her child in this rejecting, harsh and dominating way. Previous studies have stressed that the mothers of asthmatic children may have unresolved dependency problems in relation to their own mothers. In an effort to overcome these postulated conflicts between dependence and independence the child becomes a symbolic self-representation for these mothers. To some extent the present study bears this out; mothers of asthmatic children are more fearful of both rejection and domination. They score more highly on the dependency of mothers and fostering dependency scales of the P.A.R.I. than do the controls. Their need for assertion is inordinate, and they complain most frequently of the supposed wilful, stubborn behaviour of their children.

At the same time, asthmatic mothers score significantly more on the seclusion of mother, breaking the will, martyrdom, fear of harming the baby, marital conflict, strictness, suppression of aggression, avoidance of communication, suppression of sex, ascendency of mother and acceleration of development scales.

The general picture is that of the mutually engulfing parent described by Abramson (1954). He describes her—so often in his experience the mother of an allergic or asthmatic child—as the mother with preconceived notions of what her child should be like.

Offering an explanation for this phenomenon, Abramson writes:

> If the mother is immature and incapable of dealing with the physical and mental growth of her offspring in a mature way, she inevitably must fall back upon patterns which rise from her own immaturity. These patterns, so often obvious in narcissistic women who have never been prepared for the mature responsibilities of womanhood, represent an attempt to coerce the developing child into a pattern consistent with parental ideas of what the little girl should be.
>
> When possible, every act of the child is observed by and manipulated by the parent. This cannot be termed rejection, nor

can it be fully considered a compensation device for a strict, unconscious rejection, for these over-solicitous parents often openly show their rage and beat their children. ... It is the mechanism of engulfment by the parent which stifles independence, maturity and the physical and mental health of the child.

The assertive, manipulative behaviour of the asthmatic mother may be seen therefore as part of an immature emotional pattern. The mother has never achieved sufficient ego integration to cope realistically with the problems of sex, child bearing and upbringing. She defends herself from perceived threats by seclusion, deification and avoidance of all communication, she vigorously suppresses activities which may either challenge her uncertain supremacy or which evoke conflictful sexual memories. (In all these things, the asthmatic mother closely resembles the mother of the schizophrenic child studied with the P.A.R.I. by Wilson Quentin in 1961.) She is never sufficiently sure of herself to respond pragmatically to the demands of her child and she therefore uses rigid patterns to which her child must conform. Because she is narcissistically involved in the child's development, she attempts to accelerate his development and where she is unsuccessful the inherent frustrations accentuate her uncompromising attitudes. The illness further frustrates her intentions, and whilst all score more highly on the martyrdom scale than others, a number of asthmatic mothers verbalise their irritation at the child's illness.

A previous study (Margolis 1961) reported evidence to suggest that this emotional immaturity is due to an unresolved oedipus complex. The manner in which the data in the present study was analysed did not permit investigation of this point, but this clinical suggestion would certainly not be at variance with the results obtained. How then do the results obtained in this study differ, if at all, from previous clinical and empirical studies?

The first, and more obvious difference, between the results of this and many previous studies is in the stress that is placed on the assertive rather than the affection seeking needs of the asthmatic child. In contrast to some previous studies (e.g. Rogerson, Hardcastle and Duguid 1935) no evidence was found to suggest that these children were excessively concerned with the fear of losing their mother's love. In fact, they were significantly less affection seeking than the control children, and showed no statistical difference in their fear of rejection.

In contrast to the studies that saw the aetiological conflict of asthma as a conflict between the need for closeness to the mother and the need for separation (Deutsch 1955; Coolidge 1956; Monsour 1960) the conclusion of this study has been that asthmatic children show an exaggerated need for separation, and the conflict is between this need and the fear of reprisal at its fulfilment. The threat of personal inadequacy in fulfilling this need is also present.

This awareness of personal inadequacy—undoubtedly a reflection of their mother's inability to support and commend their strivings for assertion—is mirrored in the asthmatic children's general anxiety, fearfulness and lack of confidence in school. To this extent this study agrees with those of Rogerson, Hardcastle and Duguid (1935); McDermott and Cobb (1939); Gerard (1956); and Harris, Rapaport, Rynerson and Samter (1950).

No evidence could be found to support the contention that asthmatic children are excessively aggressive. Still less evidence existed for the contention (Bacon 1961) that hostile anal, urethral or sexual excretory impulses were the root cause of asthmatic attacks. Mothers of these children at no time complained of aggressive excretory behaviour, nor was a comparison of the age at which toilet training was begun and completed and the type of punishment used indicative of any excessive conflict of mother and child at this point. This is not to say that the attitude underlying the training was not more coercive on the mother's part. But to isolate one aspect of training and suggest that it was of greater importance in the causation of asthma than the general harshness of attitude seems ludicrous.

The present study would not deny that an element of hostility may exist in the asthmatic attack, both directed at the child himself (Miller and Baruch 1950) and as an attempt to punish his punitive parents (Bostock 1956). The non-accepting attitude observed in the mothers of the asthmatic children in this study would seem to justify both. These children would have ample cause to fear open hostility towards their parents, and complete justification in experiencing the emotion. Ego integration is dependent upon the gradual exerting of independence and where this natural need is thwarted, aggression against the threatening object seems the most adaptive form of behaviour. Parents in this study were seen as persecutory figures (Coolidge 1956; Alcock 1960).

The emphasis in this study has been upon the manipulative aspects of the asthmatic symptom. If the first attack was a fortuitous occurrence—dependent upon a neurological imbalance, as a result of strong, ill-co-ordinated emotion—it is thought that the child was quick to recognise the very real gains to be got from its perpetuation. Whilst it would never be argued that asthmatic attacks were produced consciously by the child—in many instances they were too frightening and disturbing—a very real element of reaction to frustration seemed to exist in their causation. As in the studies of Tuft (1957), Metcalf (1956) and Long, Lamont, Whipple and Bandler (1957), the asthma was seen to cease immediately the child was removed from its mother's side. The child's unsettledness seemed less in evidence in school than at home, a fact which might help to explain the non-existence in the Harris and Shure (1956) study of any significant difference in personality structure of asthmatic and control children as seen by their schoolteachers.

In accordance with the studies of Bostock (1956), Harris (1950), French and Alexander (1941), Gerard (1956), Sperling (1949), Coolidge (1950), Miller and Baruch (1950), Jessner (1956) and Rees (1956), mothers of asthmatic children were seen to be rejecting in their initial attitude to the child. This attitude was seen to antecede the illness and not to represent a reaction against it. In contrast to some previous studies, the subsequently perceived solicitousness of these mothers was viewed not as a guilty compensation for this rejection (Rogerson, Hardcastle and Duguid 1935; Bostock 1956), but as a further manifestation of the mother's immaturity (Sontag 1950). No statistically significant evidence of guilt existed. It was concluded that the mother tended to 'engulf' (Abramson 1954) her child as a defence against her own insecurity as a mother.

The need to maintain the child in a state of dependency was viewed not so much as a need to satisfy a love-hunger, but as a reflection of the uncertainty of the mother in handling her child. This explanation would account for the high level of aspiration found in asthmatic mothers by Cohen and Little. They concluded that it was due to maternal over-protection, but an over-protective mother would surely underestimate her child's ability lest it should fail at more realistic levels. A more adequate explanation is that asthmatic mothers become so narcissistic in their association with their children that they not only set them unrealistically high targets but dare not take cognisance of their failure. As Sears (1940) would suggest, high level goal setting reflects the insecurity of both mother and child.

The perfectionism found in asthmatic mothers by Rees (1956), their inability to handle sexual information satisfactorily (Harris 1950), their marital conflict and excessive dominance as wives (Bostock 1956) might well arise from the same source. This study has suggested that asthmatic mothers are immature, and their dominance arises from their extreme insecurity in the feminine role. This insecurity would naturally be more marked in the mothers of first children and might account for the observed preponderance, both in this study and in that of McDermott and Cobb (1939) of first children among the asthmatic population. It might also account for the larger number of males in the pre-sixteen asthmatic group (this study and Rees 1956). The postulated root of the asthmatic mother's dominance is in her psycho-sexual, particularly oedipal, conflicts (Margolis 1961). This sort of mother faced with a male first child might well find him a greater threat than she would a female child and respond in an ever more dominant manner. Unlike the Margolis (1961) study very significant differences were found in the P.A.R.I. scores of asthmatic and control mothers. The differences between results might be explained tentatively by the fact that each of these mothers was seen individually and in her own home by the author and not in groups in a hospital setting, as in Margolis' study. In hospital the mother's responsiveness may very well have been curtailed.

Specific environmental trauma were found to antecede the first attack (as they were in Bostock's 1956 study) and the possibility of asthma following any intense emotional shock rather than a specific one (Metcalf 1956) was not dismissed.

254

Discussion of Present Findings

No attempt was made in this study to explain the exact symbolism of the asthma attack. It was seen as a protest against an over-dominant environment, or an expression of frustration produced by the awareness of personal inadequacy to overcome this dominant environment. The suggestion that it might represent a 'cry for help' to the rejecting mother (Weiss 1922; Bostock 1956), was thought to be unlikely as little fear of rejection was found. More likely is the suggestion that asthma, if it must be thought of as a cry, is a cry of fear against a threatening environment (Monsour 1960) and an attempt to ward off that threat (Ibor 1956).

APPENDIX

A note on the validity of using questionnaire items 4, 5, 7, 8/9, 14/19, 17, 18 and 24, as indices of maternal rejection

Initially 'maternal rejection' was viewed by me as an attitude of hostility on the part of the mother towards an infant or child, whether in the womb or already born, which would result in maternal behaviour most likely to precipitate or increase infant or child problems.

Eight questions contained in the questionnaire were selected at the outset of the investigation (1961) as being suggestive of this maternal rejection. Each question sampled a different aspect of the mother-child relationship, and no suggestion was made as to which might be the most valid indicator of the postulated rejection.

The reasons for the selection of these items are set out below, and also comments where they seem applicable—for the suggested modification of these criteria of maternal rejection. These suggested modifications stem both from the results of studies published since the outset of this investigation and also from the results of the present study.

Basically, such modifications arise from the need to satisfy the two-fold criteria of maternal rejection, as we defined it:

(1) Underlying maternal hostility
(2) Behaviour likely to produce or increase infant problem behaviour.

Frequently we have found, during the study, that mothers behave towards their children in a manner most likely to increase their problems, without showing any real underlying hostility, e.g. a sick mother may find difficulty in accepting her pregnancy, may have complications due to her illness during the pregnancy and labour, and may fail to cope satisfactorily with the infant's problems subsequently. Yet, such a mother may basically like and want to help her child. From the child's point of view, this mother is rejecting in so far as she is unable to really satisfy his needs.

This situation seems to be the converse of the frequently observed analytic situation in which the mother compensates for her basic hostility by taking extra effort to meet the child's physical needs.

Obviously, both underlying attitude and maternal behaviour must be considered in assessing maternal rejection, therefore all the questionnaire questions used to evaluate degree of maternal rejection, have been scrutinised in an effort to see to what extent they established deviancy in both attitude and behaviour.

All nine questions showed maternal behaviours most likely to lead to problem infant behaviour. Two of the questions failed however to demonstrate validly the presence of underlying hostility.

Question 4. 'Did you have an easy pregnancy?'

Answers indicative of distress during pregnancy, e.g. excessive sickness or hypertension, were thought to indicate some degree of rejection on the mother's part.

This prediction was based on the psychoanalytic studies of Jones (1942), Robertson (1946) and Rosen (1955), which suggested that underlying hostility was mirrored in pregnancy stress. Brown (1964) has investigated the concept in a more empirical manner, and established high correlations between physical disturbance in pregnancy and anxieties over relationships with husband and baby. The most anxious mothers produce the largest number of bodily symptoms. The most significant relationship was that between pre-eclamptic toxaemia and prior maternal anxiety.

No definite conclusion could be reached in this study as to the degree to which pregnancy sickness actually symbolises maternal hostility, but a real relationship was thought to exist between high scores on the pathogenic scales of the P.A.R.I. and responses indicative of distress during pregnancy, suggesting that a real relationship between hostility and distress might exist.

The pioneer work of Sontag (1941, 1942, 1950), Pasamanick, Rogers and Lilienfield (1956) and Stott (1957, 1959) suggested that undue stress during pregnancy would communicate itself directly to the child with consequent behaviour difficulties. Again, this study would suggest that such a relationship might exist. Mothers who reported most infant problem behaviour tended to be mothers who had exhibited most pregnancy stress.

Answers to this question indicative of pregnancy stress therefore appear to us to be valid measures of maternal rejection.

Question 5. 'How did you feel about conceiving (name)? Were you pleased or was he unplanned?'

Answers indicative of an unwanted pregnancy were thought to be indicators of maternal rejection.

This assumption was based on the early studies of Fries (1936) and Benedek (1949) which suggested that admittance of unwantedness indicated maternal hostility. Also, it was felt that the rejecting attitude would result in maternal stress which would communicate itself to the developing foetus and produce deviant infant behaviour at the outset (Ferreira 1960; Lakin 1957; Wallin and Riley 1950).

As with Question 4, mothers who reported an unwanted pregnancy in this study tended to be the more pathogenic mothers, and the mothers who most frequently reported infant problem behaviour, suggesting that this question is also a valid indicator of maternal rejection. The possibility cannot be ignored, however, in retrospective studies of this kind, that answers to the question are contaminated by the mother's subsequent difficulty with the child (Coleman, Kris and Province).

Question 7. 'Were you at all emotionally upset during your pregnancy?'

Answers indicative of excessive maternal emotional disturbance during pregnancy were thought to indicate maternal rejection.

This assumption was based on studies which suggested that emotional distress during pregnancy resulted from the mother's immaturity and consequent hostility towards the child (Benedek 1949; Wallin and Riley 1950; Ferreira 1960), and studies which suggested emotional distress would tend to disturb the developing foetus (Sontag 1941, 1942; Stott 1957, 1959).

As in previous questions in this study, a relationship was found to exist between harsh maternal attitude, infant problem behaviour, and answers to this question indicative of emotional distress suggesting it to be a valid measure of maternal rejection.

Question 8/9. A combination of Question 8 'How did you find your delivery?' and Question 9 'How long did your labour take?'

Answers indicative of non-normal delivery or an over-long delivery (over twenty-four hours) were taken as indices of maternal rejection.

This postulated relationship was based on the studies of Fodor (1949), Greenacre (1952) and Jones (1942) which suggested that such over-long or complicated labours were indicative of fear of having a baby. Also considered were the studies that suggested that birth difficulties would accentuate infant problem behaviour (Frosch and Wortis 1948; Greenacre 1952; Laufer 1957; Rosenfield and Bradley 1948; Sontag 1941; Stott 1959; and Wile and Davis 1941).

I would not dispute this latter contention—greater distress in the infant was reported by mothers who had had over-long or difficult births. The possibility that mothers of problem children justify their difficulties in terms of real or imaginary birth stress is not forgotten. No independent assessment of birth trauma was possible in a study of this kind and a developmental study would be essential to really justify the conclusion that birth stress alone produces infant problem behaviour.

Since the commencement of this study, Brown (1964) noted an absence of correlations between any of his psychological variables of maternal anxiety and unwillingness to have the baby and difficulty in labour. Similarly, in this study difficulty in labour was not thought to be confined specifically to those who—on the P.A.R.I.—appeared the least accepting of mothers. There existed a slight tendency for the least accepting mothers to have the most difficulties in labour, but the relationship was not nearly specific enough for this to be thought a really valid indicator of underlying hostility.

One reason for abandoning this item as an indicator of material rejection may stem from the real fear of, and ignorance concerning childbirth in our culture. No relaxation or participation is therefore possible at the birth and the mother tenses up, increasing complications.

Question 13. 'Were you at all nervous at the thought of having to care for (name) alone, or did you like the idea?'

Answers indicative of nervousness were thought to mask maternal hostility towards the child (Ferreira 1960), and also to increase the likelihood of neural impairment of the infant as the result of pregnancy stress.

My study suggested that such answers were indeed correlated with subsequent infant difficulty, but the relationship with underlying hostility might be slight. In some instances the mother who indicated that she was nervous at the thought of handling her baby had a very practical reason for such nervousness, e.g. chronic ill health.

Question 14/19. A combination of Question 14 'How did you feed him?' and Question 19 'Did you enjoy feeding (name) yourself?'

No breast-feeding after two weeks or dislike of breast-feeding where it was established were regarded at the outset as indicating rejection on the mother's part. This position was maintained because of repeated stress (Ribble 1944, Winnicott 1947) on the importance of the feeding relationship in the development of the healthy mother-child relationship. As Winnicott has observed, breast feeding enables the infant to realise that:

> Mother continues to exist, lives, smells, breathes, her heart beats. She is there to be sensed in every possible way. She lives in a physical way, provides contact, a body temperature, movement and quiet according to the baby's needs. She provides opportunity for the baby to make the transition between the quiet and the excited state, not suddenly, coming at the child with a feed and demanding a response.

So frequently bottle feeds are short, casual affairs; sometimes the mother may even prop the bottle against the side of the pram or cot and leave the baby. Such feeds cannot be satisfying to the baby, and they certainly do not afford mother and growing infant a few minutes of tranquillity together. In this sense they may predispose mother and child to unsatisfying interactions later on.

As a measure of underlying hostility, however, answers of 'no breast-feeding' or 'dislike of breast-feeding' cannot be thought particularly valid.

Newson (1962, 1963) suggests that 40 per cent of mothers discontinue breast-feeding before two weeks of age, and only 10 per cent of mothers continue to breast-feed until six months of age. In Northern Ireland this trend away from breast-feeding appears, from conversations, to be gaining momentum. One health visitor, representing many spoken to by the author in 1963 and 1964, noted that:

> In many districts now it is very unusual to find more than one mother a year breast-feeding for six months or so. The mothers haven't the time, the hospitals don't bother to force it, and the powdered milks are so excellent that bottle feeding is no trouble.

Similarly, even where there is a will, there may not always be a way. Many of the mothers in our study reported that physical factors such as ill-health, or inverted nipples, made it impossible to breast-feed, although they would have liked to.

As might be expected from these comments, no difference was found between supposedly rejecting mothers, and supposedly accepting mothers on these questions and therefore it was concluded that at the present time, in our culture, absence of breast-feeding cannot be thought to be a valid measure of maternal rejection, even though it may decrease the possibility of a satisfactory mother-child relationship.

Question 17. 'Did you demand feed or keep to a regular schedule?'

Answers to this question suggesting rigidity of feeding schedule were thought by me to indicate maternal rejection. Such answers were thought to indicate the mother's unwillingness to deal pragmatically with the demands of her child. The results of this study appear to have substantiated this original hypothesis. Newson (1963) noted the strong trend away from 'clock feeding'. Where rigid feeding methods are maintained despite this cultural trend towards permissive feeding, we maintain that they may indicate either maternal insecurity or hostility. In both cases the non-accepting attitude would, it is thought, be sensed by the baby and might possibly increase problem behaviour.

Questions 18 and 24. 'Did you have any feeding problems whilst (name) was a baby?' and 'Did you have any special problems in his first year?'

Mothers responding 'yes' to either of these questions were thought by me to be rejecting mothers. This assumption was based on a number of studies, which indicated that a hostile maternal attitude, either before, or immediately following, birth was inevitably accompanied by reactive problem behaviour (Ferreira 1960, Fries and Lewis 1938, Escalona 1945, Stewart 1954, Klatskin 1956, Wallin and Riley 1950). In my study this contention appears to have been borne out. Where the mother appeared initially most non-accepting in attitude she also reported most infant problem behaviour. First, maternal attitude is conveyed to the foetus and rejection or hostility in pregnancy, if severe enough, will produce hyperactive infant behaviour. Secondly, mothers who are most initially non-accepting will tend to handle their infants in a harsh, non-comprehending manner, increasing any problem tendencies.

In conclusion it must be stressed that no single questions should be thought sufficient to gauge maternal rejection. The study suggests that most mothers will produce at least one deviant answer to the questions we have posed; rejecting mothers however may be isolated on the basis of the regular occurrence of such responses in a questionnaire such as the one I used. Care should also be taken to put supplementary questions to the mothers in order to better assess their underlying attitude.

BIBLIOGRAPHY

ABRAHAM, K., 'The experiencing of sexual traumas as a form of sexual activity' (1907), *Selected Papers on Psychoanalysis*, London, Hogarth, 1927, pp. 47–63.

ABRAMSON, H. A., 'Evaluation of the maternal rejection theory in allergy' *Ann. Allergy*, 1954, 12: 129.

ACKERMAN, N. W., and LEONA CHIDESTER, ' "Accidental" self injury in children' *Archives of Pediatrics*, 1936, No. 11, Vol. 43, pp. 711–21.

ALCOCK, THEODORA, 'Some personality characteristics of asthmatic children' *Brit. J. Med. Psych.*, 1960, 33, p. 133.

ALEXANDER, F., and FRENCH, T. M., *Studies in Psychosomatic Medicine*, 1948, New York, Ronald Press.

ANDERSON, E. W., KENNA, J. C., and HAMILTON, M. W., 'A study of extra-marital conception in adolescence' *Psy. et Neurologia*, 1960, Vol. 139, No. 6.

BACON, CATHERINE L., BACKETT, E. M., and JOHNSTON, A. M., 'The role of aggression in the asthmatic attack' *Psychoanal. Quart.* 1956, Vol. 26. *Brit. Med. J.*, 1959, 1: 409.

BACKETT, E. M., and JOHNSTON A. M., *Brit. Med. J.*, 1959, 1: 409.

BALL, J. C., and NELL LOGAN, 'Early sexual behaviour of the lower class delinquent girl' *J. Crim. Law and Criminology*, 1960, Vol. 51.

BAWKIN, H., 'Disturbed sexual behaviour in children and adolescents', *J. Pediatrics*, 1955, Vol. 46.

BELL, RICHARD Q., 'Retrospective attitude studies of parent-child relations', *Child Dev.*, 1958, Vol. 29.

BENDER, L., and ABRAM BLAU, 'The reactions of children to sexual relations with adults', *Amer. J. Orthopsychiatry*, 1937, Vol. 7.

BENDER, L., and SCHILDER, E., 'Suicidal pre-occupations and attempts in children', *Amer. J. Orthopsy*, 1937, Vol. 7, pp. 225–34.

BENDER, L., 'Psychopathic Behaviour Disorders in Children', *Handbook of Correctional Psychology*, 1947, New York Philosophical Library, pp. 360–77.

BENDER, L., and KRAMER, J., 'Sublimation and sexual gratification in the latency period of girls', In Eissler, *Searchlights on Delinquency*, 1948.

BENDER, L., and GRUGETT, A., 'A follow up report on children having atypical sexual experience', *Amer. J. Orthopsy.*, 1952, Vol. 22.

Bibliography

BENEDEK, T., 'The psychosomatic complications of the primary unit—Mother: Child', *Amer. J. Orthopsy.*, 1949, 19. p. 642.

BENEDEK, T., (a) 'Towards the biology of the depressive constellation', *J. Amer. Psa. Assoc.* 1956, 4. pp. 389–427. (b) 'Psychobiological aspects of mothering', *Amer. J. Orthopsy.*, 1956, Vol. 26, pp. 272–8.

BERES, DAVID, 'Clinical notes on aggression in children', *Psychoanal. Stud. of Child*, 1952, Vol. 7, pp. 241–263.

BERGMANN, THESI, 'Observations of children's reactions to motor restraint', *Nerv. chi.* 1945, Vol. 4.

BIRNBACH, S. B., *Comparative Study of Accident Repeater and Accident Free Children.* 1948, New York University Press.

BLAU, ABRAM, and HULSE, WILFRED C., 'Anxiety neuroses as a cause of behaviour disorders in children', *Amer. J. Orthopsy.*, 1956, 26. pp. 108–118.

BLOS, PETER, 'Preoedipal factors in the etiology of female delinquency', *Psychoanal. Stud. of Chi.* Vol. XII, 1957.

BLUMSTEIN, GEORGE, 'The aetiologic diagnosis of asthma in childhood', *Amer. J. Dis. Chi.* 1957, Vol. 93.

BOSTOCK, JOHN, 'Asthma: A synthesis involving primitive speech organism and insecurity', *J. Ment. Sci.* 1956, Vol. 102, pp. 559–75.

BOURDIOL, L., and PETTENATI, G., 'Reflexions à propos de 40 expertises médico-légales en matière d'attentats aux moeurs', *Ann. de. Méd. Lég.* 1961, Vol. 41.

BROWN, E. A., and GOITEN, B. L., 'Some aspects of mind in asthma and allergy', *J. Nerv. and Ment. Dis.* 1943, Vol. 98, p. 638.

BROWN, L. B., 'Anxiety in Pregnancy', *Brit. J. Med. Psych.* 1964, Vol. 37, Part I. pp. 47–58.

BUFFUM, W. P., 'The diagnosis of asthma in infants and children', *Amer. J. Dis. Chi.* 1957, Vol 93.

BURTON, LINDY, 'Three Studies of Deviant Child Development', unpublished Doctoral Thesis, 1964, The Queens University of Belfast.

CAPLAN, H., 'The role of deviant maturation in the pathogenesis of anxiety', *Amer. J. Orthopsy*, 1956, Vol. 26, pp. 94–104.

CLOTHIER, F., 'The unmarried mother of school age as seen by a psychiatrist', *Ment. Hyg.*, 1955, Vol. 39, pp. 631–46.

COHEN, LOUIS D., and SUE WARREN LITTLE, 'Goal setting behaviour of asthmatic children and their mothers for them', *J. Person.* 1950–1, Vol. 19, pp. 376–89.

COLEMAN, R. W., KRIS, E., and PROVINCE, S., 'Study of variations in early parental attitudes', *Psychoanal. Stud. of Chi.*, 1953, Vol. 8.

COLIN, M., and BOURJADE, 'Les attentants aux moeurs dans les bandes d'adolescents', *Ann. de Méd. Lég.*, 1961, Vol. 41.

COLM, HANNA, 'Children's sexual preoccupations as a reaction to difficult family relations and the parent's anxieties about sex', *J. Chi. Psychiatry*, 1951, Vol. 2, pp. 205–20.

COOLIDGE, J. C., 'Asthma in mother and child as a special type of communication', *Amer. J. Orthopsy*, 1956, Vol. 26, pp. 165–76.

COX, B., and SARGENT, H., 'T.A.T. responses of emotionally disturbed and emotionally stable children. Clinical judgements versus normative', *Data J. Proj. Tech.*, 1950, Vol. 14.

CRUICKSHANK, W. M., 'The relation of physical disability to fear and guilt feelings', *Chi. Dev.*, 1951, Vol. 22, p. 221.

DEES, S. C., and LOWENBACH, H., 'The E.E.G. of allergic children', *Ann. Allergy*, 1948, Vol. 6, p. 99.

DEES, SUSAN C., 'Development and course of asthma in children', *Amer. J. Dis. of Chi.*, 1957, p. 93.

DEKKER, E., and GROEN, J., 'Reproducible psychogenic attacks of asthma', *J. Psychosom. Res.*, 1956, Vol. 1, pp. 58–67.

DEKKER, E., PELSER, H. E., and GROEN, J., 'Conditioning as a cause of asthmatic attacks', *J. Psychosom. Res.*, 1957, Vol. 2, p. 97.

DESPERT, J. L., 'Suicide and depression in children', *Nerv. Chi.*, 1951–2, Vol. 9.

DEUTSCH, FELIX, *The psychosomatic concept in psychoanalysis*, 1953, New York, Internat. Univ. Press.

DUC, N., 'Considérations sur la criminologie et la victimologie des attentats aux moeurs (à propos de 35 cas personnels)', *Annal de Méd. Lég.*, 1961, Vol. 41.

DUNBAR, FLANDERS, 'Psychoanalytical notes relating to syndromes of asthma and hay fever', *Psychoanal. Quart.* 1938, Vol. 7, pp. 25—68.

DUNBAR, FLANDERS, 'Susceptibility to accidents', *Med. Clin.N. Amer.*, 1944, Vol. 28, p. 653.

EISNER, EUGENE, 'Relationship formed by a sexually delinquent girl', *Amer. J. Orthopsy*, 1945, Vol. 15.

EISSLER, RUTH, 'Scapegoats of society', Eissler edit: *Searchlights on Delinquency*, 1948.

ESCALONA, S., 'Feeding disturbances in very young children', *Amer. J. Orthopsy*, 1945, Vol. 15, p. 76.

FENICHEL, O., *The psychoanalytic theory of neurosis*, 1945, New York W. Norton and Co.

FERENCZI, SANDOR, 'Confusion of tongues between the adult and the child', (1932) republished *Int. J. Psychoanal.*, XXX, 1949, pp. 225–30.

FERREIRA, A. J., 'The pregnant woman's emotional attitude and its reflections on the newborn', *Amer. J. Orthopsy*, 1960, Vol. 30.

Bibliography

FIGGE, M., 'Some factors in the aetiology of maternal rejection', *Studies in Maternal Over-protection*, Smith College Stud. Work. 1932, Vol. 2, p. 181.

FINCH, S. M., 'Psychosomatic problems in children', *Nerv. Chi.* 1951–2, Vol. 9.

FITT, A. B., 'An analysis of road accidents to children in Great Britain', *Aust. J. Psy.*, 1956, Vol. 7, pp. 129–134.

FITZELLE, G. T., 'Personality factors and certain attitudes toward child rearing among parents of asthmatic children', *Psychosomatic Med.* 1959, Vol. 21.

FLECK, S., 'Pregnancy as a symptom of adolescent maladjustment', *Internat. J. Soc. Psychiat.* 1956, Vol. 2.

FODOR, N., 'The Trauma of Bearing', *Psychiat. Quart.* 1949, Vol. 23.

FRANK, 'Personality Development in adolescent girls', *Monog. for Research in Child Development*, 1951.

FRIEDLATER, F., 'Latent Delinquency and ego development', Eissler Edit: *Searchlights on Delinquency*, 1948.

FRIES, M. E., 'Factors in character development, neuroses, psychoses and delinquency. A study of pregnancy, lying-in period and early childhood', *Amer. J. Orthopsy*, 1937, Vol. 7, pp. 142–81.

FRIES, M. E., and LEWIS, B., 'Interrelated factors in development, a study of pregnancy, labor, delivery, lying-in period and childhood', *Amer. J. Orthopsy.*, 1938, Vol.8, pp. 726–52.

FRIES, M. E., 'Psychosomatic relationships between mother and infant', *Psychosomat. Med.*, 1944, Vol. 6, pp. 159–62.

FRENCH, T. M., and ALEXANDER, F., 'Psychogenic Factors in Bronchial Asthma', *Psychosomatic Medicine Monograph* No. 4, 1941. Washington National Research Councils.

FREUD, ANNA, 'The psychoanalytic study of infantile feeding disturbances', *The Psychoanal. Stud. of Chi.*, 1946, Vol. 2, p. 119.

FREUD, ANNA, 'Certain types and stages of social maladjustment', Eissler Edit: *Searchlights on Delinquency*, 1948.

FREUD, ANNA, *The ego and the mechanisms of Defence*, 1948. London, Hogarth.

FREUD, ANNA, 'The role of bodily illness in the mental life of children', *Psychoanal. Stud. of Chi.*, 1952, Vol. 7, pp. 69–81.

FREUD, SIGMUND, *Fragment on an analysis of a case of hysteria*, 1905, Vol. VII.* *Three Essays on the Theory of Sexuality*, 1905, Vol. VII.* *The Sexual Enlightenment of Children*, 1907, Vol. II.* *Psychopathology of Everyday Life*, 1914, pp. 198–209. *Psychoanalysis*, 1922, Vol. V, p. 107.* *Psychoanalysis*, 1925, Vol. III, p. 145.* *Libidinal Types*, 1931, Vol. V.* *Female Sexuality*, 1931, Vol. V.*

* The Standard Edition of the Complete Psychological Works of Sigmund Freud, 1953, London, Hogarth.

FROSCH, J., and WORTIS, S. B., 'A contribution to the Nosology of the Impulse Disorders', *Amer. J. Psychiat.*, 1954, p. 132.

FULLER, E. M., 'Injury–prone Children', *Amer. J. Orthopsy.* 1948, Vol. 18, p. 708.

FULLER, E. M., and BAUNE, H. B., 'Injury proneness and adjustment in the second grade', *Sociometry*, 1951, Vol. 14, pp. 210–25.

GERARD, M. W., 'Bronchial asthma in children', *Nerv. Chi.*, 1946, Vol. 6, p. 327.

GERARD, M. W., 'Genesis of psychosomatic symptoms in infancy', In Deutch edit: *The psychosomatic concept in psychoanalysis*, 1953, New York, Internat. Univ. Press.

GIBBENS, T. C. N., 'Juvenile Prostitutes', *Brit. J. of Delinq.*, 1957, Vol. 8.

GIBBENS, T. C. N., and JOYCE PRINCE, 'Child Victims of Sex Offences 1963', Pamphlet of the Institute for the Study and Treatment of Delinquency, London.

GOLDFARB, W., 'Psychological Privation in Infancy and subsequent Adjustment', *Amer. J. Orthopsy*, 1945, Vol. 15.

GREENACRE, P., *Trauma, Growth and Personality*, 1952, New York, Norton 328 p.

HALLECK, S. L., 'The physician's role in the management of victims of sexual offenders', *J. Amer. Med. Assoc.* ,1962, Vol. 1.

HARRIS, I. D., RAPOPORT, L., ANN RYNERSON, and MAX SAMTER, 'Observations on asthmatic children', *Amer. J. Orthopsych.*, 1950, Vol. 20, pp. 490–505.

HARRIS, M. C., and SHURE, N., 'A Study of Behaviour Patterns in Asthmatic Children', *J. Allergy*, 1956, Vol. 27, pp. 312–23.

HARTMANN, H., KRIS, E., and LOWENSTEIN, R. M., 'Comments on the formation of the psychic structure', *Psychoanal. Stud. Child.*, 1946, Vol. 2, pp. 11–38.

HARTOGS, RENATUS, 'Discipline in the early life of sexual delinquents', *Nerv. Chi.*, 1951–2, Vol. 9.

HEIMAN, M., and LEVITT, E., 'The role of separation and depression in out-of-wedlock pregnancy', *Amer. J. Orthopsy*, 1960, Vol. 30.

HENRIQUES, B., 'Child victims of sexual assault', *Mental Health*, 1961.

HOLT, R. R., 'Level of aspiration: ambition or defense?; *J. Exp. Psy.*, 1946, Vol. 36, pp. 398–416.

HONTIG, HANS VON, 'Remarks on the interaction of perpetrator and victim', *J. Crim. Law and Crimin.*, 1941,Vol. 31.

IBOR, J. J. LOPEZ, 'Problems presented by asthma as a psychosomatic illness', *J. Psychosom. Res.*, 1956, Vol. 1, p. 115.

ILLINGWORTH, R. S., 'Crying in infants and children', *Brit. Med. J.*' 1955, Vol. 75.

Bibliography

ISAACS, SUSAN, *Social Development of Young Children*, 1933, London, Routledge.

JOHNSON, A. M., and SZUREK, M. D., 'The genesis of antisocial acting out in children and adults', *Psychoanal. Quart.*, 1952, Vol. 21, p. 323.

JOHNSON, A. M., 'Factors in the etiology of fixations and symptom choice', *Psychoanal. Quart.*, 1953, Vol. 22, p. 475.

JONES, ERNEST, 'Psychology and Childbirth', *Lancet*, 1942, Vol. 242, p. 695.

JONES, ERNEST, *Sigmund Freud, Life and Work*, 1955, Vols. 1 & 2, London, Hogarth.

JESSNER, L., LAMONT, LONG R., ROLLINS, N., WHIPPLE, B., and PRENTICE N., 'Emotional impact of nearness and separation for the asthmatic child and his mother', *Psychoanal. Stud. of Chi.*, 1956, Vol. 10.

KARPMAN, B., 'Considerations bearing on the problems of sexual offences', *J. Crim. Law and Crimin.*, 1952, Vol. 43.

KASANIN, J., and HANDSHIN, S., 'Psychodynamic factors in illegitimacy', *Amer. J. Orthopsy*, 1941, Vol. 11, p. 66.

KAUFMAN, S. H., 'Aggression in the girl delinquent', *Amer. J. Orthopsy*, 1945, Vol. 15.

KEPECKS, J., MILTON, R., and CLARE MUNRO, 'Responses to sensory stimulation in certain psychosomatic disorders', *Psychosom. Med.*, 1958, Vol. 20.

KINSEY, A. C., POMEROY, W. B., MARTIN, C. E., and PAUL GEBHARD, 'Sexual Behaviour in the Human Female', 1953, p. 116. W. B. Saunders, Philadelphia and London.

KLATSKIN, E. H., JACKSON, E. B., and WILKIN, N., 'The influence of degree of flexibility in maternal child care practices on early child behaviour', *Amer. J. Orthopsy*, 1956, Vol. 26, pp. 76–93.

KLEIN, MELANIE, *Psychoanalysis of Children*, 1932, London, Hogarth.

KNAPP, P. H., and NEMETZ, S. J., (a) 'Personality variations in bronchial asthma', *Psychosom. Med.*, 1957, Vol. 19, p. 443.
(b) 'Sources of tension in bronchial asthma', *Psychosom. Med.*, 1957, Vol. 19, p. 466.

KRALL, VITA, 'Personality characteristics of accident-repeating children', *J. Abnorm. and Soc. Psy.*, 1953, Vol. 48, pp. 99–107.

LAFON, R., TRIVAS, J., and POUGET, R., 'Aspects psychologiques des attents sexuels sur les enfants et les adolescents', *Annales Médico-Psychologie*, 1958.

LAFON, R., 'Quelques propos sur le victimologie', *Annales de Médecin légale*, 1961, Vol. 41.

LAFON, R., TRIVAS, J., FAURE, J. L., and POUGET, R., 'Victimologie et criminologie des attentats sexuels sur les enfants et les adolescents', *Ann. Méd. Lég.*, 1961, Vol. 41.

LAING, R. D., *The Divided Self*, Tavistock Publications, 1960.

LAKIN, M., 'Assessment of significant role attitudes in primaparous mothers by means of a modification of the T.A.T.', *Psychosom. Med.*, 1957, Vol. 19, pp. 50–60.

LANDIS, JUDSON T., 'Experiences of 500 Children with Adult Sexual Deviation', *Psychiat. Quart.*, Supplement 1956, Vol. 30, pp. 91–109.

LANGEVELD, J., 'The form in which the allergic manifestations present themselves to the psychologist during the psychological examination of the child', *Internat. Arch. Allergy*, 1954, Vol. 5, p. 314.

LANGFORD, W. S., *et al.* Pilot Study of Childhood Accidents. *Pediatrics*, 1953, 11, pp. 405–13.

LAUFER, M. W., DENHOFF, E., and SOLOMONS, G., 'Hyperkinetic impulse disorder in children's behaviour problems', *Psychosom. Med.*, 1957, Vol. 19, p. 38.

LE SHAN, L. L., 'Dynamics in accident-prone behaviour', *Psychiatry*, 1952, Vol. 15, pp. 73–80.

LEVY, D., *Maternal Overprotection*, 1943, New York, Columbia University Press.

LINN, LOUIS, 'Psychoanalytic contributions to psychosomatic research', *Psychosom. Med.*, 1958, Vol. 20.

LITIN, E. M., GIFFIN, M. E., and ADELAIDE M. JOHNSON., 'Parental influence in unusual sexual behaviour in children', *Psychoanal. Quart.*, 1950, Vol. 25.

LONG, R. T., LAMONT, J. H., WHIPPLE, B., and BANDLER, L., 'A psychosomatic study of allergic and emotional factors in children with asthma', *Amer. J. Psychiatry*, 1957–8, Vol. 114, p. 890.

MARCUS, *et al.* 'Society for Research in Child Development', 1960 *Developmental Monograph*, No. 76, Vol. 25.

MARGOLIS, MARVIN, 'The mother-child relationship in bronchial asthma', *J. Abnorm. and Soc. Psy.*, 1961, Vol. 63, pp. 360–7.

MCDERMOTT, N. T., and COBB, S., 'Psychiatric survey of 50 cases of bronchial asthma', *Psychosom. Med.*, 1939, Vol. 1, pp. 201–244.

MENAKER, ESTHER, 'Masochism—a defence reaction of the ego', *Psychoanal. Quart.*, 1953, Vol. 22, p. 205.

MENNINGER, K., 'Purposive accidents as an expression of the self destruction tendencies', *Internat. J. Psychoanal.*, 1936, Vol. 17, pp. 6–16.

MENNINGER, K., *Man against himself*, 1938. Reprinted Harvest Books, 1963, pp. 278–93.

METCALFE, MARYSE, 'Demonstration of a psychosomatic relationship', *Brit. J. Med. Psy.*, 1956, Vol. 29, p. 63.

MILLER, HYMAN, and DOROTHY BARUCH, 'A study of hostility in allergic children', *Amer. J. Orthopsy*, 1950, 20, pp. 506–19.

Bibliography

MILLER, HYMAN, and DOROTHY BARUCH, 'The emotional problems of childhood and their relation to asthma', *Amer. J. Dis. Chi.*, 1957, Vol. 93.

MILLER, MILTON, 'Emotional conflicts in asthma', *Dis. of the Ner. System*, 1952, p. 298.

MONSOUR, K. J., 'Asthma and the fear of death', *Psychoanal. Quart.*, 1960, Vol. 29, pp. 56–69.

MORGAN, C. D., and MURRAY, H. A., 'A method for investigating Phantasies: The Thematic Apperception Test', *Archives of Neurology and Psychiatry*, 1935, Vol. 34, pp. 289–306.

MOSES, J., 'Psychische Auswinkurgen sexueller Angriffe bei jungen Mädchen', *Z. sch. f. Kinderforsch*, 1932, Vol. 40.

NEUHAUS, EDMUND, 'A personality study of asthmatic and cardiac children', *Psychosom. Med.*, 1958, Vol. 20.

NEWELL, H. W., 'The psycho-dynamics of maternal rejection', *Amer. J. Orthopsych.*, 1936, Vol. 6, pp. 576–89.

NEWSON, L. J., and E., 'Breast feeding in Decline', *Brit. Med. J,*. 1962, Vol. 11, p. 1744.

NEWSON, L. J., and E., *Infant Care in an Urban Community*, 1963, London, Allen and Unwin.

O'KELLY, F., 'Some observations on the relationship between adolescent girls and their parents', *Brit. J. Med. Psych.*, 1955, 28, pp. 59–66.

OWEN, FREYA W., 'Asthma and maternal stimuli', *Dissert. Abst.*, 1961, Vol. 22, p. 644.

PASAMANICK, B., ROGERS, M. E., and LILIENFIELD, A. M., *Amer. J. Psychiat.*, 1956, Vol. 112, p. 613.

POWELL, M., 'Illegitimate pregnancy in emotionally disturbed girls', *Smith Coll. Stud. Soc. Wk.*, 1948, Vol. 19–20.

QUENTIN, WILSON, 'Are differences in schizophrenic symptoms related to the mother's avowed attitude toward child rearing?', *J. Abnorm. and Soc. Psy.*, 1961, Vol. 63, pp. 440–2.

RABINOVITCH, R. D., 'The sexual psychopath—a symposium', *J. Crim. Law and Crimin.*, 1953, Vol. 43.

RABINOVITCH, R. D., 'Etiological Factors in disturbed sexual behaviour of children', *J. Crim. Law and Crimin.*, 1953, Vol. 43.

RAPPAPORT, H. G., 'Psychosomatic aspects of allergy in childhood', *J. Amer. Med. Assoc.*, 1957, Vol. 165, pp. 812–815.

RASMUSSEN, A., 'Die Bedeutung sexueller Attente auf Kinder unter 14 Jahren für die Entwicklung von geisteskrankheiter und charakter Anomalien', *Acta. Psychiat. Kbh.*, 1934, Vol. 9.

REES, LYNFORD, 'Physical and emotional factors in bronchial asthma', *J. Psychosomat. Res.*, 1956, Vol. 1, pp. 58–114.

Bibliography

REIFEN, D., 'The child as a victim of sexual offence', *Brit. J. of Psychiat. Soc. Wk.*, 1958, Vol. 4.

RIABOY, P., 'Prediction of recidivism in unmarried mothers', *Smith Coll. Stud. Soc. Work*, 1943, Vol. 14, pp. 267–268.

RIBBLE, M. A., *The rights of infants.*, 1944, New York, Columbia.

ROBERTSON, G. G., 'Nausea and vomiting in pregnancy', *Lancet*, 1946, Vol. 251, pp. 236–341.

ROGERSON, C. H., HARDCASTLE, and DUGUID, 'A psychological approach to the problem of asthma and the asthma-eczema-prurigo syndrome', *Guy's Hospital Reports*, 1935, Vol. 85, pp. 289–308.

ROSEN, S., 'Emotional factors in nausea and vomiting of pregnancy', *Psychiat. Quart.*, 1955, Vol. 29.

ROSENFELD, G. B., and BRADLEY, C., 'Childhood behaviour sequelae of asphyxia in infants', *Pediatrics*, 1948, Vol. 74.

R.O.S.P.A., *Road Accident Statistics*, 1963.

ROYAL ULSTER CONSTABULARY, *A statistical Analysis of road accidents in Northern Ireland*, 1963.

SARGENT, H., 'Projective Methods. Their origin, theory and application in personality research', *Psy. Bull.*, 1945.

SAUL, L. J., and LYONS, J. W., 'Psychodynamics of respiration', in *Somatic and Psychiatric Treatment of Asthma*, Edit: Abramson, 1951, Baltimore, Williams and Wilkins.

SCHAEFER, E. S., and RICHARD BELL, *The Parent Attitude Research Instrument*, (PARI) National Institute of Mental Health, Publication No. 5559, Library of Congress, Washington.

SCHAEFER, E., and NANCY BAYLEY, 'Consistency of Maternal Behaviour from infancy to preadolescence', *J. Abnorm. and Soc. Psy.*, 1960, Vol. 61, No. 1, pp. 1–6.

SCHAEFER, E. S., and RICHARD BELL, 'Development of a parental attitude research instrument', *Child Dev.*, 1959, Vol. 9, No. 3.

SCHAEFER, E. S., and RICHARD BELL, 'Development of a maternal behaviour research instrument', *J. Genet. Psy.*, 1959, Vol. 95, pp. 83–104.

SCHACTER, STANLEY, *The psychology of affiliation.*, 1961, Tavistock, London.

SCHOBEN, G. L., 'The assessment of parental attitudes in relation to child adjustment', *Genet. Psych. Mono.*, 1949, Vol. 39, p. 127.

SEARS, R. R., 'Ordinal position in the family as a psychological variable', *Amer. Sociol. Rev.*, 1950, Vol. 15, pp. 397–401.

SEARS, P. S., 'Level of aspiration in academically successful and unsuccessful children', *J. Abnorm. and Soc. Psy.*, 1940, Vol. 35.

SHAHMUGAN, T. E., 'Sexually delinquent Women and their fantasies', *Madras Psy. Soc. J. of Psy. Researches*, 1958, Vol. 11.

SHELDON, WILFRED, *Diseases of infancy and childhood*, 1951, London, Sheldon, p. 360.

SMID, A. C., and LOGAN, G. B., *Minn. Med.*, 1956, 39, p. 394.

SONTAG, LESTER, 'The significance of fetal environmental difference', *Amer. J. Obstet. and Gynae.*, 1941, Vol. 42, pp. 996–1003.

SONTAG, LESTER, 'Differences in modifiability of fetal behaviour and physiology', *Psychosomatic Med.*, 1942, Vol. 16, pp. 151–4.

SONTAG, LESTER, 'The genetics of differences in psychosomatic patterns in childhood', *Amer. J. Orthopsy*, 1950, Vol. 20, pp. 479–89.

SPERLING, M., 'The role of the mother in psychosomatic disorders in children', *Psychosomat. Med.*, 1949, Vol. 11, pp. 377–85.

SPITZ, R. A., 'The psychogenic diseases in infancy: an attempt at an aetiological classification', *Psychoanal. Stud. of Chi.*, 1951, Vol. 6, p. 255.

STEIN, MORRIS I., *The Thematic Apperception Test*, 1955, Addison-Wesley Publishing Co., Cambridge, Mass.

STEIN, M., and OTTENBERG, P., 'The role of odours in asthma', *Psychosomat. Med.*, 1958, Vol. 20, p. 60.

STENDLER, CELIA B., 'Critical periods in socialization and over-dependence', *Chi. Dev.*, 1952, Vol. 23, pp. 3–12.

STERN, E., 'Recherches sur la psychologie de l'adolescent à l'aide du TAT de Murray', *Schwieg. Z. Psycho.*, 1951, Vol. 10.

STEWART, A., 'Excessive infant crying (colic) in relation to parent behaviour', *Amer. J. Psychiat.*, 1954, Vol. 110, pp. 687–94.

STOTT, D. H., and SYKES, E. G., *Bristol Social Adjustment Guides*, 1956, University of London Press.

STOTT, D. H., 'Physical and mental handicaps following a disturbed pregnancy', *Lancet*, 1957, p. 1006.

STOTT, D. H., 'Evidence of prenatal impairment of temperament in mentally retarded children', *Inter. J. Human Dev.*, 1959, Vol. 2, p. 125.

STOTT, D. H., *The Social Adjustment of Children*, (Manual to the Bristol Social Adjustment Guides), 1958, University of London Press.

STOTT, D. H., *Unsettled Children and their families*, 1956, University of London Press.

STOTT, D. H., 'Prediction of delinquency from non-delinquent behaviour', *Brit. J. Delinq.*, 1960.

STOTT, D. H., 'Measuring Crime Proneness in children', *New Scientist*, 1962, No. 278.

STOTT, D. H., 'Thirty-three troublesome Children', 1964, (in manuscript).

SYMONDS, P., 'Inventory of Themes in Adolescent Fantasy', *Amer. J. Orthopsy*, 1945, Vol. 15.

TUFT, HAROLD S., 'The development and management of intractable asthma of childhood', *Amer. J. Dis. Chi.*, 1957, Vol. 93, p. 251.

WAGGONER, and BOYD, D., 'Juvenile aberrant sexual behaviour', *Amer. J. Orthopsy*, 1941, Vol. 11.

WALLIN, P., and RILEY, R., 'Reactions of mothers to pregnancy and adjustment of offspring in infancy', *Amer. J. Orthopsy*, 1950, Vol. 20, pp. 616–20.

WATTENBERG, W. W., and SAUNDERS, F., 'Recidivism among girls', *J. Abnorm. and Soc. Psy.*, 1955, Vol. 50.

WEBB, M. L., 'Delinquency in the making—patterns in the development of girl sexual delinquents', *J. Soc. Hygiene.*, Vol. 29, 1943

WEBLIN, J. E., 'Psychogenesis in asthma: an appraisal with a view to family research', *Brit. J. Med. Psy.*, 1963, Vol. 36, p. 211.

WEISS, J., ROGERS, E., DUTTON, C. B., and DARWIN, M. R., 'A study of girl sex victims', *Psychiat. Quart.*, 1955, Vol. 29.—based on final report on *California Sexual Deviation Research*, 1954, Vol. 20, No. 1, p. 59.

WEISS, E., 'Psychianalyse eines falles von nervoesen Asthma', *Int. Zeit f. Psychoanal.*, 1922, Vol. 8, p. 440.

WILE, and DAVIS, R., 'Relation of birth to behaviour', *Amer. J. Orthopsy*, 1941, Vol. 11.

WINNICOT, D. W., 'Pediatrics and Psychiatry', *Brit. J. Med. Psy.*, 1947, Vol. 21, p. 229.

WITTKOWER, F. W., and O'REILLY, D., Quoted in *Medicine* Edit: Garland and Phillips, 1953, p. 503, London.

WORLD HEALTH ORGANISATION, 'Report of the Advisory Group on the Prevention of Accidents in Childhood. Facts as a basis of prevention', *W. H. O. Tech. Rep. Ser.*, No. 118, 1957.

YOUNG, FLORENE, 'Responses of juvenile delinquents to the TAT', *J. Genet. Psy.*, 1956, Vol. 88.

INDEX

Abraham, H. A., 187
Abraham, K., 18, 81, 92
Abramson, 182, 188, 250, 253
Accidents
   authority hostility conflicts, 17, 20, 21
   domestic, 14
   means of gaining sympathy, 17, 21
   proneness to, 14, 22
   unconscious self injuries, 17, 18, 22
Accident involved children, 7, 13–84
   affection seeking of, 39
   aggression of, 28
   assertive needs, 22, 24, 43, 70–4, 76
   awareness of own guilt, 22, 43, 44
   control group, 37
   circumstances preceding accidents, 34, 65
   environmental stress, 24, 29, 70–4
   fear of environment, 43
   hostility of, 39, 43
   hyperactivity of, 30
   inconsequence, 39, 82–83
   mothers of, 23, 30, 54–69, 78, 82
   parent-child conflict, 51
   parent-child relationships, 49–51, 76
   parents of, 23, 28, 30
   personality needs of, 32–80

   problem behaviour, 51–53, 75
   response to T.A.T. pictures, 41–51
   review of empirical work on, 25–31
   restlessness of, 39, 40, 77
   unsettledness in school, 38–41, 75
Ackerman and Chidester, 20, 75, 81
Affection seeking needs, 39, 88. 173, 186
Aggressive behaviour, 20
Alcock, 173, 176, 178, 197, 253
Alexander, 173, 181
Anderson, 110
Aphanisis, 92, 94
Assertive needs, 7, 24, 43, 70–4, 76
Asthma in childhood, 8, 173–255
Asthmatic children
   affection seeking needs of, 173, 186
   aggression of, 177, 178, 252
   allergy and, 174, 194, 249
   anxiety, 176, 177, 186, 196, 200, 208
   assertive needs, 176, 180, 181, 185–6, 209, 219, 247, 251
   chronic illness and, 187, 202, 206, 244
   crying, and development of asthma, 174, 182, 183, 192

273